THE ECONOMY OF SCOTLAND
in its European setting
1550 — 1625

THE ECONOMY OF SCOTLAND

in its European setting

1550 — 1625

S. G. E. LYTHE

GREENWOOD PRESS, PUBLISHERS
WESTPORT, CONNECTICUT

Library of Congress Cataloging in Publication Data

Lythe, S   G   E
    The economy of Scotland in its European setting, 1550-
1625.

    Reprint of the ed. published by Oliver and Boyd,
Edinburgh.
    Bibliography: p.
    Includes index.
    1. Scotland--Economic conditions. I. Title.
[HC257.S4L9 1976]   330.9'411'05   75-31475
ISBN 0-8371-8533-5

© 1960   S. G. E. Lythe

First published in 1960 by Oliver and Boyd, Edinburgh

Reprinted with the permission of Oliver & Boyd

Reprinted from a copy in the collections of the Brooklyn Public Library

Reprinted in 1976 by Greenwood Press,
a division of Williamhouse-Regency Inc.

Library of Congress Catalog Card Number 75-31475

ISBN 0-8371-8533-5

Printed in the United States of America

PREFACE

The period covered by this book has, in the past generation, attracted the attention of both English and Continental historians, and my primary intention has been to discover how far the great Europe-wide economic tendencies were reflected in Scotland's domestic life and external relationships. In some measure the raw material was ready to hand, for since the time of William Robertson the historians of Scotland have increasingly laid bare the facts of the past, and, with W. R. Scott, Dr Grant and Dr Insh, the focus of attention has turned onto the economic affairs of the sixteenth and seventeenth centuries. With, I hope, due acknowledgment, I have re-used and reinterpreted their material to suit the plan of this book; and, in such important matters as overseas trade and relations with England, I have supplemented our meagre native data by drawing on sources outside Scotland.

I have not confined myself within any narrow definition of economic history. Even if the data were adequate, the resulting picture would reveal little more than the bones and sinews of the nation. The outer body, the thing of flesh and colour, is a compound of many elements, and its vitality is not sustained by bread alone.

Scattered over the chapters are reproduced, either verbatim or in paraphrase, a few passages which have already appeared in my contributions to *Dundee Economic Essays* (1955), the *Scottish Journal of Political Economy* (1958), and *Abertay Historical Society Publications* (1958).

It is a pleasure to make public acknowledgment of the kind help I have received. Professor H. Hamilton of Aberdeen University encouraged me from the start and gave valuable guidance. Two colleagues in this College, Professor D. F. Macdonald and Dr I. F. Gibson, read the work in various immature stages and made many suggestions for its improvement. Dr A. M. Millard of the Battersea Training College

v

allowed me to draw on her expert knowledge of the English Port Books, and Miss O'Farrell and Miss Bryant transcribed documents for me in the Public Record Office. My many conversations with Mr C. Smout of Clare College, Cambridge, were more helpful to me than he possibly suspected, and I have acknowledged in footnotes private assistance on specific points from other specialists. It would be ungracious to omit reference to my wife and daughter whose help in a thousand small ways amounted in the end to a major contribution.

I have had much encouragement and guidance from my publishers, and am particularly indebted to the members of their editorial and production departments for their pain-staking attention to detail.

The Court of my University provided financial aid towards the cost fo research, and a generous guarantee from the Carnegie Trust for the Universities of Scotland has made it possible for the work to be published without delay.

S. G. E. LYTHE

Queen's College, Dundee,
  University of St Andrews

CONTENTS

I

FOOD AND FAMINE

FOOD PRODUCTION

It is no matter of chance that so many of the Scottish poets, ranging back from Burns with his one timorous mouse to Henryson with his two garrulous mice, have dealt with the stark realities of rural life. They faithfully mirrored the true interests of the vast majority of their contemporary countrymen. In the absence of exact statistics it seems reasonable to estimate that in the seventy-five years spanned by this book not more than one Scotsman in five or six lived in surroundings which could, even by the widest definition, be called urban; and it is certain that a great many of these townsmen maintained close rural connexions and strong agricultural interests. No apology, therefore, is required to explain the priority here given to the state of arable farming, the rearing of cattle and sheep, the catching of fish and the slaying of game, and to the various forces and incidents which permanently or temporarily restricted the domestic production of the essential foods.

We are not, of course, dealing with a simple subsistence type of rural economy. Our period, as later chapters will show, witnessed significant developments in manufacturing and in mining which widened and deepened the hitherto narrow industrial sector in the Scottish economy. For a minority of Scotsmen, notably those in the coastal burghs in the east, wider economic horizons had opened: townsmen there might think of food as something to be purchased with the profits of trade or manufacturing. Nevertheless for most Scots in the time of Queen Mary and her son, the supply of daily bread remained the insistent daily concern; and even in 1625, when James died, the dominance of rural pursuits had been but mildly challenged. The strength and roots of the main trunk of the nation's economic life still lay, as they had done through the centuries, in the soil of Scotland.

How adequate was the yield of this soil to meet the country's needs? Generalisations, from traditional sayings to the seemingly objective observations of experienced travellers, can be arranged to form a verbal curve from poverty to plenty. The saying that when the Devil showed God all the countries of the world he kept his thumb over Scotland, has a genuine medieval ring to it. The foreign visitors of the fifteenth and sixteenth centuries, admittedly often from relatively advanced agricultural countries, commented almost universally on the low level of Scottish rural husbandry, but nevertheless, in Rait's phrase, gave "an indication of rough plenty."[1] Sir Thomas Craig, writing his *De unione regnorum* in 1605, and anxious to create the best impression of Scotland among Englishmen, claimed that the natural foods were plentiful and that death from famine was less common in Scotland than in either England or France.[2] At the top end of the curve we should put the notes to Speed's *Atlas* of 1627 in which Scotland is said to be a land where "fish, fowl, cattle and corn are so plenteous that it supplieth other countries in their want." Alongside these contemporary opinions must be set the very frequent direct references to dearth and famine in the burgh and national records which, taken together, give point to Boissonnade's phrase "la stérile Ecosse," a country, he says, "réputée pour sa pauvreté."[3]

The truth is that any generalisation must be invalidated by variations over time and space. The examination, phase by phase, of the latter part of the sixteenth century which we shall undertake later in this Chapter, will show how the rough plenty of one year might give place to dire scarcity in the next. Of regional variations in standards of material welfare, on the other hand, we know deplorably little. It is, of course, a commonplace of Scottish history to speak of the cleavage between Highland and Lowland, a cleavage probably more pronounced in the sixteenth century than today. "Further,"

---

[1] R. S. Rait, *History of Scotland*, 1929, p. 203.

[2] Sir Thomas Craig, *De unione regnorum Britanniae tractatus*, henceforth cited as *De unione*, tr. C. S. Terry, Scottish History Society, VOL. LX, 1909, p. 416.

[3] P. Boissonnade, "Le Mouvement commercial entre la France et les Iles Britanniques au XVIe siècle," henceforth cited as "Mouvement commercial," in *Revue historique*, CXXXIV (1920), p. 219.

wrote John Major in his *Historia Majoris Britanniae* (*c.* 1520), "just as among the Scots we find two distinct tongues, so we likewise find two different ways of life and conduct"; and in elaboration of this he distinguished between the "Wild Scots" of the north and west, and the "Householding Scots" of the Lowlands.[4]

This is not to say that the one region was better fed than the other. Within the Lowlands certain favoured regions had an enviable reputation for high agricultural productivity, and in normal times they fed the nearby towns with relative ease. It is clearly no accident that each of the four main urban concentrations in our period, Edinburgh, Dundee, Perth, and Aberdeen, embraced within its immediate hinterland at least one of these prominent grain-producing regions. All the carselands, in spite of inadequate land-drainage, were highly productive. In 1582 George Buchanan described the Carse of Gowrie as "a noble corn country," and fifty years later Lithgow, in his euphuistic style, called it "the Diamond-plot of Tay, or rather the Sister of matchlesse Piedmont."[5] The Moray district—"la petite France" in the eyes of Mary of Lorraine[6]— was, according to Buchanan, so abundant "in corn and pasturage, and so much beautified as well as enriched by fruit trees, that it may truly be pronounced the first county in Scotland." We get a close-up view of arable farming in the Banff area in the testament of that remarkable woman, Mrs Catherine Grant, reputedly the mother of thirty-six children by three husbands, but none the less "an active mettled woman who had the uncommon humour of holding several farms."[7] In 1591, when she wrote her testament, these farms were well stocked with "plough oxen," "work horses," sheep and cattle, implements, and grain in stacks. The urban growth which carried Edinburgh far ahead of all Scottish towns could scarcely have taken place without the fertility of the nearby Lothians, according to

[4] J. Major, *History of Greater Britain*, tr. A. Constable, Scottish History Society, VOL. x, 1892, p. 48.
[5] W. Lithgow, *The Totall Discourse of the Rare Adventures and Painefull Perigrinations of long nineteene yeares travayles*, henceforth cited as *Totall Discourse*, 1632, p. 498. Other evidence on the agricultural state of the Carse of Gowrie is collected in L. Melville, *The Fair Land of Gowrie*, 1939.
[6] Quoted by Boissonade, "Mouvement commercial," p. 219.
[7] *An Account of the Antiquities of the City of Aberdeen with the price of grain and cattle from 1435 to 1591*, n.d. pp. 109-10.

Boece "the maist plentuus ground of Scotland";[8] and if the Lothians farms proved inadequate, Edinburgh could call on those of the Merse, another area "plentifull of corne."

Though no comparable regions of high natural productivity existed in the Western Isles or in the Highlands proper, it was claimed that, by primitive methods pursued with persistent vigour, some remarkable results were achieved. In the two contemporary accounts of the Western Isles, one by Donald Monro in 1549,[9] the other by an unknown hand and dated by internal evidence as between 1577 and 1595,[10] the phrases "inhabit and manurit" (tilled) and "fertill and fruitfull" repeatedly occur. In Eigg "everie boll of aittis [oats] will grow 10 or 12 boilis agane"; in Lewis barley yielded from sixteen-to twenty-fold; in Lismore the yields were equally remarkable; North Rona, inhabited by simple people, was "scant of ony religione," but abundant "of corne." In little St Kilda, though "thay use na pleuchis, but delvis thair corn land with spaiddis," they could pay their dues in grain: small wonder that their "daylie exercitation" was "maist in delving and labouring the ground" and that, however great the military emergency, no field worker was allowed to leave his isle.

Notwithstanding the depth of mutual suspicion between the peoples of the two main zones of Scotland, some social intercommunication took place at all levels, from the sons of chiefs who stayed in Lowland towns as students or hostages, to Matthew Thomesoun, "hielandman fiddler," who, at Glasgow in 1612, escaped conviction for assaulting "ane young damesall" only to be put in the stocks as an "idill vagabound." The extent of legitimate economic intercourse cannot, however, be easily assessed. As we shall see presently, there is abundant evidence of the southward movement of cattle and horses, skins and hides, and the classic "gap" towns, Perth, Stirling, and Dumbarton, fulfilled traditionally the dual function of fortress

---

[8] H. Boece, *The History and Chronicles of Scotland*, 1536, translated by John Bellenden, 2 vols., 1821. This, and the numerous subsequent quotations, are taken from the "Cosmographie and Description of Albion" which appears in VOL. I of the *History*, pp. xvii-lxiv. The substance of this is reprinted in P. Hume Brown, *Scotland before 1700 from Contemporary Documents*, henceforth cited as *Scotland before 1700*, 1893, pp. 64-104.
[9] D. Monro, "Description of the Western Isles of Scotland, called Hybrides," printed in Hume Brown, *Scotland before 1700*, pp. 238 ff.
[10] Printed as App. II to W. F. Skene, *Celtic Scotland*, 1890.

and market. The activities of Perth merchants—traceable for example in the Inverness burgh records—typify the economic function of a market town at the gateway to the Highlands. Occasionally, as in 1555, the Privy Council issued a special dispensation to permit the burghs of the south-west coast to send food north, and again in 1566 the Council expressed pious sentiments about the obligation on each of the zones to relieve the other's necessities by the transfer of "the excrescence and superflew frutis."[11]

According to Sir Thomas Craig, there were times when the glens sent cheese southwards, "which," he says, "is often used, and without injury to health, when the supply of cereals is short."[12] It is, however, difficult to believe that in normal conditions the Highland zone was able to make much contribution to the relief of cereal shortages elsewhere. The clan system, with its constant feuds, its vague concepts of landownership, and its emphasis on military preparedness and activity, was ill adapted for the expansion of arable farming even if the terrain in the Highlands had been favourable. In his supreme function as military leader, the chief aimed at increasing his following, and irrespective of the economic resources at his disposal he would receive disordered and clanless men—"broken men" in the language of the time—who went to swell the numbers living off his clan territory. Such a system, planted in the generally barren soil of the north, was hardly likely to produce grain surpluses. In short, in the absence of strong evidence to the contrary, we shall proceed on the assumption that grain markets were normally localised, and the consequent regional variations in supply, price, and diet must therefore be accepted as inevitable but imponderable qualifications to any generalisation.

Looking at Scotland as a whole, we can see that food production was limited by an unhappy combination of political instability, periodic invasion, uncertainty of tenure, and methods of cultivation already obsolescent elsewhere. The dislocation of rural life by invading forces was all too familiar in the southern half of the country. There is a pathetic reference to

---

[11] *Register of the Privy Council of Scotland*, henceforth cited as *R.P.C.*, 1st ser., vol. I, 1545-69, ed. J. H. Burton, 1877, p. 471.

[12] *De unione*, p. 447.

it in the testament of Sir Patrick Hepburn of Waughton (1547) in which, after setting out his bequests, he indicated the modifications necessary "gif England destroyis our corne and cattall."[13] Destruction of this kind was familiar to men of Hepburn's generation. Two years earlier, in 1545, the English commander, Hertford, had obeyed his king's instructions with vigour and enthusiasm in razing 243 "villages" in the counties of Berwick and Roxburgh, while, operating with the same zeal, the English Wardens of the Marches claimed to have seized over 10,000 cattle and 12,500 sheep and to have fired expanses of standing corn.[14] The English occupation of Broughty Ferry Castle in 1547, the struggle between them and the French for Leith in 1559-60, the French foray into Fife in 1559, all meant plunder and the destruction or seizure of local food resources.

On balance, however, the economic loss from invasion was, in the long run, less than that from the lawlessness and internal strife which bedevilled Scotland until the later part of the reign of James VI. Geography was on the side of the lawbreaker; Scotland was no exception to the universal rule that the hill-dweller preys on the lowlander:

Quod God to the Hielandman, "Where wilt thou now?"
"I will doun to the Lawland, Lord, and there steal a cow."

The opening lines of the Psalm cxxi can have had little personal meaning for the sober farmer of Strathmore. Geography, too, lay beneath the old Scottish tradition of baronial insubordination which continued strongly into the sixteenth century with its royal minorities and its weak central administration; and into this furnace of political discord fell the volatile fuel of religious controversy. Political anarchy and governmental weakness provided scope for private vengeance, and widespread destruction must have been wrought in the settlement of private feuds in times like those of the Huntly Rising of 1561 or the early 1590's when, as Robertson says, "universal licence and anarchy prevailed to a degree scarcely consistent with the preservation of society."[15] In such times the scenes witnessed by the Lass wi' the Muckle Moo cannot have been peculiar to the traditionally unruly parts.

---

[13] Printed in *Miscellany of the Bannatyne Club*, VOL. III, 1855, p. 289.
[14] W. Robertson, *The History of Scotland During the Reigns of Queen Mary and King James VI*, 1794, VOL. I, pp. 113-6.
[15] *Op. cit.*, VOL. II, p. 210.

The dislocation of peaceful farming in the Borders was, down to the middle years of the reign of James VI, aggravated by the unhappy relations between England and Scotland to which we shall return in Chapter VII. The Western Isles and the adjacent Western Highlands were tormented by the regional problem of the Lordship of the Isles and its relationship to the Scottish Crown. Though the independent Lordship was formally abolished in the closing years of the fifteenth century, so late as 1545 Donald Dubh raised a force of 8,000 men and 180 galleys and accepted the suzerainty of Henry VIII. So long as the Lordship had persisted, regional loyalty to the Lord had provided a measure of stability, but once it was destroyed a tangle of bitter rivalries rose to the surface. Throughout the sixteenth century the "danting" (pacification) of the Isles was a major task for Scottish rulers, a task which they could undertake only by playing one group against another with fearful consequences in blood and destruction.

On the mainland north of the Highland Line, social life was rarely entirely stable, and the basis of local conflict was often economic: disputes about grazing rights or fertile straths, pressure of population against limited resources. Casualties were grim when men were locked in close conflict with the battle-axe and the two-handed sword: at Blar-na-Leine in 1544, for example, only a handful of Frasers survived out of a force of 300; and the wholesale plunder of livestock—over 7,000 head were lifted from Glenurquhart in 1545—meant bitter hardship to the entire community.[16] Nevertheless it would be misleading to suggest that the entire manpower of the Highlands was constantly under arms. The exemption of field-workers from military service which existed, as we have seen, in some of the Isles, may not have been universal on the mainland, but there are indications that the aggressive spearhead in local fighting consisted of clansmen who can, not unfairly, be regarded as semi-professional soldiers. In any event much of the routine farming work was done by women and children, and the operations involving an all-out effort—sowing, haymaking, and harvesting—were concentrated into fairly short periods of the year.

[16] This paragraph is based on W. R. Kermack, *The Scottish Highlands*, 1957, pp. 124-5.

In every part of Scotland social unrest and political instability were reflected in insecurity of tenure from the highest to the lowest levels. As great houses rose or fell, so their cadets and followers acquired or lost land, and this uncertainty served as a fatal disincentive to progressive estate management. It is true that in our period the modern system of feuing was gaining ground, and where it was adopted the laird or the farmer secured perpetual tenure, but the older forms of kindly tenure, the short lease and so on, continued to regulate the relations between most superiors and tenants. None of these old methods provided the security essential for the introduction of advanced husbandry or for long-term planning in land utilisation. When Lithgow, in his rhyme "Scotland's Welcome to her Native Sonne and Soveraigne Lord King Charles," put the question:

Ah, what makes my Countray looke so bare?

and gave his own answer:

But only that the Land-Lords set their land
From yeare to yeare, and so from hand to hand,

he was simply versifying what John Major had said a hundred years before about the reluctance of insecure tenants to build houses, plant hedges and trees and dung the land.[17] In these conditions no revolution in farming methods or in field layout could be expected. Apart from some instances of afforestation, Scotland generally was untouched by the new spirit in estate management which was sweeping contemporary England. No assault was made on the great expanses of moss and bog which could have been brought into cultivation by the drainage techniques of a Vermuyden. Blaeu's map of Fife, incorporating material collected by Timothy Pont ($c.1560$-$c.1630$), shows about twenty lochs and lochans, some as big as the present Loch Leven, and there must have been thousands of acres of adjacent low land too wet for arable farming. Scotland generally continued down to the eighteenth century to labour under restrictions on her grain-producing capacity, to tolerate a primitive and inefficient field system, and to employ implements and methods of husbandry long outdated in the more technically advanced and socially progressive countries.

[17] Major, *History of Greater Britain*, p. 31.

It appears, therefore, that Scotland did not, indeed could not, make the best use of her relatively limited arable land; and, as we shall see later, over long periods she lived on such narrow margins that any disturbance, whether by human or by climatic agency, caused alarm. It must also be remembered that by no means all the grain was used for food, though its diversion to other purposes, especially in times of shortage, was opposed by the burghs and the Council. Ale-making, an expanding industry, produced little protest, but at Inverness in 1569 and 1574 the making of "brogat"—another malt liquor— was banned "for awoiding of derth," and in 1567 the Burgh Court there set a rigid limit to the number of aquavitae pots which might be employed in the town.[18] Nevertheless the making of whisky—*uisge beatha* in the Highlands—had certainly increased since about 1500 when the small doses supplied by the surgeon-barbers of Edinburgh were medicinal in the unequivocal sense of the term.[19] By the 1570's Bishop Lesley could write that whisky was commonly drunk in the west instead of wine, and references to it occur repeatedly in burgh records as far apart as Ayr and Inverness; in 1579 the Estates were alarmed about the excessive use of malt for whisky-making; in 1585 the Countess of Argyll found, no doubt with equal alarm, that her accustomed supply was not available in Bute; and, according to Fynes Moryson, by the end of the sixteenth century whisky was among Scotland's exports to Ireland.

The system of arable farming commonly pursued—the agricultural historians' "infield-outfield"—meant that a very limited amount of land was continuously and intensively tilled; while, of the rest, isolated patches were cropped until they reached exhaustion and then were abandoned to revert to a state of nature. The consequence was that even in the Lowlands much potentially arable land was in fact rough pasture, which, as we turn to consider the extent of stock-rearing, must be reckoned alongside the vast stretches of natural grazing land in the Southern Uplands and in the Highlands and Isles.

[18] *Records of Inverness: Burgh Court Books 1556-86*, henceforth cited as *Inverness Records*, New Spalding Club, 1911, pp. lxxix and 154.
[19] These sentences on whisky are drawn from R. Scott-Moncrieff, "Note on the early use of aqua vitae in Scotland," in *Proceedings of the Society of Antiquaries of Scotland*, henceforth cited as *P.S.A.S.*, L (1915-16), pp. 257 ff.

B

Intelligent use was made of both hill and glen pastures by the very general practice of transhumance, whereby the flocks— tended often by women and girls—spent the summer months at the shielings (the summer pastures) and returned to the valley homesteads in the autumn. Stock-rearing was the appropriate rural employment in a country where, in the conditions we have discussed, more intensive land utilisation was impossible, and stock represented wealth for the highest as well as for the lowest.

The scale of sheep-farming in the southern shires, a legacy of the medieval abbeys, is indicated by the flocks of up to a thousand head which grazed in Tweeddale.[20] The sheep population of the Highlands and Isles has almost certainly been underestimated: admittedly their wool exports were small, but so were their sheep, and in any event much of the wool was woven locally. The common breed bore some resemblance to the modern Soay sheep, and already in the sixteenth century St Kilda was famous for its sheep, "fairer and greiter, and larger tailled, than in any uther ile about."[21] But though wool and mutton and ewes' milk played a great part in the daily life of the northern and western regions of the country, their reputation as stock-rearing areas rested more on cattle. Climatic conditions in the west generally produced lush pasturage, though perhaps not everywhere so "nurischand" as in Tiree where the "ky abundis sa of milk that thai are milkit four times in the day"; and from these western pastures cheese and butter were sent to Glasgow and Dumbarton. In the northern and central Highlands, beef cattle and horses could be reared on rough pasture with a minimum of supervision, and any surplus could be transported on the hoof east to Inverness or south to the Lowlands. Sir Walter Scott's picture of the Highlanders, "driving their bullocks, as Vergil is said to have spread his manure, with dignity and consequence," is accurate in substance if not in embellishment. In 1565-6, for example, the Privy Council heard with sympathy the complaint of certain Highlanders who alleged that they had been molested

[20] *The Historie of Scotland, wrytten first in Latin by . . . Jhone Leslie and translated into Scottish by Father James Dalrymple . . . 1596*, henceforth cited as Lesley, *Historie*, ed. E. G. Cody, Scottish Text Society, 1888, VOL. I, pp. 18-19.
[21] These remarks on stockfarming are based on Monro, "Description of the Western Isles," and the account in Skene, *Celtic Scotland*, App. II.

in their habitual practice of driving their "ky furth of Ergyle to be sauld in the lawland" at the markets of Perth, Stirling, Dumbarton, and Renfrew.[22] Even more convincing is the evidence collected by Canon R. C. MacLeod[23] showing how a spectacular rise in the annual value of the MacLeod estates in Skye and Glenelg began during the chieftainship of Rory (1596-1626). The last clan war in which the MacLeods were engaged ended in 1601, and within a very few years their kinsmen and tenants had created a flourishing traffic in live cattle to the south.

So far however—indeed right down to 1707—droving to England provided only a minor outlet for the products of all these pastoral activities. Transhumance ensured the resting of the home pastures while the animals were on the hills, but in spite of the hardiness of the cattle—Lesley said that those of Argyll and Ross "nevir thair heid sett undir the ruffe . . . how deip saevir [soever] be the snawe, how long saevir the frost ly"[24]—the sustenance of great herds throughout the winter was impossible. Heavy slaughtering in the late autumn of "mart" cattle was therefore the normal practice: Lesley also describes how the cattle of Carrick (south Ayrshire) were fattened and sent "through all partes of the realme," where, "being slane, thay ar poudiret, or with salte ar seasoned . . . to be keipet frome corruptione . . . as swyne fleshe is uset in uthir cuntries."[25] The annual export from Scotland of over half a million hides and sheep skins was by no means exceptional,[26] indicating butchery on the grand scale and alone representing—on the average—one carcass for consumption by each human inhabitant.

Lesley's reference to "swyne flesh" prompted him to add that this was a food in which "our cuntrie peple hes lytle plesure."[27] While it is true that the pig never penetrated the rural economy of Scotland as it did elsewhere, it was common enough in the towns to become a public nuisance and a menace to health and

[22] *R.P.C.*, VOL. I, pp. 470-1, and *Collectanea de Rebus Albanicis*, Iona Club, 1847, pp. 151-3.
[23] *The Book of Dunvegan*, ed. R. C. MacLeod, Third Spalding Club, 1937, VOL. III, p. 246.
[24] Lesley, *Historie*, VOL. I, p. 31.   [25] *Op. cit.*, p. 32.
[26] Calculated from *Rotuli Scaccarium regum Scotorum, The Exchequer Rolls of Scotland*, henceforth cited as *Exchequer Rolls*, 1908, VOLS. xx-xxii, ed. G. P. McNeill, passim.   [27] Lesley, *Historie*, VOL. I, p. 32.

good-neighbourliness. At Inverness, according to evidence before the Burgh Court in 1579, the owners of pigs failed to keep them confined, suffering them "to offend thair nychbouris nycht and day in wrutting and eitting of thair cornis and gerse, tending thairbe to rais occasioun of discord."[28] The Burgh Council of Edinburgh in 1605 directed its Lockman to patrol, armed with sword and staff, and to "hald the swyne of the hie gate,"[29] and when King James in 1608 urged various reforms on the Convention he specifically recommended the clearing of middens and of swine from the streets of the burghs.[30]

In the upland stock-rearing regions the shielings were the frontier belt between the realm of the herdsman and the realm of undomesticated nature. When Boece was writing in 1527 he could say that wolves were "richt noisum to the tame bestiall in all partis of Scotland except ane part thairof namit Glenmores";[31] but the damage they did was serious only in the northern counties where, according to Lesley in 1578, "nocht only invade thay scheip, oxne, ye and horse; bot evin men, specialie women with barne, outragiouslie and fercelie thay ouirthrowis."[32] Lesley's statement, at least as far as the word "oxne," is substantiated by incidental references in the Inverness Court Book which show that in winter-time the wolf would come dangerously close to human habitations. The fox —the "tod" in sixteenth-century Scots—was a universal pest. In one of his excursions into improbability Boece describes how the farmers of Glenmore out-guiled the fox and secured immunity for their stock by mixing a proportion of fox flesh with the food of their "fowlis or uthir smal beistis,"[33] but elsewhere the habitual toll of poultry was paid annually. There were slight compensations, for along with the pelts of the marten, the weasel and the badger, fox skins found a ready market "amang uncouth merchandis."

The monarch of the country's wild life, the deer, represented a valuable supplementary source of food. Peder Swave,

[28] *Inverness Records*, p. 275.
[29] *Extracts from the Records of the Burgh of Edinburgh*, henceforth cited as *Edinburgh Records*, VOL. VI, 1604-26, ed. M. Wood, 1936, p. 17.
[30] *Records of the Convention of the Royal Burghs of Scotland*, henceforth cited as *Convention Records*, VOL. II, ed. J. D. Marwick, 1870, pp. 253-4.
[31] Hume Brown, *Scotland before 1700*, p. 83.
[32] Lesley, *Historie*, VOL. I, p. 29.
[33] Hume Brown, *Scotland before 1700*, p. 83.

Danish Ambassador to the court of James V, tells a somewhat far-fetched tale of how the "wild Scot," spurred on by hunger, "would outstrip a stag in swiftness of foot, overtake and kill it, and so sustain life."[34] The more orthodox and less exhausting method of capture was the "tinchel" into which herds of anything up to a thousand head were gradually coralled by a host of beaters and dogs, though, not, says Lesley, "without gret danger baith of men and dogs."[35] Similarly fowl of all sorts, and their eggs, were a variant and reinforcement to diet. Contemporary writers testify to their abundance: the capercailzie, "maist acceptable" to those "quha eitis her"; the bustard, "in taste nocht unlyke the pertrik" (partridge); hawks, waterfowl, the heathcock, pheasants, and partridges; larks so common that in 1570 twelve sold for a French sou. To the nutritive value of the birds was added the commercial value of feathers, either plucked from their bodies or filched from their nests.

The food resources of the land were supplemented by the river and sea fisheries which, in several ways, occupy a distinct place in the national economy. Though local disturbances or the unruliness of clansmen might embarrass fishermen—in 1597 for example they dared not venture among the Western Isles for the hostility of the McLeans[36]—yet the fish normally continued to live and multiply. And whereas the yield of the land had not greatly changed for centuries, the sea fisheries had been enormously enriched by the migrating herring, which had moved from the approaches to the Baltic and, as Hitchcock said in 1580, rose "out of the deepes on both sides of Scotlande,"[37] offering a rich harvest to those with the skill and daring to gather it. By our period the wealth of the Scottish fishing grounds was already renowned. Fish, wrote Major, was far more abundant around Scotland than around England, and he regarded it as proof of "Divine Wisdom" that a country which lacked sunshine should have the "greater store of fish."[38]

[34] Swave's account of Scotland is printed (in Latin) in *Aarsberetninger fra det Kongelige Geheimsarchiv*, ed. W. F. Wegener, Copenhagen 1865, VOL. III, pp. 232 ff. A modern translation appears in P. Hume Brown, *Early Travellers in Scotland*, henceforth cited as *Early Travellers*, 1891, pp. 55-8.

[35] This summary of 16th-century fauna is drawn from Lesley, *Historie*, VOL. I, pp. 39-40, and from H. Yule, "Jerome Cardan's Travels in Scotland," in *The Geographical Magazine*, Sept. 1874, pp. 240 ff. [36] *R.P.C.*, VOL. III, p. 124.

[37] Quoted in *Tudor Economic Documents*, edd. R. H. Tawney and E. Power, 1924, VOL. III, p. 246. [38] Major, *History of Greater Britain*, p. 32.

But plentiful supply was matched by heavy demand. It is of course true that the native fisherman monopolised the rivers and firths, but on the open sea his craft and gear looked amateurish alongside those of the Dutch. There were always facilities and opportunities for exporting fish, so that the domestic consumer found himself in competition with the foreign buyer, who, especially if he were a Dutchman, would offer sound currency and a cash and carry transaction.

In theory at least the fish merchant's choice between domestic and export markets was not determined simply by prevailing prices. A series of statutes and Privy Council orders from 1540 to 1587[39] provided that home requirements must be met before export could begin, but laudable as was the motive behind it was, the application of this policy of "plenty" must have strained the capacity of any sixteenth-century Scottish administration. Though there were limits to the extent to which fish could be substituted for other foods, the case for diverting it to the home market was obviously greatest in time of general famine; and it is significant that in 1585-7, when the general food position was critical, fish exports to at least one major overseas market—the Baltic—fell to zero.[40] On the other hand in 1594-8, when the famine was of comparable severity, the decline in fish exports was much less pronounced, and David Wedderburne, the Dundee merchant whose account book survives, seems to have been exceptionally active in consigning fish both to the Baltic and to Flanders.[41]

The relatively well-to-do, from the burgess in Dunbar or Perth to the chief in Skye, could enliven his diet and embellish his table with exotic foods and drinks brought into Scotland mainly from France and the Low Countries. In our studies of these branches of Scotland's trade we shall encounter apples and figs, prunes and preserves, onions by the ton, wine by the shipload. These were the frills; the national staple items of food were locally produced grain and flesh, locally captured

[39] Conveniently summarised in A. M. Samuel, *The Herring: its Effect on the History of Britain*, 1918, pp. 88-9.

[40] This, like all subsequent generalisations about the Baltic trade, is based on *Tabeller over Skibsfart og Varetransport gennem Øresund, 1497-1660*, henceforth cited as *Sound Toll Registers*, ed. N. E. Bang, Copenhagen 1922.

[41] *The Compt Buik of David Wedderburne, Merchant of Dundee*, henceforth cited as *Wedderburne Compt Buik*, ed. A. H. Millar, Scottish History Society, VOL. XXVIII, 1898, pp. 68, 71, 72, 98, 132.

game, and locally landed fish. Contemporary writers agreed that in the bulk of Scottish households, bread in some form was the staff of life. Thus both Major and Lesley emphasised the role of oats in the life of country people; Major indeed described the oat bread of the time and quoted a recipe for "bannoka."[42] Fynes Moryson said that "the Scots . . . vulgarly eate harth Cakes of Oates, but in Cities have also wheaten bread,"[43] and the Glasgow University dietary of 1602 stipulated bread, either wheaten or oaten, for professors and students at every meal.[44] In his *De unione regnorum*, written three years later, Sir Thomas Craig said: "we eat barley bread as pure and white as that of England and France, our servants are content with oatmeal which makes them hardy and long-lived. The greater number of our farm hands eat bread of peas and beans. . . . Any other they consider will weaken their strength."[45] Furthermore, as we shall demonstrate later in this chapter, the coincidence of heavy grain shipments from the Baltic in Scots vessels with reports of crop deficiencies in Scotland suggests a high rigidity of demand for grain.

It is clear, in short, that the predominance of cereals in the Scottish diet is not—as is sometimes thought—a phenomenon peculiar to the generations after 1707. On the other hand we have already assembled enough evidence to demonstrate the importance attached to flesh and fish which were eaten regularly by the wealthier, and at least sometimes by all but the poorest. Consequently any event, either human or climatic in cause, which reduced the country's production of either grain or flesh was likely to set up strains at almost every level in the economy from the domestic to the national.

FAMINE AND THE GRAIN TRADE

And in the seven plenteous years the earth brought forth by handfuls. . . . And the seven years of plenteousness were ended . . . and the famine was over all the face of the earth.

The translation of the forty-first chapter of Genesis placed no strain on the credulity of Lancelot Andrewes and his fellow-scholars, for even in the relatively genial south of England

[42] Major, *History of Greater Britain*, pp. 7-12.
[43] Hume Brown, *Early Travellers*, p. 89.
[44] *R.P.C.*, VOL. VI, p. 452.   [45] *De unione*, p. 417.

empty bellies and lean kine were still a bitter reality. In Scotland the recurrence of famine or near-famine had been one of the few certainties in those unpredictable times which extended from Flodden to the middle years of the reign of James VI. Though James no doubt escaped the discomfort of personal hunger, he could not have failed to see its mark on the faces of his countrymen and to hear its voice in the streets of his towns. The impact of food shortage was so widespread throughout the entire economy that repetition of the theme in later chapters calls for no apology. Whether our concern is with changing prices, as in Chapter III, or with the composition of the Eastland trade, as in Chapter V, the level of Scottish food output is a dominant note. What follows here is an attempt, based on statistical and literary sources, to describe the main fluctuations down to about 1600: thereafter, apart from the early 1620's, a combination of better harvests and political stability ensured a more reliable and stable level of domestic food production.

Our period opens badly. In 1550-2 there was alarm about the food supply, especially in Edinburgh whose normal granary, the nearby Lothians, had been ravaged during the recent English invasions.[46] In 1550 the Privy Council issued sumptuary regulations prescribing the maximum number of dishes to a meal with, of course, ample concessions to the higher social ranks; and these regulations were followed in 1551 and '52 by the familiar bans on forestalling and on the export of foodstuffs.[47] By 1553 grain prices had so far returned to normal that the Edinburgh housewife's 4d. bought twice as much bread as it had done in the three previous years,[48] but flesh of all sorts remained dear and it is unlikely that this hardship was immediately removed, for the winter of 1554-5 was exceptionally severe. "The great snaw," wrote a man who lived through it, "began on Yowl da and ilk da fra that furth mayr and mayr snaw without ony thryfft quhyl the xvii day of Januar."[49] Then, after a short break, it snowed and froze again until the end of February, with great mortality among horses, cattle, sheep, and goats in the Highland region.

---

[46] *R.P.C.*, VOL. I, p. 115.   [47] *Op. cit.*, pp. 94-6, 137.
[48] Calculated from the burghal assessed prices, see below, p. 110.
[49] "The Chronicle of Fortirgall," printed in *The Black Book of Taymouth*, ed. C. Innes, Bannatyne Club, 1855, p. 124.

The 1560's similarly opened badly. The effects of the fighting around the Forth and in the north-east were aggravated by severe winters in 1560[50] and 1562[51] with great loss of stock, especially sheep. Official proclamations against the hoarding of grain and the eating of flesh in Lent may have helped,[52] but meal prices in 1563 were still abnormally high and the carriage of grain out of the Baltic in Scottish ships reached a tonnage only twice exceeded in the rest of the century.[53] Temporary relief came with a good harvest in 1564, so that the price of meal in the Highlands was only a third of what it had been a year before—in which, as the Dean of Lismore wrote, "ye ma se the Grace of God."[54] But the respite was brief, for 1565 was a bad year with dear food in Western Europe generally.[55] Scotland had "evil weather" at harvest time, and as early as November alarm about grain deficiency produced a flow of proclamations banning the export of food.[56] Unlike 1563, there is no evidence of unusual imports: perhaps the Continent had none to spare. The later 1560's were not much happier, for in 1567 the Privy Council was again expecting dearth, since the grain had, "at Goddis plesour," been "plagit and split with weit";[57] exports were again banned, and Edinburgh at least had the additional trial of pestilence.[58] Hunger and pestilence, "twoo buddes of the same tre" as Harryson called them in 1547, were social tribulations to aggravate the problems confronting Mary and Bothwell.

The regency of Moray, on the other hand, seems to have had the benefit of relative plenty. European food prices generally were low; the Scottish records are silent about weather and crops, and silence generally implies satisfaction; there is no indication of any substantial food imports. But the severe winters of 1571 and '72,[59] coupled with the general anarchy of English invasion and civil war in Scotland, ushered in another phase of shortage which lasted certainly to 1573[60] and probably

[50] R.P.C., VOL. I, pp. 200-1.
[51] Compota Thesauriorum regum Scotorum, Accounts of the Lord High Treasurer of Scotland, henceforth cited as Accounts of Lord High Treasurer, VOL. XI, ed. J. Balfour Paul, pp. xxxviii, 172.   [52] Op. cit., p. 253; R.P.C., VOL. I, p. 201.
[53] Sound Toll Register for relevant years.   [54] "Chronicle of Fortirgall," p. 132.
[55] W. Beveridge, "Weather and harvest cycles," in The Economic Journal, XXXI (1921), p. 449.
[56] Accounts of Lord High Treasurer, VOL. XI, p. 436; R.P.C., VOL. I, p. 402.
[57] R.P.C., VOL. I, p. 571.   [58] Edinburgh Records, VOL. III, pp. 253-5.
[59] "Chronicle of Fortirgall," p. 137.   [60] Op. cit., p. 140.

to 1575, when, in spite of the high food prices on the Continent, shipments of grain from the Baltic were still abnormally heavy. Thereafter, apart from 1578, Morton's administration seems to have been facilitated by favourable social conditions. Indeed in 1576-7 the Council was saying that while in times of shortage Scotland had received "large help and support of victuallis out of the eister seyis [the Baltic], France, Flanderis and England," she was now in a position to extend the like good-neighbourliness to them.[61] The next year the tune quickly changed and foreigners were encouraged to bring in food, but the shortages seem to have been local.[62] At all events European prices were reasonably low, so that even when shipments to Scotland rose the strain on her economy was tolerable.

Then followed seven fat years. From 1579 to 1585 grain imports from the Baltic—the main emergency source—were negligible and, in spite of the Raid of Ruthven and the power politics of the nobles, the nation's internal life remained relatively stable. The tide began to turn in 1584 with the reappearance of the plague. From West Wemyss, where it had been "brocht hame frae flanderis be marinars," it was conveyed to Leith by "Malvio Curllis dochter out of Kirkcaldy."[63] Its incidence can be traced in the sanitary precautions—elementary attempts at isolation and so on—taken by the east coast burghal authorities;[64] and Calderwood's estimate of 20,000 dead in Edinburgh, though a palpable exaggeration, indicates the impression made by the disaster on the mind of a man, who, as a boy of ten, had survived it.[65] More reasonable mortality figures, but none the less formidable in relation to the populations of the time, are 1,400 or 1,500 for Edinburgh, perhaps 400 for St Andrews, perhaps 300 for Kirkcaldy.[66] These congested old towns, their narrow wynds and timber

---

[61] *R.P.C.*, VOL. II, pp. 588-9.
[62] *R.P.C.*, VOL. II, p. 680; *Extracts from the Council Register of Aberdeen*, henceforth cited as *Aberdeen Council Register*, ed. J. Stuart, VOL. II, Spalding Club, 1848, p. 30.
[63] *Edinburgh Records*, VOL. IV, pp. 413, 445; *Gleanings from the Records of Dysart*, ed. W. Muir, 1862, p. 40.
[64] E.g. *Kirkcaldy Burgh Records*, henceforth cited as *Kirkcaldy Records*, ed. L. Macbean, 1908, pp. 91-8.
[65] D. Calderwood, *The History of the Kirk of Scotland*, Wodrow Society, 1843, VOL. IV, p. 377.
[66] *Kirkcaldy Records*, p. 37; James Melville, *Autobiography and Diary*, ed. R. Pitcairn, 1842, p. 222; D. Moysie, *Memoirs of the Affairs of Scotland, 1577-1603*, Bannatyne Club, 1830, pp. 53-4.

houses full of stink and corruption, bred and nourished disease.
How far the plague spread beyond their gates to sweep the
countryside and dislocate rural production is a matter of guesswork: all one can say with safety is that a phase of very acute
food shortage came hard upon its heels.

The first warnings of impending famine (the word is not too
strong) come in 1585 with the promulgation of fresh restrictions
on meat-eating in Lent because of the dearth of all kinds of
flesh.[67] For the next two years the evidence of severe food
shortage is entirely conclusive: the catch of herring in the lochs
and off the Isles was much below average,[68] corn stacks were
to be threshed without delay, and no grain was to be hoarded
or exported.[69] The 150 per cent rise in wheat prices in Paris
and London[70] shows that the Scottish conditions were by no
means unique around the North Sea. But as so often happened,
the eastern Baltic ports, drawing on the great hinterlands of
eastern Germany and Poland, saved the day. Because of
affairs at home the Dutch could not exploit this situation with
their customary efficiency,[71] but the Scots, like the English and
French, made a tremendous maritime effort. In 1587, 124
Scottish ships entered the Baltic, well over twice the average
of the adjacent years, and 80 of them went in ballast. All
returned laden, 80 from Danzig, the rest from Königsberg, and
the 1,817 lasts of grain they carried westwards through the
Sound is much the highest annual total in our period.[72] Unfortunately there is no means of determining how much of this
grain was in fact brought to Scotland. In June of that year the
King was informed of the great fleet of Scottish vessels in the
Baltic, and he heard with considerable alarm that many of the
shippers were proposing to transport their cargoes to foreign
ports "for thair greter advantage and commoditie."[73] In view
of this information he instructed Sir Patrick Waus, his ambassador in Denmark, that no Scots grain ship should be

---

[67] *R.P.C.*, VOL. III, p. 722.   [68] *Op. cit.*, VOL. IV, p. 243.
[69] *Op. cit.*, VOL. IV, pp. 74, 84, 116, 123.
[70] A. P. Usher, "General course of wheat prices in France, 1350-1788," in
Review of Economic Statistics, XII (1930), p. 161; W. Fleetwood, *Chronicum preciosum,
or an Account of English Money*, 1707, p. 123.
[71] A. E. Christensen, *Dutch Trade to the Baltic about 1600*, The Hague 1941, p. 86.
[72] *Sound Toll Register* for 1587.
[73] *The Correspondence of Sir Patrick Waus*, ed. R. V. Agnew, 1887, VOL. II, pp.
401-2.

allowed to leave Elsinore unless the skipper undertook to come direct to Scotland; and it may be that the accompanying threat that offenders should be "handillit as thai mereit" sufficed to bring the whole fleet to its native ports. At all events the King's anxiety confirms the other evidence of the severity of the shortage of food in Scotland.

Thenceforth to 1594 the food situation was reasonably good with general European prices and Baltic exports low. Locally a "dearth of vivers" might cause alarm—it did in Edinburgh in 1588[74]—and in 1591 the Privy Council thought too much was being exported for safety;[75] but such alarms amounted to little until 1594, which heralded a four-year phase of genuine national shortage. A combination of bad weather and the mustering of troops for action against the rebellious lords delayed the ingathering of the 1594 harvest,[76] so that before the end of the year the Dundee magistrates were ruling that nobody buy "within the water of Tay and libertie of ys Burgh mor than whilk may serve for the furnishing of his oun house."[77] Thenceforth the frequency of Privy Council consultations on dearth indicates that the food position remained very critical until 1598.[78] Scotland was, of course, by no means alone in this misfortune. Fleetwood, in the *Chronicum preciosum*, records very high wheat prices in England—"our sins (as Mr Stow says) deserving it."[79] Likewise wheat in France was dear throughout the whole '90's,[80] so that once again the Scots had to join the queue of vessels loading rye and wheat at Danzig, Königsberg, and Stralsund: indeed the Scottish shipping effort of 1595-7 is comparable with that of 1587. Burghs joined with private traders in buying grain: thus the Aberdeen bailies in 1596 imported 318 bolls of rye at £8 the boll and 35 lasts (each about 18 or 19 bolls) of rye meal at £7 the boll.[81] Had they come earlier these years of dearth might well have undermined the support on which James and the Protestant Church rested;

---

[74] *Edinburgh Records*, VOL. IV, p. 533. [75] *R.P.C.*, VOL. IV, p. 589.

[76] *Op. cit.*, VOL. V, p. 163.

[77] *Burgh Laws of Dundee with the History, Statutes, and Proceedings of the Guild of Merchants and Fraternities of Craftsmen*, henceforth cited as *Burgh Laws of Dundee*, ed. A. J. Warden, 1872, p. 45. [78] *R.P.C.*, VOL. V, pp. 221, 243-4, 292, 306.

[79] Fleetwood, *Chronicum preciosum*, p. 123.

[80] Usher, in *Review of Economic Statistics*, XII (1930), pp. 161-2.

[81] W. Kennedy, *Annals of Aberdeen*, 1818, p. 185. These, and all the other Scottish prices and wages quoted in this book, are in terms of the Scottish national currency of the period.

but—apart perhaps from the tumult in Edinburgh in 1596—there is little sign of the social tensions so often generated by scarce and dear food. Nevertheless the experience bit deeply into the minds of contemporaries: years later men spoke in sorrowful recollection of the "great dearth of 1595."[82]

The deduction from this chronological survey down to the end of the sixteenth century is that the adequacy of Scotland's domestic grain production was finely poised, so dependent on favourable climatic, political, and social conditions that any serious disturbance in any of them involved the nation in recourse to outside supplies and all that that entailed in the way of external payments. Especially in times of general West European shortage, these outside supplies came primarily from the Baltic which, throughout our period, was the emergency granary for all the North Sea countries. In the main these relations between Scotland and the Baltic grain producers were strictly commercial, but those with France, Scotland's second external supplier, were influenced by diplomatic and dynastic considerations. So Mollat,[83] writing of the *congés d'exportation de blé* granted, shortly before our period, to the Duke of Albany, says: "La politique, comme la cœur, a ses raisons: il faut nourrir les gens du duc d'Albany." Boissonnade suggests that France regularly provided food: "Il n'était pas rare que la stérile Écosse en tout temps, et même la plentureuse Angleterre en temps de disette, eurent recours à nos froments et à nos farines."[84] Until the latter part of the period England had no such interest in succouring the Scots, indeed the evidence of food shipments from England often reflect strained relationships. We know, for example, that the export of peas via Lynn to Scotland was the indirect cause of a riot in Huntingdonshire;[85] and in 1579 John Hudson of York had to take proceedings for the recovery of £100 for wheat supplied to Thomas Kay of Crail, warning Scots merchants generally that they will "find less credit and furtherance when the like occasion of necessity of victuals may occur hereafter."[86] As relationships

---

[82] *R.P.C.*, vol. vi, pp. 57, 82, 314, 368.
[83] M. Mollat, *Le Commerce maritime normand à la fin du moyen âge*, Paris 1952, p. 326.
[84] Boissonnade, "Mouvement commercial," p. 219.
[85] Petition of the inhabitants of Yaxley, quoted in *Tudor Economic Documents*, VOL. I, p. 144.
[86] *R.P.C.*, vol. iii, p. 102.

improved, however, the Scots came to look on East Anglia as a more generous source of food, and, as we shall see in our study of Anglo-Scottish trade, by the early 1600's fairly substantial amounts of grain were being carried to Scotland in returning salt ships.

Some part, probably a small part, of the imported grain was later re-exported. In 1598, for example, some of the grain passing outwards through the Edinburgh customs is specified as "German rye" and "Danskyn wheat." During the dearth of the early 1620's William Dick and William Wilkie imported so heavily that by 1624 they had a surplus available for re-export, some of which, to their dismay, ultimately fell into the hand of Dunkirk privateers.[87] True exports were officially regarded with disfavour unless there was a glut at home, or unless the exports were destined for the purchase of such essential imports as Norwegian timber.[88] But some of Scotland's best grain country—the Lothians, the Carse of Gowrie, the Moray coastlands—lay in the close hinterland of one or other of the chief ports, and news of attractive prices in France or Spain must have diverted some Scottish grain, legally or otherwise, from the home market. There certainly seems to have been a substantial export of Scottish grain in the 1610's[89] which were, with a few exceptions, years of good harvests. Rye and oats were shipped to Boston (Lincs.) in 1615-16, and when Taylor, the "Water Poet," visited Leith in 1618, he was "credibly informed" that the equivalent of 320,000 English bushels of wheat, oats and barley had been shipped from there in one year to Spain, France, "and other forraine parts," besides smaller amounts from almost every "portable towne" from Dunbar to Aberdeen.[90]

The tentative conclusion is that life in Scotland in the closing years of King James's reign was easier and safer than it had been when he was a boy. James had given the country

---

[87] *State Papers and Miscellaneous Correspondence of Thomas, Earl of Melros*, Abbotsford Club, 1837. The letter relating to Dick and Wilkie is reprinted in Hume Brown, *Scotland before 1700*, p. 283.

[88] R. Chambers, *Domestic Annals of Scotland from the Reformation to the Revolution*, henceforth cited as *Domestic Annals*, 1858, VOL. II, p. 71.

[89] See below, p. 220.

[90] J. Taylor, *The Pennyles Pilgrimage, or The Moneylesse Perambulation of John Taylor, alias the King's Majesties Water-Poet*, 1618, and in *The Works of John Taylor*, ed. C. Hindley, 1876. The sections relating to Scotland are reprinted in Hume Brown, *Early Travellers*, pp. 104-31, and the passage here quoted occurs on p. 112.

internal stability and external security: manpower was no longer dissipated in domestic feud, the perpetual state of warfare on the Borders had ceased, the royal writ was earning respect even in the Highlands and Isles, landowners and tenants were becoming more secure, farmers could sow and harvest with confidence, sheep and cattle could graze in safety. Social life was shifting onto a firmer basis. There was still poverty, but mass famine and mass destruction were slipping into the mists of memory.

II

ENTERPRISE AND EXPANSION

THE BASES OF ECONOMIC GROWTH

There is general agreement among historians that between the reign of Henry VIII and the Civil War England experienced industrial changes so considerable that the more courageous writers—following the lead of Professor Nef—now employ the caption "Industrial Revolution" beneath their picture of economic affairs in this period. The strong centralised government of the Tudors and early Stuarts gave England internal stability and a positive economic policy. The impact of the Reformation, on both thought and the distribution of material wealth, strengthened the drive towards capital accumulation and weakened the shackles on enterprise. The great upward heave of prices, coupled with the abundance of labour, encouraged the producer of goods by the prospect of higher gain.

The extent to which the same kind of stimuli operated in Scotland can be determined only in part. The statistical material is quite inadequate for any close analysis of the financial rewards to enterprise, and comparison with England must, therefore, proceed on more general lines. In one important respect the timing of the expansive phase was inevitably different, for—and it must be a recurrent theme in this book—it was not until the later part of the reign of James VI that Scotland attained any real degree of internal political stability; indeed from the point of view of political life the Scotland of the sixteenth century is more comparable to the England of the Wars of the Roses than to the England of Elizabeth I. As Sir James Fergusson pointed out in the Andrew Lang Lecture at St Andrews in 1956, but for the names of the characters, Shakespeare's *Macbeth* might have been regarded as a tragedy set in the Scotland of the sixteenth century.

The relationship between political conditions and economic progress was not far removed from that which Hobbes was to analyse in his *Leviathan* of 1651. What, he said, is consequent to any time of open conflict is similarly consequent to any time when men live with no security other than their own strength. "In such condition there is no place for Industry; because the fruit thereof is uncertain; no commodious building; no Instruments of moving; . . . and the life of man . . ."[1]—but to complete the familiar quotation might be to press the analogy too far. This internal instability and external insecurity was recognised by sapient Scotsmen as the curse of their land. Thus in *The Dreme of Schir Dauid Lyndesay* the poet asks:

> Quhat is the cause our boundris bene so bair?

and:

> Quhareof dois proceid our pouertie?

And the inevitable answer follows: lack of good government, lack of universal justice, and the threat of war. Scotland was later than most of her neighbours in offering the elementary conditions for economic growth, and in devising a national economic policy powerful enough to overawe sectional interests yet positive enough to stimulate enterprise.

An attempt to assess the impact of the Scottish Reformation on the rate and character of economic growth involves some consideration of both its material and its ideological aspects. It is a reasonably secure proposition that the secularisation of Church property—a potent force for change in England—was, in the short run at least, less decisive in Scotland. On the eve of the Scottish Reformation the Church still predominated among the owners of land—some would put her share at almost one-half[2]—but the working relationship between the Church and the tillers of the soil was far removed from the textbook medieval pattern. A substantial part of Church property was held *in commendam* by a relatively small number of men, many of whom were merely titular clerics; and, since the levying of the "great tax" under James V, ecclesiastical owners had

---

[1] T. Hobbes, *Leviathan, or the Matter, Forme and Power of a Commonwealth*, 1946 edn., p. 82.

[2] A. R. Macewen, *A History of the Church in Scotland*, 1913, VOL. I, p. 413.

C

resorted increasingly to feuing as a device for raising money.[3] Under the original Reformation settlement of 1561-2, one-third of the revenue of the Old Church was allocated to the Crown and the New Church, while the remaining two-thirds were left with the "auld possessouris" for life—two-thirds for the Devil and one-third between God and Devil, as Knox summarised it.[4] As the old possessors died off, their titles were granted by commendation or some similar arbitrary arrangement to the nobles who happened to be in royal favour at the moment. "Commendations," Dr Grant writes, "might be likened to a sort of medium of exchange in the struggle for power,"[5] and much of the old ecclesiastical property certainly changed hands often as families rose and fell in royal favour. In short, stability of ownership, essential for economic development, was conspicuously absent, and it was only after the legislation of 1587 that any improvement in conditions of tenure became even likely.

In the opinion of an impressive body of historical writers, these direct material results of the Reformation were less influential than the contemporary spread of the "Protestant ethic." The specific question is easily put: how far did the Calvinist character of the Reformed Church facilitate—or even encourage—the spread of private capitalism? Archdeacon Cunningham, who liked neither capitalists nor Presbyterians, had no doubts about the answer. "Calvinism," he wrote, "is a form of Christianity which gave its sanction to the free exercise of the commercial spirit and to the capitalist organization of industry"; and again: "The strict ecclesiastical discipline, which was reared in Scotland, does not appear to have been much concerned with attempting to check extortion or greed of gain."[6] The Scottish ministers, it has been argued, culled the Book of Proverbs for texts to justify capitalism; they tolerated harsh systems of poor relief and impressment of

[3] R. K. Hannay, "On the Church lands at the Reformation," in *Scottish Historical Review*, henceforth cited as *S.H.R.*, XVI (1919), p. 53.
[4] Knox, *History of the Reformation in Scotland*, ed. W. C. Dickinson, 1949, VOL. II, p. 29; *R.P.C.*, VOL. I, introduction, p. cxvii.
[5] I. F. Grant, *Social and Economic Development of Scotland before 1603*, henceforth cited as *Social Development*, 1930, p. 240.
[6] I have drawn here on W. Cunningham, *The Growth of English Industry and Commerce*, VOL. II, PART I, 1919; M. Weber, *The Protestant Ethic and the Spirit of Capitalism*, 1930; and especially on H. M. Robertson, *Aspects of the Rise of Economic Individualism*, 1935.

labour into conditions of virtual slavery; they were more concerned with the suppression of promiscuous dancing than with the promotion of social justice; they came dangerously near to identifying prosperity with godliness.

To all these charges there are answers. Knox himself, far from condoning the exploitation of the poor, explicitly stated that the poor (along with the ministers) "must be sustened upoun the chargeis of the Churche"; and he went on to condemn those who had oppressed "the lauboraris and manuraris [tillers] of the ground."[7] It can, indeed, be maintained that the failure of the Reformed Church to implement these charitable injunctions lay in its financial incapacity, not in its harshness of doctrine. Its attitude to usury is perhaps a more useful test. This is a theme which cuts across the activities of both Church and State, and we shall return to it later in our consideration of policies: suffice it here to say that the Scots ministers learned their Calvinism from progressive Continental communities where free use of money was the heartbeat of business life. Calvin's own attitude to usury was far from one of unqualified approval,[8] and though the Scots ministers took no firm stand against interest payments in respectable commercial circles, they were not condoning something peculiar to Scotland or to any comparable nation.

Indeed according to its apologists, Presbyterianism contributed little, and that only indirectly, to the economic expansion of Scotland. Honesty in business transactions, it is said, was encouraged by the watchful eye of the Kirk Session, and the intimacy which it assured enabled men to form a more exact estimate of the credit-worthiness of their neighbours. By its educational activities—on which Knox put great stress[9]—the Kirk helped to develop the abilities of the youth of the land, thus improving their prospects in the professions and in business. But the once-popular facile theory of the wholesale encouragement of private capitalism by the Calvinist Churches has been sadly buffeted: indeed—for Scotland at any rate—a diametrically opposite theory can be advanced. Thus W. L. Mathieson, after citing instances of the Scottish ministers'

---

[7] *The Works of John Knox*, ed. D. Laing, Wodrow Society, 1846, VOL. II, p. 221.
[8] J. Calvin, *De usuris responsum*, Geneva edn. 1617, col. 488.
[9] Knox, *Works*, VOL. II, pp. 208-12.

protests against trade with Iberia, their attitude to the export of food, their attempt to make Monday a holiday so that the Sabbath might be kept holy, and their efforts to establish fasts, concludes that "such a Church can hardly claim to have promoted the interests of trade." On the contrary, he says, "the religious spirit . . . was the most serious of all obstacles to industrial progress."[10]

There is danger in all branches of historical study in relying over-much on the microscope. The Reformation was itself of such magnitude that its lasting effects must be sought rather in the panorama. So Carlyle, in his lecture on "The Hero as Priest": "This that Knox did for his Nation, I say, we may really call a resurrection as from death. . . . The people began to live . . . Scotch Literature and Thought, Scotch Industry; James Watt, David Hume, Walter Scott, Robert Burns; I find Knox and the Reformation acting at the heart's core of every one of these persons and phenomena; I find that without the Reformation they would not have been."[11] But in the present study our range is limited and our vision myopic: it would be hard to demonstrate that the integrative and stimulating force of Presbyterianism had much effect on the material life of Scotland down to the death of King James VI.

Until the last twenty-five years of his reign the rate of change in the economy of Scotland was seriously retarded by recurrent pestilence and famine. Of the second half of the sixteenth century, Barbé calculated that plague years in the aggregate "covered at least a third of the whole period," and went on: "pestilence and dearth must be taken into account as one of the main causes to which the poverty of the country must be attributed."[12] We have already considered the intensity and frequency of famine. The relevant deductions here are that famine normally involved the diversion of scarce currency to the buying of food overseas; it invariably meant high prices for foodstuffs and a consequent fall in demand for other goods: it plunged the community into pessimistic gloom, sapping confidence and destroying initiative. Even if every other factor is

---

[10] W. L. Mathieson, *Politics and Religion, a Study in Scottish History 1550-1695*, 1902, VOL. I, pp. 202-3.

[11] T. Carlyle, *Heroes and Hero Worship*, World's Classics edn., 1904, p. 146.

[12] L. A. Barbé, *Sidelights on the History, Industries, and Social Life of Scotland*, 1919, p. 305.

favourable, hunger and sickness will kill industrial enterprise. The one factor continuously favourable was the abundance of manpower, though just how great the population was nobody can say: estimates for 1550-1600, for example, range from half a million to a million.[13] Contemporaries, especially in the later years of James VI, had no doubts either about the abundance of people or of their increase. In the 1580's L. von Wedel had observed that the Scots "have children without number,"[14] but it needed a Scot to say why. "Our women," wrote Sir Thomas Craig in 1605, "do not indulge themselves with wine, exotic foodstuffs and spices from distant lands, so harmful to the womb, hence the more readily do they conceive."[15] Twenty years later Sir William Alexander, though less explicit on the biological causes, was no less confident about the buoyancy of Scotland's population;[16] and these contemporary opinions are reinforced by the later calculations of William Kennedy, who, employing local baptismal and burial registers, calculated that the natural increase at Aberdeen between about 1560 and the early 1600's was of the order of thirty per cent.[17]

Furthermore it is significant that, in spite of mortality from plague, famine, and violence, we hear persistently in the sixteenth century of a surplus of labour in the country. The prevalence of pauperism, a recurrent theme in the works of the sociologist-poets of the period, is proved by the attention paid to it by both the burghs and Parliament.[18] The unruly vagrants and the fearsome beggar bands, familiar to students of Elizabethan England, had their counterpart in the "idill lymmaris and harlottis falslie calling thame selffis egiptianis,"[19] who roamed Scotland, extorting food and money, robbing and threatening, and bringing panic to isolated farms and clachans.

The data are inadequate for any definitive statement of the

[13] E.g. in G. N. Clark, *The Seventeenth Century*, 1931, p. 8; P. Hume Brown, *Scotland in the time of Queen Mary*, 1904, p. 52.

[14] "Journey through England and Scotland in the years 1584 and 1585," printed in *Transactions of the Royal Historical Society*, IX (1895), pp. 223-70.

[15] *De unione*, p. 416.

[16] Sir Wm. Alexander, *An Encouragement to Colonies*, 1624, reprinted in *Royal Letters, Charters, and Tracts relating to the Colonization of New Scotland and the Institution of the Order of Knights Baronets of Nova Scotia, 1621-1638*, henceforth cited as *Nova Scotia Charters*, ed. D. Laing, Bannatyne Club, 1867, pp. 38 ff.

[17] Kennedy, *Annals of Aberdeen*, p. 188.

[18] G. Nicholls, *A History of the Scotch Poor Law*, 1856, pp. 6-7.

[19] Act anent Beggaris, 1593. *Acts of the Parliament of Scotland*, henceforth cited as *A.P.S.*, VOL. IV, ed. T. Thomson, 1816, pp. 42-3.

economic well-being of the working population. That the pure
wage-earner represented only a small fraction needs little emphasis: most family men had some source of income other than
the money wage, indeed in some sectors of the community the
money wage itself was the exception. Furthermore even where
the cash nexus was normal, the prevalence of piece-work makes
exact comparison difficult. What, for example, was represented
in terms of hours and effort by the £2. 0s. 0d. paid in 1607 by
the Edinburgh Dean of Guild to "ane man for bering of the
lyme to the Stepil upon his heid"?[20] Where wages were by the
day or week and comparison is possible, some suggestive differ-
entials emerge. Thus between about 1560 and the early 1600's
the top-grade craftsmen of Edinburgh seem to have enjoyed a
threefold increase in money wages. The supply of skill in the
working of stone and metal had not outrun the demand for it.
On the other hand the unskilled, the victim of abundant labour
supply, increased his money wage over the same period by no
more than about sixty per cent.

If we set these movements in money wages alongside contemporary trends in the price of such essentials as bread, candles
and beer, the deduction can be made that whilst the purchasing
power of the skilled underwent little significant change, that of
the unskilled deteriorated substantially. In theory these conditions should have stimulated the expansion of industries
employing low-grade labour, and should have encouraged
parents to apprentice their offspring to skilled trades.

The concept of the "economic man" implied in this kind of
reasoning is, however, of limited validity in relation to the
Scotland with which we deal. Sir Thomas Craig, unwilling as
he was to decry his own people, admits that "our Countrymen
choose to live in idleness, nay even in poverty, than to apply
themselves to any gainful Trades; because by dealing in them
they falsely reckon the honour of their Birth to be impaired and
stained."[21] Twenty years later, Sir William Seyton similarly
emphasised the strength of this mental barrier to economic
expansion. In his report to the Scottish Council in 1623 on the

[20] The following details of payments are drawn from *City of Edinburgh Old
Accounts*, VOL. I, *Bailies' Accounts 1544-66*, ed. R. Adam, 1899; VOL. II, *Dean of
Guild's Accounts 1552-67*, ed. R. Adam, 1899; and from *Edinburgh Records*, VOL. VI,
especially App. XXI.
[21] Sir T. Craig, *The Right of Succession to the Kingdom of England*, 1703 edn., p. 429.

development of manufactures, he said that hitherto the country had forgone "the benifeitt thairof almaist in the greattest pairt by our sluggishness . . . not being ashamed to mak our countrey be called poore."[22]

Yet in a very real sense this disinclination to apply the nation's abilities to regular industrial employment was no more than a symptom of the chronic malady of internal instability from which Scotland had long suffered. In spite of the opposition which his religious policies aroused, the adult James VI went a long way towards effecting a cure. The power of the Scottish Crown, which we shall examine more fully in the next chapter, was never more effective than between the Union of the Crowns and the death of King James. Always more at home with the pen than with the sword, James's attitude towards his great subjects became notably more resolute when he could address them from the safety and comfort of Theobalds, three hundred English miles south of the Border.

By the early 1600's a measure of respect was at last being extracted even from the "peccant" parts of the kingdom—the Isles, the Highlands, and the Borders. Thus though the attempt in 1598 to overawe the MacLeods of Lewis by the planting among them of a group of Fife lairds came to nothing, in 1610 the island was granted to Seaforth who resolutely set about the peaceful development of its fisheries.[23] Almost simultaneously the Band of Icolmkill (Iona), to which the chiefs were induced to agree, provided a basis for a more orderly way of life in the Western Isles generally, and promised to terminate the chaos which had existed there since the overthrow of the traditional Lordship in 1494. On the Highland fringe, the MacGregors, whose geographical location made them a potential threat to the Lowlands, were outlawed after the Battle of Glen Fruin in 1603. As we shall see in a later chapter on relations with England, within two decades after 1603 the special problem of the Borders ceased to exist. The thoroughness of this process of pacification must not be exaggerated. The feuds of centuries did not evaporate overnight; loyalty to clan or family was not suddenly displaced by loyalty to King;

---

[22] *R.P.C.*, VOL. XIII, pp. 773-7.
[23] W. C. Mackenzie, "The Fife Adventurers," in *The Book of the Lews*, 1919, pp. 55 ff.; and id. *History of the Outer Hebrides*, 1922, p. 293.

yet this resolute move towards a more stabilised and centralised society clearly established an environment more favourable towards economic development.

It is, furthermore, of obvious significance that after the turn of the century natural conditions were generally more favourable. Mortality was certainly heavy in 1607-8[24] with a new scourge which baffled the physicians but which—if a contemporary Dundonian's account is accurate—must have been typhus;[25] rough weather and floods in the autumn of 1621[26] ushered in two years of domestic crop shortages.[27] But on the whole those who grew to manhood in the last two decades of King James's reign knew little of the threats to life which had darkened the previous generation. The crude test is the state of the grain market. In the 1590's annual shipments of grain by Scotsmen from the east Baltic had averaged 563 lasts a year; for 1601-10 the corresponding average was 211, and for 1611-20 only 111;[28] and even when imports were required the cost was moderate. Good Prussian rye, which had been 175 guilders a last in the later 1590's and was to be 190 guilders in 1624, was selling in Amsterdam in many of the intervening years at 100 guilders or less,[29] and as we shall see in Chapter III this adequacy of grain supply was reflected in the unwonted steadiness of bread prices in the Scottish burghs. As, therefore, Scotland was faced with no serious external payments for grain, and as in some years she had a surplus for export, her overseas trading position was immediately strengthened. Furthermore —and perhaps more importantly—as the spectre of famine withdrew, men's hearts were lightened, their confidence was enlarged, and their vision widened.

Simultaneously we can detect a quickening and a broadening of the mental activities of the nation. In the generation which spanned the Scottish Reformation the keenest brains had been occupied in religious and religio-political controversy; but by

[24] For evidence of its impact on a single town see A. Maxwell, *The History of Old Dundee, narrated out of the Council Register*, 1884, pp. 372-80.
[25] Peter Goldman, "Margaretae Iacchae matris suae . . . Lachrymae," printed in *Delitiae Poetarum Scotorum*, 1627. Also R. C. Buist, "Peter Goldman's Description of the Desolation of Dundee," in *British Medical Journal*, 12 March, 1927.
[26] Calderwood, *History of the Kirk of Scotland*, VOL. VII, p. 513.
[27] *R.P.C.*, VOL. XII, pp. 598-9, 605, 703; VOL. XIII, p. 129.
[28] *Sound Toll Registers* for the years quoted.
[29] N. W. Posthumus, *Inquiry into the History of Prices in Holland*, Leiden 1946, VOL. I, p. 573.

1600 attention was shifting to wider fields: secular, academic, and utilitarian. The state of the educational institutions provides a touchstone. Though Knox's laudable plans for universal schooling did not at once receive the statutory backing they deserved, the Church herself took steps—for example at the General Assemblies of 1563 and 1571—for the "planting" of schools in the northern counties, and elsewhere schools were founded or revived from the wreckage of the Reformation.[30] The spirit was even more manifest in the vitality of university life. St Andrews, the witness of blood and fire in the days of Beaton and Wishart, resumed its proper function as a fount of pure scholarship under George Buchanan and Andrew Melville, for as Mr Cant writes, "if there is controversy about Melville as a churchman, there can be none about him as a scholar and educationalist."[31] The humane influence of St Andrews was diffused through the land. It sent Robert Rollock to institute classes in the new College in Edinburgh, founded in 1582 and later to acquire university status. Managed by the Burgh Council, the Edinburgh College stimulated immense local pride and quickly attracted substantial local financial support.[32] Though—in common with most young institutions —it suffered from a rapid turn-over of staff (one Regent of Humanity had to be deposed for "furnicatioun"), the Edinburgh College was being actively developed in the early 1600's with the building of a library and the creation of additional teaching posts in divinity, mathematics, and metaphysics. At Glasgow, where the University had survived the Reformation in poor shape with a handful of students at loggerheads with the town, a series of benefactions from the 1570's onwards made possible the appointment of more regular teachers, and, as at Edinburgh, considerable building work was afoot in the early 1600's.[33] Similarly at Aberdeen the grounds and properties of the pre-Reformation friars were devoted in 1593 to the foundation of Marischal College, a supplement and independent rival to the older King's.[34]

[30] J. Grant, *History of the Burgh and Parish Schools of Scotland*, 1876, pp. 78-80. For a specific instance see *Kirkcaldy Records*, p. 71.
[31] R. G. Cant, *The University of St Andrews*, 1946, p. 55.
[32] A. Grant, *The Story of the University of Edinburgh*, 1884, VOL. I, Ch. IV *passim*; *Edinburgh Records*, VOL. VI, pp. 135, 138, 155.
[33] J. D. Mackie, *The University of Glasgow*, 1954, pp. 87-8.
[34] G. D. Henderson, *The Founding of Marischal College*, 1947.

"It is significant," writes Professor Nef, "that Kepler, who must have known of James I's visit to the observatory of Brahe in Denmark in 1590, should have thought enough of the king's scientific interests to dedicate to him *De harmonice mundi* in which the great scientist announced his third law of motion."[35] The secular and practical application of intellectual effort is illustrated—on different moral planes—by the work of men such as Napier of Merchiston and Alexander Seton. Napier's logarithms and his multiplication device (commonly called "Napier's bones") represented major aids to the further progress of science and mechanics, which, by 1600, was impeded by the complexity and labour of numerical calculations. In mechanical ingenuity, Napier's proposals at least echo those of Leonardo himself. The list of his "secrett inventionis, proffitabill and necessary for defence of this Iland," shows that in the 1590's he had devised such formidable instruments of war as a mirror capable of burning enemy ships at a great range, a war chariot with a revolving gun turret, and a piece of artillery which, when tested in a field in Scotland, killed all the livestock in the vicinity.[36] Seton, the alchemist, left his native Fife in 1602 to blaze a gilded trail from Holland to Poland. Everywhere the story was the same: the heated crucible containing base metal, the pinch of mysterious powder added by Seton, the residue of pure gold. Imposter he must have been, but nobody in the history of alchemy ever imposed more brilliantly.[37]

On a level of fame only slightly lower were Napier's fellow-workers in the realm of mathematics: John Craig, who also communicated with the famous Danish astronomer Tycho Brahe; and James Hume, who apparently originated the story that Napier was driven to mathematics by gout. With Kinloch, Low, Liddell, and others Scottish medicine too was, by 1600, becoming a specialised craft with a scientific bias. Thus Kinloch's *De hominis procreatione* makes him the first Scottish writer on obstetrics, though like most of his contemporaries his medical skill had been acquired in Paris or Leiden.[38] Legal

[35] J. U. Nef, "The genesis of industrialism and modern science," in *Essays in Honor of Conyers Read*, ed. N. Downs, 1953, p. 253.
[36] W. R. MacDonald, *The Construction of Logarithms*, 1889, p. xv; M. Napier, *Memoirs of John Napier of Merchiston*, 1834.
[37] E. J. Holmyard, *Alchemy*, 1957, pp. 218-27.
[38] R. C. Buist, "Dr David Kinloch (Kynalochus) 1559-1617," in *British Medical Journal*, May 1926; A. H. Millar, *Roll of Eminent Burgesses of Dundee*, 1887, pp. 92-4.

studies were also advancing on specialised lines. Sir Thomas Craig, on whose political works we draw frequently, is in fact distinguished primarily for his *Jus feudale*; and William Welwood's *The Sea Law of Scotland* was the first independent treatise on this branch of law written in Britain, preceding Selden by a generation.[39] Deep and irrational prejudices certainly remained—one need only cite the attitude towards witchcraft—but over a wide range intellectual movement was free and fertile. The personification of that freedom, Thomas Urquhart of Cromarty, was growing towards manhood in the closing years of King James.[40] His energies swinging effortlessly from mathematics via a translation of Rabelais to a plan for a universal language, he died, wholly appropriately, in a fit of uncontrollable mirth on hearing the news of the restoration of Charles II.

Like Napier and Seton, Urquhart came from the ranks of the lairds and landed gentry, to whom the more stable political conditions offered a release from anxiety and an opportunity for wider activities. Direct economic results can be detected when progressive members of these classes added industrial enterprise to their traditional landholding function. We shall see later how great landed families were prominent in coal-mining; how Archibald Campbell, brother of the laird of Lawers, was involved in a herring-curing project; how Lord Erskine actively employed a patent for leather-tanning; and how Sir George Hay established glassmaking and iron-smelting works. In a closely allied field of enterprise, the land-owner might provide the initiative: thus in 1612 the Burgh Council of Edinburgh, "understanding that my lord Merchell [Marischal] hes begun ane guid wark in making of ane sub-stantious bulwark at the Staynehyve [Stonehaven] verray proffitabill to all sailleris," and hearing that Aberdeen had contributed generously thereto, authorised a grant of 400 merks from Edinburgh's own funds.[41]

On balance the corporate burghs, both individually and as members of the Convention of Royal Burghs, were heavily on the side of conservatism. By and large the townsman had his capital tied up in goods, houses, or ships; his economic thinking

[39] Scottish Text Society, *Miscellany Volume*, 1933, pp. 38-80.   [40] J. Willcock, *Sir Thomas Urquhart of Cromartie*, 1899.   [41] *Convention Records*, VOL. II, pp. 302, 320.

was encased in tradition; neither mentally nor financially was he equipped for great adventures. There were, of course, a few exceptions. Thus a string of entries in the Edinburgh Council Register for the years around 1620 reveal the progress of a purely local project, sponsored by the town and pretty generously supported, to establish a manufactory of fine woollen stuffs at St Paul's Work.[42] It was nothing if not ambitious, for, guided by a few foreign weavers and manned by selected paupers, the manufactory was intended to produce cloth to displace the imports from the highly-skilled textile towns of the Low Countries.

More conspicuously there were occasional townsmen, who, coming from the most conventional burghal background, tore ruthlessly through the conventional barriers against private enterprise. Nathaniel Udward (often "Uddert" to his neighbours) typifies this spirit.[43] Son of a former provost of Edinburgh, he outraged the town by failing to enter himself on the burgess roll and by insisting on living in the socially inferior Leith—in the eyes of Edinburgh a mean uncultured outport. His name crops up with almost unfailing regularity in connexion with the various industrial monopolies in the last two decades of the reign of James VI, especially in the controversies over the soap monopoly, where his determined individualism was most sharply demonstrated. When powerful burghal protests against his monopoly of the home market threatened to reopen the ports to soap from the Low Countries, he secured from the crown a reversion of the office of Conservator of the Staple at Veere and thereupon "delt with the soapemen thair that they sould sell no soape bot to him," to the end that he "micht exact from his Ma. liedges quhat prices he list."

The burghs did not mince their words. In a statement of grievances to the Privy Council in 1624, they related how Udward had been bankrupt "for great soumes of money" and had suffered imprisonment for debt at Bordeaux, being released only by the compassion of his creditor; how he never settled to any trade like a respectable burgess, but was "lyke ane rolling stone now heir now thair leiving upoun projects";

---

[42] *Edinburgh Records*, VOL. VI *passim*; *R.P.C.*, VOL. XII, p. 337.
[43] Udward's activities can be traced through *R.P.C.*, VOLS. VIII-XIII, and through *Edinburgh Records*, VOL. VI, especially App. XXXIII.

how he had secured the appointment at Veere without the burghs' approval; how, within a few weeks of appointment, he was in financial trouble, bringing the high office of Conservator into disrepute. Nevertheless Udward had the better of them. His title as Conservator was legally valid, and it cost the burghs 6,000 merks to persuade him to give it up. Perhaps he was an anachronism, perhaps his plausible tongue and ready money commanded the ear of the King. Certainly he was—in Burns's phrase—the man of independent mind, at once an irritant and a stimulant.

In all industrial techniques Scotland had much to learn, and the nations with which she had old-established contacts had much to teach. The inflow of foreign skill, and of some foreign capital, was not surprisingly a concomitant to each surge of domestic enterprise. Since the early years of the sixteenth century Germans, Flemings, Frenchmen, and Englishmen had brought to Scotland their skills in the mining of precious metals, and, less readily perhaps, their capital for mining and extractive enterprises. A wide variety of foreign talent entered Scotland from the 1590's to the Civil War. Thus Erskine's tannery project hinged on the skill of English immigrant craftsmen; Udward proposed to bring in Dutch weavers to demonstrate improved methods of linen weaving; in 1604 Alexander Hunter was sent "in name of the haill burrowis to Ingland and to the Law Cuntreyes . . . for hamebringing of Flemyngs and utheris for making of braid claithe . . . and uther stuffis sic as ar maid in Flanderis of our Scottis woll."[44] In 1618 William Dickson, "indweller of Delph," arrived in Edinburgh and offered to bring five more families of wool-cloth makers;[45] as we shall see English skill was employed by Hay in his iron-works; and a Venetian expert was imported to advise on glass-making. In the 1580's and '90's Eustatius (or Gustathius) Roghe or Roche, a Flemish "medicinar," bestrides the realm of Scottish industrial enterprise almost as manfully as Udward a generation later. We shall encounter him in precious metal mining and in salt production; he had a "skilful disposition" to "excogitat" various devices for saving fuel;[46] and his success in persuading Dundee brewers and dyers to pay a royalty for the use of his

[44] *Convention Records*, VOL. II, pp. 107-9, 117.
[45] *Edinburgh Records*, VOL. VI, pp. 198-202.   [46] *A.P.S.*, VOL. IV, p. 187.

new furnace suggests a bargaining ability of no mean order.[47]
It was through these foreign specialists that Scotland participated in the European advance in industrial technique.

THE INDUSTRIAL RESPONSE

For this purpose the manufacturing industries can be divided
into two groups: the traditional and the novel. Among the
traditional industries, cloth-making in its various branches has
obvious priority; for though, as we shall see in our studies of
external trade, Scotland was still mainly a producer of primary
goods, her coarse cloth had for a long time entered certain
European markets, and her gild and country cloth-makers met
most of the country's own day-to-day needs. The furtherance
of the wool cloth industry occupied the attention of all the
official bodies in both central and local government, and
though their policies were by no means invariably consistent or
compatible, the underlying industrial aims are apparent. An
adequate supply of raw material was a first essential; therefore
from time to time the export of raw wool was banned. The
native cloth was liable to "grite abuisses and imperfectiounes";
therefore alien craftsmen were imported to teach better
methods, and fresh regulations were made about quality and
quantity. The existing pattern of the industry was not always
sufficiently flexible for it to accept the new technique and
absorb the new craftsmen; therefore it was sometimes necessary, by licence or patent, to establish a new form of organisation. Some of the wool cloth was exported in the unfinished
state, and much of the linen as yarn; therefore attempts were
made to extend and improve the finishing trades and to reach
improved linen-weaving.

The better-informed contemporaries, such as Sir Thomas
Craig, realising the dangers of undue reliance on primary
goods as a means of purchasing imports, advocated the expansion of cloth production. The means to this end, as we
have just seen, were various and in general laudable, but their
application encountered serious difficulties. The existing
industry fell into two clearly defined sections: the burgh gilds
which generally made the better cloth, and the scattered
country weavers who generally made the coarser plaids and

[47] Maxwell, *History of Old Dundee*, pp. 285-6.

hodden grey. Both sections were riddled with traditional practices, both were suspicious of innovation at the hands of foreigners, and the town weavers especially were keenly jealous of their privileges. The experiment of bringing in Flemings—some via Norwich, some direct from Leiden—and spreading them over a number of cloth-making burghs was a typical failure; they were unhappy at being split up among strangers, their reception by the burgh authorities was often frigid, and the survivors seem to have re-congregated at Bonnington in 1609 and to have worked there as an isolated group.[48] There is, in brief, no indication that the Scottish textile industries were experiencing either the rapid technical improvement or the penetration of capitalist organisation which characterised the parallel industries in England in the Tudor period.

Nevertheless Scottish textile production as a whole constituted, by the Scottish standards of the time, an industry of considerable stature, which catered for the bulk of domestic requirements and which, in its chosen lines, was competing by the later years of James VI to an increasing extent in overseas markets. For wool manufacture Scotland had the initial advantage of an abundance of fleeces, though, if contemporary English opinion is to be trusted, the quality was low. Most of this wool was converted, by the most elementary processes, into one or other of the coarse fabrics which clothed the typical Scot and which penetrated outside markets, especially those of north-west Europe. Alternatively wool was made up into knitted goods by processes involving little more than the manual dexterity of the women. While knitted goods were primarily for home use, they appear regularly, and sometimes prominently, in the country's exports in the early 1600's as stockings, notably those which the 1612 Book of Rates called "woollen hois maid in Leith wynd."[49] By the 1620's various kinds of wool hose were being shipped from Leith alone at anything up to 13,000 or 14,000 pairs a year, many of them to England.[50]

The prominence of flax in the catalogue of goods imported

[48] T. Pagan, *The Convention of the Royal Burghs of Scotland*, 1926, pp. 207-8.
[49] Printed in *The Ledger of Andrew Halyburton, Conservator of the Privileges of the Scotch Nation in the Netherlands 1497-1503*, ed. C. Innes, 1867, p. 279.
[50] "The Entress of Ships, Guidis and Geir transportit at the port of Leith, 1627-28," MS in General Register House, Edinburgh.

from the Baltic indicates that linen manufacturing already occupied a prominent place in the Scottish economy. Importing merchants broke up bulk, parcelling out the lint in small lots to scores of local housewives. Thus in 1600 David Wedderburne, under the heading "The Compt of my Lynt and the selling thairof. Persons addebrit to me thairfor . . ." lists the parcels, mainly of two or three stones each, distributed to "Mr Alexander my brothers wyf," "David Strathauchin skipperis wyf," and twenty-four others, as well as a couple of broken packages kept for his own wife.[51] The yarn not required for local use was sold directly or indirectly to the gildsmen, in whose ranks there was already clear differentiation. Thus at Dunfermline in 1596 the Weaver craft distinguished between its prosperous members who bought yarn in quantity both for their own looms and for export, and the "remanent brethren" who were "heavily hurt and prejudiced" thereby.[52] Similarly some regional specialisation can be detected: in 1613 Dunfermline was making "good dornicks for table and bed";[53] but, to judge from the export records, the staple flax fabrics were harden, twill, and ticking. The last named, because of its very tight weave, was ideal for mattress and cushion covers; and as Scotland also had an abundance of feathers, it is not surprising that the making of cushions, bed coverlets, and the like, became a significant ancillary occupation.

A characteristic of all "mercantilist" states was an anxiety to broaden and diversify their industrial structure. Scotsmen were keenly aware of the need for this in their own land, but again implementation was hampered by suspicion, conservatism, and the conflict of interests. The scheme advanced by the ubiquitous Udward for the establishment of soap-works encountered these obstacles in full measure. Hitherto soap had been imported, mainly from the Low Countries and the Baltic, and Scotland as a whole had a poor reputation for cleanliness and hygiene. "The ladies," wrote a visitor in 1617, "are of opinion that Susanna could not be chaste, because she bathed so often";[54] and Brereton, twenty years later, had to hold his

[51] *Wedderburne Compt Buik*, pp. 161-2.
[52] D. Thomson, *The Weaver's Craft*, 1903, pp. 74-5.   [53] *Op. cit.*, p. 88.
[54] *A Perfect Description of the People and Country of Scotland*. The authorship is in some doubt; see A. Mitchell, *List of Travels and Tours in Scotland, 1296-1900*, 1902, pp. 44-5. The pamphlet is reprinted in Hume Brown, *Early Travellers*, pp. 96-103.

nose when he entered some of the buildings in Edinburgh.[55] Udward, in his application for a patent in 1619, was disposed to blame the soap rather than the people; for, he said, "strangeris . . . may not abide the stinken smell of the naprie and lynning clothes wachin with this filthie saip."[56] The patent of monopoly, permitting him to erect a soap-works at Leith, was followed in 1621 by a ban on imported soap, coupled with the prescription of maximum prices for that made in Scotland.[57] This experiment in controlled monopoly failed, however, to satisfy some of the influential burghs. Edinburgh complained about the damage done to its import trade, Dumfries complained against the cost of overland transport from Leith; and in response to these protests Udward's immunity from overseas competition was made conditional upon his ability to produce soap as good and cheap as that procurable in Flanders.[58]

The drive to establish glass-making, another sign of the growing urbanity of Scotland, is closely parallel to the contemporary attempts to raise the output and standards of the English glass industry. Both sand and kelp (from which alkali could be extracted) abounded around the Scottish coasts, and there are slender references to the production of fairly sophisticated glassware at Falkland as early as 1506-7.[59] The first step in the formal establishment of a glass industry was, however, delayed to the end of the sixteenth century, when a licence was granted to one of the Bowes family (Sir Robert Bowes was Elizabeth's ambassador to Scotland) who in 1592 also acquired the wide rights in England formerly held by Jacob Verzelini.[60] No evidence of actual manufacture under formal arrangements is forthcoming until the appearance of a second licencee, Sir George Hay (later the Earl of Kinnoull), whose rights were confirmed by Parliament in 1612.[61]

In glass, as in soap, the monopolist's first aim was to displace imports; and within a short time Hay's works at Wemyss (Fife)

[55] Sir W. Brereton, *Travels in Holland, the United Provinces, England, Scotland and Ireland, 1634-5*, henceforth cited as *Travels*, ed. E. Hawkins, Chetham Society, 1844, p. 103.
[56] *R.P.C.*, VOL. XII, p. 106.   [57] *Op. cit.*, VOL. XII, pp. 503-6.
[58] *Op. cit.*, VOL. XII, pp. 516-9; VOL. XIII, pp. 157, 162, 167, 294; *Convention Records*, VOL. III, pp. 163, 168, 172.
[59] *Accounts of the Lord High Treasurer*, VOL. III, pp. 161, 192.
[60] E. W. Hulme, "English glass-making in the sixteenth and seventeenth centuries," in *The Antiquary*, XXX (1894), pp. 210 ff.; XXXI (1895), pp. 68 ff.
[61] *A.P.S.*, VOL. IV, p. 515.

D

was making "braid" or window glass claimed to be as good as that hitherto imported from Danzig.[62] Bottles and table-glass presented greater technical problems: to help solve them specimens of English glass were procured as models,[63] and a Venetian craftsman was introduced to demonstrate the methods employed by the world's finest glass-makers.[64] The fairly substantial export of coarse drinking-glasses from Scotland to London in the mid 1620's suggests that the innovation had succeeded;[65] though as in England there was concern about the amount of wood fuel used by the glass-makers, and radical proposals were made for a general return to lattice windows and earthenware vessels.[66] Though the whole story is disappointingly obscure, one can only conclude that the coal-using furnace, which was certainly coming into use in England after about 1611, did not penetrate Scotland until considerably later. Nor is the subsequent history of the Wemyss works much clearer. It is known that Sir Robert Mansell, the English glass monopolist, was alarmed at Scottish competition; and in 1619 only a vigorous plea from the Scottish Privy Council prevented the English from classifying Scottish glass as "foreign" and so excluding it from English markets.[67] Mansell seems to have pursued the monopolist's recognised tactics: if you cannot exclude foreign competitors, buy them up. By some means he acquired control of the Wemyss plant, and it has been suggested that, to strengthen his English interests, he allowed Scottish production to fall off.[68]

It is a short mental step from drinking-glasses to their intended use. Notwithstanding the general popularity of wine —to which we shall return later—Scotsmen had long shown a liking for ale and beer. Small-scale brewing for domestic use went back to the brewhouses of medieval abbeys and castles: by 1598 Fynes Moryson found that "the better sort of citizens brew ale, their usuall drinke," which, he added, "will dis-

[62] *R.P.C.*, VOL. XII, pp. xv-xvii, 428, 439.
[63] *Op. cit.*, pp. 439-41.
[64] A. and N. L. Clow, *The Chemical Revolution*, 1952, p. 26.
[65] Exchequer and King's Remembrancer, Port Books, henceforth cited as Port Books, MSS in Public Record Office; E/190/31/5.
[66] J. A. Fleming, *Scottish and Jacobite Glass*, 1938, p. 5.
[67] J. U. Nef, *The Rise of the British Coal Industry*, 1932, VOL. I, p. 182.
[68] Clow, *Chemical Revolution*, p. 27.

temper a stranger's bodie."[69] Whether or not the stricture was justified, he was technically correct in speaking of ale, for this home-made drink was brewed without hops, and hitherto the genuine beer had been imported from England or the Continent. As a first step towards remedying this weakness in Scottish beverage production, Edinburgh in 1596 set up a Society of Brewers,[70] and in 1619 bought equipment from Danzig.[71] Within a few years hops were appearing among imports from England, and by the 1630's the "common brew-house" in Edinburgh was a local showpiece of considerable dimensions. According to Brereton it supplied the need of the city in both ale and beer and had the "greatest, vastest leads, boiling keeves [vats] and cisterns" he had ever seen.[72]

The evidence of other industrial innovations is largely fragmentary. Especially after the Reformation there was a striking increase in printing and publishing in the country—no less than nine Scottish editions of Sir David Lindsay's works appeared between 1558 and 1614[73]—and the establishment of paper-mills would seem a natural corollary. All we know, however, is that a paper-making licence for nine years was conferred in 1590 on Peter Groot Heres and his partners.[74] A small-scale pottery works, making jugs and butter-tubs, was established at Blackfaulds in 1595, and twenty years later "Lord Kinelevin" had a patent for making pots and clay pipes.[75] A single reference in 1619 indicates that sugar refining was at least contemplated.[76] Native production of munitions was the active concern of governments with "mercantilist" leanings: two patents were issued in 1617-18, for the making of sulphur, saltpetre, and powder, one to Walter Heddesley, the other to Andrew Gray;[77] and Professor Nef believes that gunpowder mills were operating in Scotland in the 1620's.[78] Nonetheless when the Burgh Council of Edinburgh was busy overhauling the town's defences in 1625 it arranged with Sir

---

[69] *An Itinerary Written by Fynes Moryson, Gent, . . . containing his ten yeares travell through . . . Germany . . . England, Scotland and Ireland,* henceforth cited as *Itinerary,* 1617. The references to Scotland, scattered in the original work, are mainly reprinted in Hume Brown, *Early Travellers,* pp. 80-90.
[70] *Edinburgh Records,* VOL. V, p. 213.
[71] *Op. cit.,* VOL. VI, p. 187.   [72] Brereton, *Travels,* p. 105.
[73] Mathieson, *Politics and Religion,* VOL. I, p. 208.
[74] *R.P.C.,* VOL. IV, p. 452.   [75] Clow, *Chemical Revolution,* p. 29.
[76] *R.P.C.,* VOL. XII, pp. 77, 91-2.   [77] *Op. cit.,* VOL. XI, pp. 275, 306, 322.
[78] Nef, *Rise of the British Coal Industry,* VOL. I, p. 185.

William Dick to procure powder to the value of £500 sterling "ather at Londoun or the low cuntreyis."[79] Tanning was much more widespread. Sir James Balfour's note,[80] under the year 1620, that "the first tanning of lether in Scotland begane this zeire by his Maiesties especiall directione," must relate to Lord Erskine's patent under which hides were tanned by "landward barkers" into what the burghs regarded as very inferior leather.[81] Tanning on a substantial scale had existed long before: the burgh records—notably at Inverness—are full of references to it, and before 1600 whole cargoes of bark were arriving at Scottish ports from England.[82]

The expansion of iron-smelting was retarded by the shortage of wood fuel and by the official policy of preserving woodlands. In the very early 1600's, for example, alarm was caused by a proposal to set up "irne mylnis" (blast furnaces) in the Highlands; in response legislation forbade the "making of irne mylnis in ony woddis or forrestis, or destroying the tymmer thairof." Commenting on this, the Privy Council said: "as we understand, their is not ane irne mylne within this cuntrey, and the little quantitie of irne that is maid heir is only wroght with scroggis [scrubwood], boughis, and brancheis . . . and cuttingis of tymmer which can serve no other use."[83] The implication —that iron was made in small "bloomeries"—is substantiated by quasi-archaeological investigations which have revealed many small sites of indeterminable age scattered throughout the Highlands.[84]

The one plant definitely established in our period was at Letterewe, where bog-ore and timber were both locally available. On this site Sir George Hay, the promoter of the Wemyss glass-works, established a colony of Englishmen skilled in making iron and casting guns, and through his influence in high places (he was to become Lord Chancellor of Scotland) he secured in the early 1600's exemption from the bans on the

---

[79] *Edinburgh Records*, VOL. VI, p. 284.
[80] *Annales of Scotland*, henceforth cited as *Annals*, in *Historical Works*, ed. J. Haig, 1825, VOL. II, p. 79.
[81] *Convention Records*, VOL. III, pp. 141-2; *R.P.C.*, VOL. XII, pp. 189-93.
[82] E.g. "Ane Buik contenand the Intress of Schippis . . . at ye port of Dundie," henceforth cited as Dundee Shipping Lists, printed up to 1618 in *Wedderburne Compt Buik*, and after 1618 in MS in Dundee City Archives.
[83] *A.P.S.*, VOL. IV, p. 408; Hume Brown, *Scotland before 1700*, pp. 274-5.
[84] W. Ivison Macadam, "Notes on the ancient iron industry of Scotland," in *P.S.A.S.*, IX (1887), pp. 89-131.

use of timber and a licence to sell his iron anywhere in the country regardless of established local trade practices.[85] As production expanded local ore proved insufficient, and supplies of haematite were imported, some from Ulverston in Cumberland. The iron from Letterewe is said to have been of high quality, but after 1621 there is no further documentary reference to the plant there, and the supposition is that it closed down on the expiry of Hay's lease in 1626.

The wide range of the established secondary metal trades is illustrated by the membership of a typical Hammerman Gild, in which the brethren might range from goldsmiths and pewterers via gunmakers and sword-slippers to plain blacksmiths. By 1600 the goldsmiths of Edinburgh, notably Heriot and Foullis, occupying small shops in the shadow of St Giles', were among the wealthy ones of the land, prominent royal creditors, and active in municipal affairs. Their craft, which had suffered with the Reformation, revived with the rising urbanity of the burgesses and re-entered the ecclesiastical market after the Act of 1617 which required each parish to provide itself with Communion plate.[86] The Scottish sword-slippers enjoyed so high a reputation that, without abusing history, Scott could make his armourer hero in *The Fair Maid of Perth* decline Errol's offer of "my good Spanish sword" and rely instead on a two-edged blade of his own forging. The origin of the famous Ferara swords presents a seemingly insoluble problem. They long remained in use—indeed one fell from the grasp of the dying Alastair Macdonald at Culloden—but of Andrea Ferara himself "nothing is certainly known . . . beyond the excellence of the blades that bear his mark."[87] The story of the cave workshop in the Highlands is—apparently— charming economic mythology. Against these traditions of sword-making must be set the solid fact that swords were still imported to Scotland: they appear in quantity in the Aberdeen Customs for 1614,[88] and small lots were often sent from London after the Union of the Crowns. In fact Scotland clearly failed

---

[85] *A.P.S.*, VOL. IV, pp. 515, 686. I am indebted to Dr I. F. Gibson for allowing me to read his unpublished Ph.D. thesis on the history of the Scottish iron and steel industry.

[86] *A.P.S.*, VOL. IV, p. 534. I. Finlay, *Scottish Gold and Silver Work*, 1956.

[87] J. Drummond and J. Anderson, *Ancient Scottish Weapons*, 1881, p. 19.

[88] Aberdeen Customs, King's College Library, MS M.70.

to achieve the normal "mercantilist" aim of self-sufficiency in armaments. There was talk of munition production, and it goes without saying that Nathaniel Udward had a patent in the 1620's;[89] but when the Bishops' War came in 1639 Scotland still looked to her familiar Continental sources for arms and munitions.

As later chapters will show, Scotland continued throughout our period to import a wide range of miscellaneous metal goods for civilian use. Nevertheless the rising level of imports of iron in the crude state, especially from Sweden in the opening decades of the seventeenth century, must reflect an increasing amount of smith-work in Scotland. Demand came from all elements of society: from the salt-master whose cash sales to the Dutch enabled him to install bigger iron evaporating pans; from the main towns, notably Edinburgh, where, according to Dr Marguerite Wood, municipal activity in building reached a level between 1603 and 1626 not surpassed until the late eighteenth century;[90] from, at the bottom of the scale, the housewife whose flax yarn paid for a new oatcake girdle from the smithy at Culross.

COAL AND SALT PRODUCTION

"In this country," wrote Estienne Perlin in 1552, "the people warm themselves with coals."[91] In so far as outcrop coal had been worked in the days before the Wars of Independence, coal-mining could be classed as a traditional element in the Scottish economy. Locally, especially in the Lowland districts familiar to foreign tourists, production from surface workings was considerable. Thus in the late 1540's the Queen's "maister coilyear" had an agreement with the lessee of the "larde of Caldouris heucht" near Stirling for the supply of coal at 16d. for as much as two horses could draw.[92] Kirkcaldy had regulations about taking coal from the burgh muir,[93] and there are

---

[89] *R.P.C.*, 2nd ser., VOL. II, p. 338.

[90] *Edinburgh Records*, VOL. VI, Introduction, pp. xxxii ff.

[91] E. Perlin, *Déscription des royaulmes d'Angleterre et d'Écosse*. Paris 1558. The English translation in *Antiquarian Repertory*, IV (1784) is reprinted in Hume Brown, *Early Travellers*, pp. 71-9.

[92] *Extracts from the Records of the Royal Burgh of Stirling, 1519-1666*, henceforth cited as *Stirling Records*, ed. R. Renwick, Scottish Burgh Records Society, 1889, p. 46.

[93] *Kirkcaldy Records*, p. 70.

similar references at Glasgow and elsewhere.[94] But it was not until well on in the reign of James VI that Scotland joined in the technical revolution in coal-mining already under way in England and Flanders. This involved the technique of deep mining, which called for relatively great capital resources and was therefore conditional on reasonable political stability. Exceptionally the initiative and capital came from a burgess—thus Thomas Hunter in 1609 sought the consent of the Edinburgh Burgh Council "to mak sinks and air hoillis for wynning of coill" at Newhaven[95]—but generally the mainspring was the landed proprietor, a Dundas, an Elphinstone, an Elcho, or a Bruce.[96] No other group in Scotland could have borne the time-lag and the risks inherent in deep mining, while the continuity of ownership from father to son and the political influence of these families gave the industry an enviable stability and strength.

The show-piece of Scottish mining, near Culross Abbey Church, was a starred item for every tourist in Scotland. Lord Walden, in 1614, "went touardis Culross to sie Sir George Bruce's coill workis"; unfortunately, "the wind being verie loude, he was exceiding seike at sea" on the way back to Edinburgh.[97] Three years later the King himself paid his celebrated visit when, according to legend, he suffered one of those visions of sudden death with which his apprehensive mind was haunted.[98] The next year, John Taylor, "alias the King's Majesties Water-Poet," was there and wrote a graphic description of the mine. This "unfellowed and unmatchable worke," as he called it, was distinguished by having two entries, one from the mainland, one from an artificial island built for the purpose in the Forth. The underground workings, which had then been operated for nearly thirty years, extended more than a mile below the bed of the river "with many

[94] *Extracts from the Records of the Burgh of Glasgow*, VOL. I, 1563-1642, henceforth cited as *Glasgow Records*, ed. J. D. Marwick, Scottish Burgh Records Society, 1876, p. 70.
[95] *Edinburgh Records*, VOL. VI, p. 56.
[96] R. W. Cochran-Patrick, *Early Records relating to Mining in Scotland*, henceforth cited as *Mining in Scotland*, 1878; Dundas Papers, in Historical Manuscripts Commission, *Third Report*, 1872, p. 414; Elphinstone Papers, in Historical Manuscripts Commission, *Ninth Report*, 1883, p. 195.
[97] "Progress of My Lord Walden's Journey in Scotland," printed in *Miscellany of the Bannatyne Club*, VOL. III, pp. 209-11.
[98] *Statistical Account of Scotland*, ed. Sir J. Sinclair, 1796, VOL. X, p. 144.

nookes and by-wayes." What a place, said Taylor, for the Gunpowder Plotters, or, better still, what a place for storing beer![99]

Deeper mining and greater output raised a whole series of problems of ventilation, drainage, and haulage. To some extent these were eased for British mine-owners by the great technical advances in Continental mining now made available in treatises such as Georg Agricola's *De re metallica* of 1567. At Culross the seepage of estuary water presented a special drainage problem, to overcome which Bruce installed a great horse-driven chain pump, on which thirty-six constantly moving buckets raised the water and discharged it onto surface conduits. An indication that surface transport was receiving attention in Scotland is provided in the application for a monopoly placed before the Privy Council by Thomas Tulloch in 1606.[100] Tulloch claimed that he had spent the greater part of his life among "uncouth nations," acquiring the knowledge of making and operating engines and works for the transport of coal. Very likely he had seen working examples of the kind of tramway for coal trucks illustrated in Muenster's *Cosmographia universalis* of 1550. The Council gave him the sole right to use his devices in Scotland provided they were of a type "nocht knawin in this kingdome at na tyme before."

But continued dependence on water-borne transport confined extensive mining to the coastlands of the Forth, south Fife and Ayrshire. An oblique indication of the value placed by the mine-owners on sea-borne trade is given by Sir James Balfour, who says that in 1621 those around the Forth "put markes and becons on all the crages and blind rockes upone ther auen charges."[101] All the evidence suggests that the overall volume of coal exports rose appreciably in the later sixteenth century and sharply in the generation before the Civil War; and Professor Nef's statistics,[102] while admittedly speculative, can be accepted as wholly consistent with other data:

Scottish Coal Exports (annual averages in modern tons)

1551-60	1,000
1591-1600	7,000
1631-40	60,000

[99] Hume Brown, *Early Travellers*, pp. 115 ff.
[100] *R.P.C.*, VOL. VII, p. 278-9.   [101] Balfour, *Annals*, VOL. II, p. 83.
[102] Nef, *Rise of the British Coal Industry*, VOL. I, p. 84.

The concentration of ownership in a few influential families encouraged concerted action, especially among the Lothians group, who, besides enjoying the usual export opportunities, had the great Edinburgh market at their doorstep. By manipulating their measures, so it was alleged before the Council in 1621, they applied price discrimination against local consumers. In November of the previous year, meeting at the house of Janet Lawson of Fawside "under pretext . . . to have dynnit with hir," they agreed that their prices should be "hichted" by a shilling a load and that henceforth they "sould all keepe ane constant and uniforme pryce"; but the Council denounced the ring and punished the leading participants.[103] On the other hand the owners generally were conspicuously successful in securing exemption from export restrictions, and through the Act of 1606 they secured legal sanction for a labour system in coal-mines and salt-pans which amounted to little short of serfdom.[104] The Act was but one of a series enabling employers to impress labour, and there are grounds for thinking that it was not strictly enforced until the time of the Civil War. Yet its very existence proves the political weight of the mine-owners, and it must have been a formidable stick for them to brandish in the face of recalcitrant labour.

The making of salt was closely linked in Scotland with the mining of coal. Both are traceable to small beginnings in the Middle Ages and both underwent rapid expansion in the later sixteenth century. Both occupied roughly the same coastal areas and were associated with landed estates; the availability of coal was a major element in the increase in salt-making; both coal and salt strengthened and diversified Scotland's exports. As we shall see in our survey of French trade, Scotland was a heavy salt importer; and the dislocations in the French salt industry in the later decades of the sixteenth century powerfully reinforced the urge to extend domestic production in Scotland. But the salt produced by traditional methods from the sea-water around the Scottish coasts was not a perfect substitute for Bay salt, for the presence of traces of muriated magnesia rendered it slightly bitter to the taste, so that fish- and flesh-curers were reluctant to use it. Furthermore, for

[103] *R.P.C.*, vol. xii, pp. 418, 434; Nef, *Rise of the British Coal Industry*, vol. ii, p. 394. [104] *A.P.S.*, vol. iv, p. 286.

reasons only too obvious to residents in Scotland, simple solar evaporation was normally incapable of producing salt on any commercial scale. The success of the Scottish industry in overcoming these disadvantages stemmed from the enterprise of a few individuals, who introduced better techniques and erected coal-fired evaporating pans on sites well adapted both for the supply of coal and for the despatch of salt to the main Scottish and foreign North Sea markets.

It is not surprising that Queen Mary, coming from a country where salt figured largely both in the national economy and in royal finance, immediately took steps to organise the industry in Scotland.[105] The recipient of her patent, an Italian named Angelo Manelio, was certainly importing workers and equipment in 1564, but his personal participation was brief and undignified. Vigorously pursued by the English for a debt he owed to a London merchant, he was bankrupt by the end of the year and, with a writ hanging over his head, he completed his disgrace in the eyes of the Queen by fighting a duel with one of the Court secretaries. Nevertheless the interest of the Crown in the salt industry was resumed by James VI, notably in his arrangement with Eustatius Roche in 1588.[106] Tempted by Roche's promise to make better salt and "griter quantity nor hes been bifore" by methods sparing of fuel, and to allocate a proportion of the profit to the Crown, James added a salt-making monopoly to the mining monopoly which Roche already held.

The successive salt monopolists, from Manelio in the reign of Queen Mary to Udward in the early days of Charles I, based their claims on the introduction of new techniques whereby quality and quantity of output would be improved and dependence on imports reduced, coupled with direct financial gain to the Crown by profit-sharing or royalties. As their effective participation was normally brief, and details are lacking, it is impossible to assess their individual contribution to the industry's expansion. Nevertheless the overall trend in output was clearly upwards. As early as the 1580's, when the English salt trade was in verbal turmoil over Thomas Wilkes's

---

[105] E. Hughes, *Studies in Administration and Finance, 1558-1825*, 1934, pp. 33-4, 39.
[106] *A.P.S.*, VOL. IV, pp. 156, 182.

patent, the threat of Scottish competition was a constant controversial weapon;[107] by the early 1600's the Dutch were substantial customers, and, especially after 1622, direct exports to the Baltic were rising fast. Within the industry itself the conventional division of the salt between the "masters" (the pan-owners) and the "makers" (the operatives) ensured that the home market, served by cadgers who bought from the makers, participated in the expanding production. The scale and technique of the industry in the mid-1630's is indicated by the observations of Sir William Brereton. At one salt-works near Edinburgh he saw iron evaporating pans 18 ft. long by 9 ft. broad—larger, he said, than the famous pans at Shields in England; and to express the multitude of pans along the coasts of the Forth and East Fife he piled "infinite" upon "innumerable."[108]

THE MINING OF PRECIOUS METALS

We are inclined to envisage the later sixteenth century as a period in which the economy of Western Europe was deluged by a glittering torrent of precious metal from Central and South America. As we shall show elsewhere, there is little evidence of this torrent having reached Scotland: indeed scarcity of bullion was a chronic problem to her rulers in both the sixteenth and the seventeenth centuries. It is not surprising, therefore, that strenuous if disjointed attempts were made to exploit such seams of gold and silver as lay within the country. The tradition of substantial amounts of Scottish gold having been found in the early sixteenth century, is, in large measure, substantiated both by contemporary writers and by the Mint records. Boece, for example, describes "ane riche mine of gold" in Clydesdale, though he says that by unskilful handling output had declined.[109] In 1540, 130 ounces of gold—"lucrati in mora de Craufurd et terris de Coreheid"—was coined into the famous bonnet pieces,[110] and about the same time a comparable quantity was used in making the Scottish Regalia.[111] It is

---

[107] Hughes, *Studies in Administration and Finance*, pp. 47-9; *Tudor Economic Documents*, VOL. II, p. 260.

[108] Brereton, *Travels*, p. 98.

[109] Hume Brown, *Scotland before 1700*, p. 80.

[110] "Account of James Kirkcaldy of Grange," printed in R. W. Cochran-Patrick, *Records of the Coinage of Scotland*, henceforth cited as *Coinage*, 1876, VOL. I, p. 60.   [111] *Op. cit.*, p. xlvii.

plain that the gold, on Crawford Muir at any rate, was alluvial, for Lesley says "we mycht esileir cal it a golde strand,"[112] and a letter of 1568 to the Governor of the English Company of Mines Royal refers to "Crawford Moor in Scotland where the gold washes are."[113]

The production of precious metals was a royal prerogative, but as Scotland lacked the native skills for prospecting and refining, her rulers were forced to call in foreigners and often foreign capital.[114] In 1526 a long-term grant of mining rights was made to a group of Germans and Dutchmen headed by Joachim Hochstetter, a man whose family prestige in Augsburg had almost rivalled that of the Fuggers and Welsers; and in 1539 further specialists were brought to Scotland from Lorraine. Crawford Muir was near enough to the Border for rumours of its gold to reach English ears, both through official channels and "through the rumour and bruit of Scotsmen in Carlisle upon the market days," and from Carlisle the name and fame of Crawford Muir reached the English and German mining prospectors in the Lake District.

Though the middle years of the sixteenth century were scarcely opportune for firm commercial agreements in Scotland, there was, by the 1560's, a good deal of official and unofficial prospecting. Thus, in 1566, Thurland (of the Company of Mines Royal) wrote to Cecil: "Sir, here has been with Mr Cornelius de Vos, a Scot and an English merchant, and brought in a napkin certain sand from Crawford Moor": he went to urge Cecil and Elizabeth to negotiate with the Scottish Queen lest she sell the rights to some "foreign prince or merchant strangers." After a survey of the hills of Clydesdale, de Vos returned to Edinburgh with specimens of gold, the allure of which was likened by a contemporary "unto a woman's eye, which intiseth hir joyes into hir bosome."

This was enticement not easily to be resisted. In 1568 de

---

[112] Lesley, *Historie*, p. 17.

[113] This and the subsequent extracts from the correspondence of members of the Company of Mines Royal are taken from M. B. Donald, *Elizabethan Copper*, 1955, pp. 85-8.

[114] The details are taken from S. Atkinson, *The Discoverie and Historie of the Gold Mynes in Scotland*, henceforth cited as *Gold Mynes in Scotland*, 1619, reprinted by the Bannatyne Club, 1825; and from W. R. Scott, *The Constitution and Finance of English, Scottish and Irish Joint-Stock Companies to 1720*, henceforth cited as *Joint-Stock Companies*, 1910, VOL. II, Div. IV, Sect. ii.

Vos obtained from the Regent Moray a nineteen-year licence for the Crawford Muir mines, sold his own shares in the English Company of Mines Royal, and formed a new company in Scotland.[115] Its five shareholders—de Vos and Petersen, who were aliens, and the other three who were Scots—raised £5,000 Scots, partly in money, partly in grain and meal; and by the autumn of the same year de Vos was writing to Daniel Hochstetter (son of the Joachim mentioned above) asking him to receive samples of gold dust via Dumfries Haven, to assay it, and to send him skilful workmen. Though in one month the company produced eight ounces of gold for the Mint, its ultimate success seems doubtful. At all events it was re-organised in 1576 under a fresh licence to Abraham Petersen, the same as had held shares in de Vos's company, and now justifiably known as "Grey-beard Petersen" for his ability to tie the ends of his beard round his waist.[116]

Virtual silence follows until 1583, when an entirely fresh grant was made bestowing almost all Scottish metal-mining rights on the Fleming, Eustachius Roche.[117] Within a few years he was exporting lead ore in fair quantity, but from the point of view of the Crown the grant was a plain failure. Roche failed to pay his royalties and by the early 1590's a number of suits was being entered against him, his reputation falling so low that his rights were annulled by Act of Parliament in 1592.[118] Instead a Crown Office, the "Mastership of the Mines," was established for the future control of the country's precious metal resources.

It is at this point that Bevis Bulmer, whose association with silver and lead in Scotland can be traced back to the later 1560's, becomes a central figure in gold prospecting. He does not appear in the *Dictionary of National Biography*, yet, in the words of H. M. Robertson, "in his own time he was the accepted Croesus amongst industrial speculators."[119] By 1597 he was associated in partnership with Thomas Foullis, the Edinburgh goldsmith, to whom James had granted a twenty-one-year monopoly of all mining rights in Lanarkshire.[120]

[115] Donald, *Elizabethan Copper*, p. 87.   [116] Scott, *Joint-Stock Companies*, p. 408.
[117] *A.P.S.*, VOL. III, p. 368.   [118] *Op. cit.*, p. 556.
[119] For details of Bulmer I have drawn heavily on H. M. Robertson, "Sir Bevis Bulmer," in *Journal of Economic and Business History*, IV (1931), pp. 101 ff.
[120] *A.P.S.*, VOL. IV, p. 84; *R.P.C.*, VOL. V, p. 117.

Bulmer established himself at Glengonner, where his house remained until the nineteenth century with an appropriate couplet carved in the masonry above the doorway:

> In Wanlock, Elwand, and Glengonar
> I wan my riches and my honour.

In these valleys around Leadhills he employed, in summertime, up to 300 men, and he certainly won a fair amount of gold, some of which was stolen and some—to better effect— made into a porringer with a laudatory inscription as a present for Queen Elizabeth.

His temporary withdrawal from Scottish gold prospecting at the end of the 1590's is entirely in character. Bulmer was restless; he normally had an assortment of irons in the fire and any fresh news might deflect him from one project to another. Perhaps he lost faith in a district where "the theeves that burst in . . . cutt his purse bottom cleane away"; more likely he was short of capital. At all events, after a phase of intense activity in England farming the sea-coal tax and propounding a grand design for reorganising the tin production of the Stanneries, he returned to Scottish affairs with a plan to provide new capital for gold-mining. In an audience with James he proposed the creation of twenty-four "Knights of the Golden Mynes," or "Golden Knights," each of whom should subscribe £300 sterling for the title and the honour. The King's English advisers seem to have killed the project: only one Knight was created, Sir John Cleypoole, though from this time (1604) Bulmer himself regularly appears as "Sir Bevis."[121]

According to Stephen Atkinson, author of the *Discoverie and Historie of the Gold Mynes in Scotland* and Bulmer's right-hand man in many of his undertakings, Bulmer accepted the rebuff with Christian resignation. Yet neither he nor James was prepared to abandon Scottish gold without another effort, and between 1603 and 1606 both Bulmer and George Bowes enjoyed a measure of financial support from the King while they dredged the burns on Crawford Muir and wrote disparaging letters about each other.[122] Bulmer was clearly the more accomplished in both forms of activity, and was still receiving

---

[121] Atkinson, *Gold Mynes in Scotland*, pp. 45-6. In *R.P.C.*, VOL. VIII, p. 23 he is "Sir Bewys Bilmure, knyght."
[122] Cochran-Patrick, *Mining in Scotland*, pp. 103 ff.

a royal subsidy in 1606 when a miner, Sandy Maund, carried to him a Leadhills a sample of "red metal" from Hilderstone, near Linlithgow. Once it had been assayed and proved rich in silver, Bulmer switched his activities from the possibility of gold to what seemed the certainty of silver.

Scottish silver production long preceded the Hilderstone discovery. Its history is inextricably interwoven with that of lead-mining. Lead ore occurred fairly widely, both in the hills of the mainland and in some of the Western Isles where, according to Donald Munro's survey of 1549, it was worked in Islay and Lismore.[123] Partly because of its extreme malleability and partly because of the relative scarcity of copper, lead was highly esteemed in its own right, and it is likely that much of the Scottish ore was reduced to sheet lead without regard to its possible silver content. Down at least to the early 1600's there was no equipment in Scotland for extracting silver from the ore,[124] and much of the lead ore exported from Scotland underwent the more sophisticated methods of refining known and practised in England and Flanders. The scale was considerable. Thus in 1562 John Acheson and his partners were authorised to export 20,000 stones of ore, and three years later the Earl of Atholl had a similar licence for twice that quantity from Glengonner and Wanloch.[125] That this was no passing phase is proved by the average annual value of "leid urris" exported between 1611 and 1614, which was almost as great as that of coal and nearly twice that of linen cloth.[126]

A new chapter in Scottish silver production opened with the discovery at Hilderstone. Once Bulmer heard of the new mines "he rested not," says Atkinson, "until he had named them, calling one pitt or schafte there, God's Blessing, because of the wonderful works of God that he had seene."[127] For a mining prospector, Bulmer was a singularly pious man. His original position at Hilderstone is difficult to determine because the property belonged to Sir Thomas Hamilton who, in 1607,

[123] Printed in Hume Brown, *Scotland before 1700*, p. 245.
[124] Scott, *Joint-Stock Companies*, p. 410.
[125] Cochran-Patrick, *Mining in Scotland*, pp. 4-9.
[126] *Report on the Manuscripts of the Earl of Mar and Kellie preserved in Alloa House*, Historical MSS Commission, 1904, henceforth cited as *Mar and Kellie Papers*, pp. 70-4. The table of Scottish exports is reprinted in Hume Brown, *Scotland in the Time of Queen Mary*, pp. 226-30.
[127] Atkinson, *Gold Mynes in Scotland*, p. 47.

became "Master of the Metals"; and until the end of 1607 he and Bulmer held seemingly conflicting royal authorisations.[128] By the spring of 1608 the position was clarified: Hamilton made a glowing report to the English Privy Council, holding out the prospect of some £500 sterling clear profit each month. Samples of the Hilderstone ore had been tested with excellent results in the Tower of London;[129] and in return for compensation Hamilton yielded his interest in the mine to the King.[130] Thereupon, by warrant under the Great Seal of Scotland, Bulmer was appointed to the office of "Magister Minerarium argenti Scotie" for life.[131] In fact his active participation at Hilderstone seems to have lasted only two years, and in 1613 the lease passed to an entirely fresh partnership, consisting of Sir William Alexander (later of Nova Scotia fame), the goldsmith Foullis, and a Portuguese, Paulo Pinto.[132] Two years later Bulmer died on Alston Moor in Cumberland, a prospector to the end.

As the surviving Hilderstone Accounts[133] relate mainly to payments for running the mines, it is not possible to estimate the financial outcome of the undertaking. By contemporary Scottish standards it was clearly on a substantial scale, for the weekly payroll in some periods—such as December 1608—included sixty-one operatives for the mines alone. To judge by the results of various assays carried out in the Tower Mint in the second half of 1608, the silver yield must have varied a great deal. Atkinson claimed that some of the best ore had produced £80 sterling worth of silver a ton, but that generally the richest had been extracted before Bulmer took sole charge; and that the leaner ore subsequently raised was not worth sending to London, though it might be refined at a profit in Scotland.[134] Whatever the precise motive, melting and fining plants were set up both at Leith and near the mines, where water

---

[128] *A.P.S.*, VOL. IV, p. 391; *Registrum magni sigili regum Scotorum, The Register of the Great Seal of Scotland*, henceforth cited as *Register of the Great Seal*, VOL. VI, ed. J. M. Thomson, 1890, p. 685.
[129] Atkinson, *Gold Mynes in Scotland*, pp. 47-8.
[130] Robertson, in *Journal of Economic and Business History*, IV (1931), pp. 114 ff.
[131] *Register of the Great Seal*, VOL. VI, p. 753.
[132] *R.P.C.*, VOL. X, pp. 15-17, 146, 221.
[133] "Accounts of Money Disbursed by the Lord Treasurer on the Silver Mine at Hilderstone, 1608-13," MS in General Register House, Edinburgh; Cochran-Patrick, *Mining in Scotland*, pp. 141-57.
[134] Atkinson, *Gold Mynes in Scotland*, pp. 46-8.

from Linlithgow Loch was harnessed to operate a "fining mill."[135]

The persistence of these Scottish searchings for gold and silver is another indication of that fixation on treasure which characterised much of the economic thinking of the period. It was an age when, as Harrison said of England in the 1570's, "great store and plenty of treasure" came to those peoples who, by legitimate access or by forceful intervention, could tap the immense gold and silver resources of the Iberian empires. In their striving to keep abreast, those whose economies were less mature, and whose naval strength was less formidable, sought to acquire treasure either by establishing a favourable trade balance—as some of the Baltic nations seem to have done—or by prospecting diligently within their own frontiers. A consideration of the state of Scotland's coinage, which we undertake in the next chapter, immediately reveals the urgency which prompted prospecting in Scotland. Her misfortune was that in almost every instance the ores lay in small and scattered pockets, the working and transport costs were relatively high, and at all relevant times she had to rely on the skill and honesty of alien technicians. Yet experience of failure could not kill the hope of ultimate success. Rulers and prospectors went ahead, buoyed by the hope that one day they would "come forth on some conspicuous hilltop, and, but a little way farther, against the setting sun, descry the spires of El Dorado."

THE SEA FISHERIES

Though in technique and marketing organisation the Scottish fisheries were sadly behind the Dutch, the scale of operations in the sixteenth century was by no means negligible. An incidental entry in the Aberdeen Register of Births runs: "The fuft day and sact Januar yeir of god 1587, cayme and arivit in the red of Aberdeen ouitt of lochbruin [Loch Broom] of scottis schipis, ane hundreth sailis . . . lyk was not sene in mone yeiris afore."[136] While Pedro de Ayala, writing in 1498, had exaggerated in claiming that the quantity of Scottish fish was "so great that it suffices for Italy, France, Flanders and England,"[137]

---

[135] Chambers, *Domestic Annals*, VOL. I, p. 412.
[136] Printed in *Analecta Scotica*, ed. J. Maidment, 1832, VOL. I, p. 286.
[137] De Ayala's letter about Scotland is printed in *Calendar of Letters, Despatches, and State Papers relating to the Negotiations between England and Spain*, VOL. I, ed. G. A. Bergenroth, 1862, pp. 160-1.

E

it is certain that fish from Scottish waters was widely consumed throughout Western Europe. Had he lived a century later, de Ayala must have noted particularly the popularity of Scottish herring in the Baltic lands, whose purchases were rising in the reign of James VI until by the 1620's they had reached a level of six or seven million fish each year.[138] How greatly fish contributed to Scottish exports in the early part of our period is a matter of guesswork: what is certain is that the annual yield of £100,000 from herring and of £50,000 from salmon in 1611-14 represented about one-fifth of the total value of the nation's visible exports.[139]

On both east and west coasts the organisation of the sea fisheries conformed to a common pattern with the burghs as pivots, collecting, packing, and forwarding the fish which came to them from nearby waters, from the Western and Northern Isles and from the sea lochs. For the burgh of Ayr it is possible to trace the main stages through the transactions recorded by John Mason in his Notarial Notebook.[140] Local merchants agreed with fishermen to receive "merchandibill" herring, "sufficientlie packit, upoun the key of the said burgh." In the next stage the same merchants arranged with skippers to deliver "Ilis herring" or other fish at La Rochelle or Bordeaux. Normally all went smoothly, but occasionally trouble arose, as when "Nichols Geilis, Frenchman," complained to the Privy Council that two burgesses of Ayr had failed to implement their undertaking to deliver 9½ lasts of herring at La Rochelle.[141] At the ports of the Clyde and of the east coast the same organisation and sequence of operations prevailed. In each of them the narrow shore and confined streets were full of the sights and smells of the fish trade. Fish was handled by the typical merchant as a normal part of his mixed business. Thus one of the first entries in the Dundee Shipping Lists (for December 1580) relates to the arrival of the *Marie Jhane* "fra the Ilis laident wit herings" for nineteen local merchants.[142] The importance of barrels for fish is reflected in the prominence of

[138] *Sound Toll Registers*. I have taken a "last" of herring to be 12,000 to 13,000 fish (A. M. Samuel, *The Herring*, p. 75).

[139] *Mar and Kellie Papers*, pp. 70-4.

[140] "Notarial Notebook of John Mason, Clerk of the Burgh of Ayr, 1582-1612," henceforth cited as Mason, "Notarial Notebook," printed in *Archaeological and Historical Collections relating to Ayrshire and Galloway*, VOL. VI, 1889, pp. 223 ff.

[141] *R.P.C.*, VOL. III, p. 326. [142] Dundee Shipping Lists, p. 197.

the coopers: they ranked seventh among the Glasgow crafts in 1604[143] and their raw materials—staves from Scandinavia and iron hoops from Flanders—appear among the regular imports.[144] Furthermore, as we shall see later, the demand for salt for preserving and packing influenced the pattern both of Franco-Scottish trading and of the Scottish extractive industries.

Nevertheless there was a growing awareness of the more progressive methods and organisation in the fishing industries of rival nations. Men of experience such as Captain David Vaus saw the need for more capital and better techniques,[145] while Sir Thomas Craig maintained that a major benefit of the Union of 1603 would be realised "if the English were to introduce their faculty of commercial organisation (wherein we confess ourselves their inferiors) and to adventure capital" in the Scottish fisheries.[146] Scotsmen were equally familiar with the well-organised fisheries of the Dutch: Dutch fleets came annually in great strength to Scottish waters, the Earl of Seaforth introduced a number of Dutch families to Lewis in his attempt to develop Stornoway as a fishing port,[147] and John Keymor, writing on the general commercial situation about 1620, specifically advocated the copying of Dutch fishery methods.[148] These hints and suggestions elicited a considerable response in official circles in Scotland. While action took in part the negative form of restricting the facilities available to foreign fishermen, there were more constructive measures for better discipline in the fishing fleets,[149] for standardisation of packing,[150] for improved methods of curing red herring,[151] and for peaceable fishing among the Western Isles.

The basic problem, the recasting and organisation of the sea fisheries generally, proved more difficult. The burghs, some of the northern chiefs, and some ecclesiastical dignitaries, claimed extensive rights over both fisheries and landings and formed a complex of local vested interests hostile to any con-

[143] I. F. Grant, *Social Development*, p. 413.
[144] Dundee Shipping Lists, *passim*.
[145] *De unione*, p. 454.   [146] Ibid.
[147] W. C. Mackenzie, *The Book of the Lews*, pp. 69 ff.
[148] J. Keymor, "Policies of State Practised in various Kingdoms for the encrease of Trade," henceforth cited as "Policies of State," Edinburgh University Library, Laing MSS, Div. II, No. 52 ff. 22-4.
[149] *Convention Records*, VOL. II, pp. 326-8, 349, 404.
[150] *Op. cit.*, pp. 12, 242, 436; *R.P.C.*, VOL. X, pp. 578-9.
[151] *Convention Records*, VOL. III, pp. 26, 31, 67.

certed system. Yet if the Scots were to compete effectively with the Dutch, a strong unified organisation with ample capital and State backing was essential. No effective steps in this direction were taken until the early years of Charles I, when a joint Anglo-Scottish Commission produced an ingenious plan for a parent body, The Society of the Fishery of Great Britain, with semi-autonomous regional subsidiaries.[152] The confirmatory Scottish Act[153] clearly contemplated that the Scottish subsidiaries should be based on burghs and regions, an obvious sop to the existing vested interests. The results fell dismally short of expectations. The Association of the Lord Treasurer, set up in 1632, was the first of a series of undertakings designed to operate the Lewis fisheries, all of which failed in the face of active local opposition and the steady loss of boats and tackle at the hands of islanders and visiting Dunkirkers.[154]

Rivalry in home waters, coupled with the rising demand for fish-oil for lighting and for soap-making, directed attention to the prospects of more distant fishing grounds. The first sign of an organised project comes in 1617, when Sir James Cunningham and others were incorporated as the Scottish East India and Greenland Company[155] (the "Muscoviane Indiane Companie" in the Edinburgh Council Register),[156] with powers to operate in the Indies, the Levant, Greenland, and Russia. The existence of this Company was a plain threat to the English East India and Muscovy Companies, which immediately drew together in opposition to the patent. The immediate attraction of the enterprise for Scotland lay in the prospect of whale oil, and Cunningham promptly began fitting out a whaling expedition; but nevertheless there was considerable resistance to the scheme from the Scottish burghs, which, added to the London pressure, induced the King to cancel the patent.[157]

---

[152] Scott, *Joint-Stock Companies*, VOL. II, pp. 361 ff; *Calendar of Letters and State Papers, Domestic*, henceforth cited as *Cal. S. P. Dom., Charles I*, ed. J. Bruce, 1863, VOL. V, pp. 53-4.

[153] *A.P.S.*, VOL. V, p. 222; *R.P.C.*, 2nd ser., VOL. IV, pp. xviii-xxiii.

[154] Scott, *Joint-Stock Companies*, VOL. II, p. 369; J. R. Elder, *The Royal Fishery Companies*, 1912, is valuable on the legal issues involved.

[155] Scott, *Joint-Stock Companies*, VOL. II, pp. 55-6, 104.

[156] *Edinburgh Records*, VOL. VI, p. 156.

[157] Scott, *Joint-Stock Companies*, VOL. II, p. 55.

No project was ever dead so long as Nathaniel Udward lived. Seven years after the cancellation of Cunningham's patent, Udward petitioned the Scottish Council for leave to fish in Greenland waters "for provisioun of oiles . . . for the mentenance of his soap workis." Subject, the Council said, to the same facilities being available to all other Scotsmen, there was no reason why Udward's petition should not be approved.[158]

In the light of the foregoing survey of manufactures, mining, and fishing, we may now attempt an overall assessment of the extent to which Scotland's domestic economy in the early seventeenth century was responding to the more stable environment. Secondly we may see how this period fits into the wider pattern of Scotland's economic history. The triumphs were plainly in coal and salt, in which the abundant raw materials could be exploited by local landed capital, and for which there was a keen European demand. In the traditional industries, still dominated by the gild, there was an awareness of shortcomings and some attempt to rectify them; but change in technique encountered the kind of resistance shown by the Scottish tanners who refused by the dozen to receive the "authorised instructions" provided for them under Lord Erskine's patent,[159] and changes in industrial organisation similarly met with opposition from the entrenched burghs. Though the pressing need for modernisation was repeatedly urged upon them, neither the textile nor the fishing industry experienced any rapid influx of new capital or of leadership powerful enough to overawe these conservative elements. In the appearance of new industries we can detect an awareness of developments outside Scotland and an anxiety to substitute home-made for imported goods, yet the extent of achievement in this field—in the short run at least—remained relatively slight.

The data at our disposal are altogether too fragmentary to justify any very bold conclusions about fluctuations in the level of Scottish industrial activity as a whole. The only consecutive series available, derived from the Sound toll registers,[160]

---

[158] *R.P.C.*, VOL. XIII, p. 692.
[159] See above, p. 44; *R.P.C.*, VOL. XIII, pp. 5-9.
[160] S. G. E. Lythe, "Scottish trade with the Baltic, 1550-1650," in *Dundee Economic Essays*, ed. J. K. Eastham, 1952, pp. 63-84.

relates to the shipment of certain industrial raw materials by Scotsmen from ports within the Baltic Sea. The following table displays an index of annual average shipments of iron and flax and hemp for each decade (or part-decade where the registers are defective) from the 1560's to the Civil War, employing the average for 1590-99 as 100.

	Iron	Flax and Hemp
1562-69	65	156
1574-79	87	123
1580-89	66	94
1590-99	100	100
1600-09	113	84
1610-19	87	59
1620-29	205	176
1630-39	298	300

Using this table, with a constant eye to its limitations, along with the available literary evidence, we can at least suggest an outline pattern of the likely course of industrial fluctuation. It would be difficult to justify Hume Brown's belief that "during no period of the national history had the Scottish people taken such a forward step in material well-being" as in the reign of Queen Mary.[161] There are, however, abundant indications that the Scottish craft gilds, after a relatively late start, advanced rapidly in status and influence. Thus at Stirling in 1545 it was agreed that "four personis of the wisest" among the craftsmen should hold office on the Burgh Council and be eligible to serve as bailie.[162] At Aberdeen the craftsmen were edging themselves into town government, and by the "Common Indenture" of 1587 they secured certain of the privileges hitherto confined to members of the Merchant Gild.[163] At Dundee craft representation on the Burgh Council remained trivial until after 1600—indeed the relatively high proportion of craftsmen on the Perth Council was cited by Dundonians as evidence of their own town's superiority;[164] but even at Dundee the crafts were closing their ranks for battle. The Union among the Trades of 1581 was the first blast of the trumpet.[165]

It can, therefore, at least be suggested that in about the third quarter of the sixteenth century the medieval industrial

---

[161] P. Hume Brown, *History of Scotland*, 1911, VOL. II, p. 92.
[162] *Stirling Records*, p. 41.   [163] Kennedy, *Annals of Aberdeen*, p. 150.
[164] Maxwell, *History of Old Dundee*, p. 29.   [165] *Burgh Laws of Dundee*, pp. 247-9.

organisation achieved its maturity. The nation was torn by political instability and religious controversy; but the upward movement of prices was not yet disruptive and, in so far as raw material imports can be taken as a guide, it looks as if a reasonably stable level of industrial production was maintained until the later 1570's.

From about 1577-8 these imports were appreciably lower, confirming the conventional opinion about the depressed state of Scottish burgh life at the time,[166] and pointing to the debilitating effects of the harvest failures which, as we saw in Chapter I, came with disastrous regularity in each of the three closing decades of the century. Partly in consequence, and partly because of chaotic currency management, commodity prices staggered violently upwards, destroying confidence and disrupting traditional relationships in every sector of the economy. If the arrival of James's bride had not been delayed by storms in the autumn of 1589, she would almost certainly have embarrassed her bridegroom by reaching his capital before his wedding garments were ready. "Surely," commented the English Ambassador, "Scotland was never in worse state to receive a Queen, for there is not a house in repair."[167] It was as well that Princess Anne brought a coach from her native Denmark.

Recovery from this depressed condition was, at first, slow and uneven: sharp rises in imports of iron and textile raw materials in 1598-9 and in 1608 are matched by equally sharp slumps in 1601-3 and 1611-14; and dislocations in the Baltic area precipitated a general rise in most of these raw material prices. Meanwhile, however, the administrative and political condition of Scotland was improving daily, population and the labour force was growing apace, food was relatively plentiful, the revolution in domestic prices had shed its violence and had become a healthy stimulant to enterprise. It remained only to revitalise and recast the country's industrial system, a task which, as we shall see in Chapter III, occupied the attention of the King, most official bodies, and a group of energetic private individuals.

The effects became apparent as the reign of James VI drew

towards its close. Dr Marguerite Wood, in her introduction to the volume of *Extracts from the Records of the Burgh of Edinburgh* for 1604 to 1626, says that "the tranquillity of the closing years of James VI's reign is reflected in the history of the Burgh. The inhabitants, relieved from all external claims, save by taxation, seem to have devoted themselves to trade and to have prospered exceedingly."[168] Similarly Professor Pryde has shown how, at Ayr, the annual revenue to the Common Good, which averaged £200 to £300 in the mid-sixteenth century, fluctuated wildly in the last quarter of the century, but after 1600 never fell below £1,000 and on three occasions before 1625 actually exceeded £2,000.[169] The raw material import index reveals a great upsurge of activity beginning about 1619, and there is no indication that Scotland suffered any recession comparable to that in England in the early 1620's. Nor—and this is all the more significant in the light of earlier experience—did the crop deficiencies and the heavy grain purchases abroad in 1622-3 put any lasting damper on expansion: indeed the level of raw material shipments from the Baltic for the 1620's was almost three times as high as in the previous decade.[170]

Charles I succeeded to a Scotland whose economic life was entering a vigorous and expansive phase, displaying a dynamic quality not hitherto perceptible. Extrapolation in human affairs is notoriously dangerous, yet the persistence of this buoyancy through the 1630's demands the conclusion that, for Scotland at any rate, the Civil War was an economic disaster of the first magnitude.

WESTWARD EXPANSION: IRELAND AND NOVA SCOTIA

Though the proposition that the Scottish nation has given the world nothing more valuable than its own children is founded on the experience of the past two centuries, the history of the Scot abroad reaches back to a more remote period. In describing Scotland's economic links with various European regions between 1550 and 1625 we shall see how groups of Scots were engaged in all manner of pursuits: the apothecary saving life in Sweden, the mercenary taking life in Holland; the pedlar

---

[168] *Edinburgh Records*, VOL. VI, p. lx.
[169] *Ayr Burgh Accounts, 1534-1624*, ed. G. S. Pryde, Scottish History Society, 3rd ser., VOL. XXVIII, 1937, p. liii.
[170] *Sound Toll Registers* for the relevant years.

shivering in the damp of the Pripet Marshes, the merchant basking on the quayside at Bordeaux. Directly or indirectly, the thrust behind emigration was generally economic. Lithgow could describe Poland as "a Mother and Nurse for the youth and younglings of Scotland, who are yearely sent hither in great numbers": they found there the "fatnesse" lacking at home.[171] It is, of course, true that after the Reformation currents of religious bitterness stimulated the flow of emigration: Ninian Winzet left Scotland after his disputations with Knox to become abbot of St James's Monastery at Ratisbon; scions of faithful Roman Catholic families went to colleges in Flanders or France for secular or clerical education; non-conforming Protestants escaped to Holland or Geneva from the discipline of James VI.

It is, however, significant that in this period of enormously widened geographical horizons the Scots continued to look and move towards the familiar European territories rather than across the oceans. Dr Insh, the authority on the earliest Scottish colonial ventures, contrasts the Elizabethan Englishman's craving for voyaging and discovery with the disaster which forms the inevitable climax of most contemporary Scottish sea poems.[172] The Breton sailor's prayer

> Oh Lord, have mercy upon me,
> Thy sea is so great
> And my ship is so small,

might have come from the lips of a Scotsman. And yet Fynes Moryson could write, in 1598, that "since the Scots are very daring, I cannot see why their marriners should not be bold and courageous, howsoever they have not hitherto made any long voyages, rather for want of richcs than for slothfulnesse or want of courage."[173] The explanation is more likely to be economic than psychological. We see elsewhere that internal conditions in Scotland for much of the sixteenth century were conducive neither to the accumulation of capital nor to long-term commercial thinking. Scottish external trade was operated on the assumption of short voyages and a rapid turn-over of stock, and consequently involved relatively little com-

---

[171] Lithgow, *Totall Discourse*, p. 422.
[172] G. P. Insh, *Scottish Colonial Schemes, 1620-1686*, 1922, p. 14.
[173] Hume Brown, *Early Travellers*, p. 87.

mercial risk and only the most elementary credit arrangements. Long voyages to distant lands would have called for greater resources than those of the typical Scots merchant, and the joint-stock company, that epitome of capital accumulation and permanency, was comparatively unfamiliar to Scotsmen. Furthermore a voyage lasting several months would upset the régime of the merchant whose mixed business demanded his continuous personal attention, and it might expose his ships and cargoes to the perils of late autumn and winter storms. So, when Tucker visited Glasgow in 1655, he was told that certain Glaswegians had "adventured as farre as the Barbadoes"; but having sustained losses "by reason of theyr goeing out and comeing home late every yeare," they had discontinued the voyages.[174]

Nevertheless as the reign of James VI went on, Scotland became a more promising springboard for external enterprise. Socially the country became more stabilised, so that fathers and husbands no longer feared to leave their families; the wars with England were over, so that energies hitherto mobilised for military requirements were now free to seek other outlets. By about 1600 the plantation of the nearest available territory —Ireland—became a major Scottish project. The links between Ireland and the western fringes of Scotland, forged by a common heritage of myth and magic and by affinity of blood and language, had been kept strong by continuous human contacts. Moved by poverty or clan conflict, Islesmen, especially Macdonalds, had for centuries hired themselves to Irish chiefs as temporary or permanent mercenaries: indeed it was the prospect of a dowry of brawny redshanks that drew the eyes of O'Neills and O'Donnells towards Scottish brides. The continued arrival in Ireland of galley-loads of Islesmen remained a menace to English policy there to the end of Elizabeth's reign, and Scottish skippers—with "great villany" according to the English—were running arms from the Clyde to the Irish "rebels" in the 1570's and '80's.[175] Yet especially

---

[174] T. Tucker, "Report upon the settlement of the revenues of Excise and Customs in Scotland, A.D. 1656," henceforth cited as "Report," printed in *Miscellany of the Scottish Burgh Records Society*, 1881, p. 26.

[175] "A Speciall Direction for Divers Trades," printed in *Tudor Economic Documents*, VOL. III, p. 207; G. A. Hayes-McCoy, *Scots Mercenary Forces in Ireland, 1565-1603*, 1937, *passim*.

after the Reformation there was no firm bond of fellowship or sympathy between the Lowland Scot and the Catholic Irishman: the mass of Scots agreed with King James that Ireland was a "proper dependance" and that anarchy there threatened the stability and security of England and Scotland alike. Consequently the Lowland Scot felt no compunction in sharing with Englishmen in the dispossession of Irishmen and in the seizure of their lands. The colonisation of Ulster was, in short, quite distinct from the age-old infiltration of Ireland by fighting gallowglasses and redshanks from the Western Isles and Highlands.

Before 1612 the entry of Scotsmen into Ireland—other than that of traders and seamen—was illegal under an Irish statute of Philip and Mary;[176] but as Ireland became increasingly regarded as a territory for exploitation her domestic statutes were ignored. Settlement by Lowlanders on a significant scale began shortly after 1600. During the troubles with the O'Neills (the family of the Earl of Tyrone who claimed the Kingdom of Ulster), Con O'Neill was imprisoned in Carrickfergus Castle. His wife sought the help of Hugh Montgomery, Laird of Braidstone in Ayrshire, whose relative, Thomas, regularly traded with Carrickfergus. A rosy glow of romance now warms the dull landmarks of economic history. Thomas Montgomery made love to Miss Dobbin, daughter of the keeper of the Castle, and "during the love-making and wine-drinking which somewhat discomposed the discipline there,"[177] Con escaped. Negotiations then began between the O'Neills and the Montgomerys regarding the future of certain of the O'Neill lands, and, after the intervention of James Hamilton at his Court, the King agreed that roughly the northern part of County Down should become available for English and Scottish colonisation. Miss Dobbin's affairs progressed equally satisfactorily. She became Mrs Thomas Montgomery.

The Scottish families mainly involved—the Montgomerys and the Hamiltons—entered upon the project with resolution. The district at their command had been rendered virtually barren by the ravages of recent fighting, so that the colonisation which began in 1606 was essentially a process of rural

---

[176] *The Statutes at large, passed in the Parliaments held in Ireland*, ed. W. Ball, 1786, VOL. I, p. 274.   [177] J. Harrison, *The Scot in Ulster*, 1888, p. 9.

resettlement. Fortune smiled on the pioneers. Good grain harvests in the early years encouraged them to send home favourable reports; the "potato"—possibly our artichoke—was immediately cultivated;[178] more settlers arrived; within a few years small market towns were appearing, and, on lands leased from the Lord Deputy, the area of Scottish plantation soon outran its original bounds.[179] The Scots, in other words, were helping to inaugurate that reconstruction of the Irish economy which occupied the first four decades of the seventeenth century.[180]

Meanwhile the major plantation of Ulster was beginning. Under the first plan an area of nearly four million acres was to be carved up into medium-sized estates for Englishmen and Scots, and in 1609 the Scots Privy Council was inviting applications.[181] In subsequent re-surveys the total area was so drastically reduced that only 81,000 acres was available for the fifty-nine Scottish "adventurers" ultimately selected.[182] Though some were Court favourites who promptly sold their allocations, on the whole the King wisely chose Galloway men who already had contacts with Ireland and whose kinsmen and retainers were likely to follow them on the short crossing.[183]

In fact, geographical proximity is the key to the popularity of this first Scottish adventure in colonisation. The pioneers' stocks could be readily replenished from home—"In a fair summer season, twice sometimes thrice a week, they were supplied from Scotland"[184]—while friends and relatives crossed regularly from Stranraer to attend Newton market with the produce and gossip of Galloway. Within a generation, however, the prospects and profits of Ireland were attracting Scotsmen from further afield, especially those whose stomachs rebelled against swallowing the religious policy of James and Charles I. When Brereton was at Irvine in 1636 he was told

---

[178] R. N. Salaman, *The History and Social Influence of the Potato*, 1949, pp. 222-3.
[179] C. Maxwell, *Irish History from Contemporary Sources, 1509-1610*, 1923, p. 203.
[180] G. O'Brien, *The Economic History of Ireland in the Seventeenth Century*, 1919, *passim*.
[181] *R.P.C.*, VOL. VIII, pp. 267-8.
[182] After 1609 the enterprise was controlled from London. The relevant extracts from English official papers are reprinted in *R.P.C.*, VOL. VIII, pp. lxxxviii ff., VOL. IX, pp. lxxix ff.
[183] *Op. cit.*, VOL. IX, pp. lxxix ff.
[184] *Op. cit.*, VOL. X, pp. 28, 531, 566; Montgomery MSS, quoted in Maxwell, *Irish History from Contemporary Sources*, p. 302.

that in two years "above ten thousand persons . . . have left the country wherin they lived, which was betwixt Aberdeen and Ennerness [Inverness], and are gone to Ireland."[185] On some days, they told him, as many as three hundred had sailed from Irvine on a single tide. The pressure of "social inconvenience," of high rents, and of unpopular religion, had no doubt increased in the first third of the seventeenth century. Perhaps for the first time in recorded history civilian Scots were leaving their native land in masses and in a sense of mingled sorrow and anger.

Down to the time of this more general migration, Scotland's trade relations with Ireland had not been of great dimensions. The economies of the two were basically similar: both were essentially raw material producers with a light superstructure of simple industries. So while Fynes Moryson in 1613 "found the state of Ireland much changed . . . all the North was possessed by new colonies of English, but especially of Scots,"[186] he was clearly not impressed by the volume of trade with Scotland. The exchange of Scottish fish, coal, and aquavitae for Irish yarn, hides, and silver which Moryson outlined is confirmed by the scattered mercantile entries in the Notarial Notebook of John Mason of Ayr.[187] But as the Scots planters became established trade naturally developed both in volume and variety, and the townspeople of Ayr told Tucker in the 1650's that before the Civil War they had maintained a "pretty trade" with Ireland.[188] Coal had certainly featured in this expansion. In spite of the shallowness of the approach, small open boats—some as small as four tons—came to Glasgow for coal; while through Irvine and Ayr—both more accessible to bigger vessels—Ayrshire coal competed actively with Cumberland and Welsh in the Irish market.[189]

These Irish openings, coupled with the more regular trade which resulted from the pacification of the Western Isles, contributed materially to the expansion of the ports of the Clyde and the south-west generally. Each had its private problem in the later sixteenth century. Dumbarton, for example, suffered heavily from flooding. Its rival, Glasgow, was striving to

---

[185] Brereton, *Travels*, p. 119.
[186] Moryson, *Itinerary*, PART III, BK iii, p. 299.
[187] Mason, "Notarial Notebook", *passim*. [188] Tucker, "Report," pp. 27-8.
[189] Nef, *Rise of the British Coal Industry*, VOL. I, p. 109; Tucker, "Report," p. 26.

recover from the dismemberment of its pre-Reformation
ecclesiastical structure and from the damage it had suffered in
the civil wars of the reign of Queen Mary and of the regencies.[190]
So long as the Hamiltons were involved in fighting, Glasgow
was in peril. Its citizens who mustered with Moray to fight at
Langside in 1568 earned praise and fame, but two years later
the avenging Hamiltons were again in the town and, though
it was saved, the ensuing devastation of Clydeside can only
have aggravated local economic dislocation. But its immediate
mercantile rivals, Renfrew and Dumbarton, were no more
sheltered, and Lesley was certainly right in calling Glasgow
"the maist renouned mercat in the west, honorable and
celebrate."[191] Its genuinely overseas trade—for example with
France—was in part a by-product of its old ecclesiastical links,
and the expansion of nearer markets came opportunely to
accelerate recovery. The trade with Ireland and the Isles,
because it was local and could be conducted in small vessels,
enabled the Glasgow merchants to progress in wealth and
experience, and encouraged them to devise plans which, as the
seventeenth century went on, were to result in the building of
a deep water outport and the improving of the waterway of
the Clyde.

Until the early 1600's the trans-Atlantic enterprise, in which
Glasgow's commercial genius found its ultimate expression, had
scarcely taken on the substance of a dream. Trade and settlement in remote and savage territories called for the leadership
of visionaries, backed by appropriate economic resources, and
surrounded by an aura of confidence. It was not, as we have
seen, until about 1600 that these qualities were at all readily
available in Scotland, but by the closing years of King James's
reign Scotland was at last able to look out beyond the narrow
seas. Invitations to launch forth were plentiful and optimistic.
John Mason's *Brieffe Discourse of the New-found-land*, addressed
in manuscript to Sir John Scott of Scotstarvet, was published
in Edinburgh in 1620.[192] Four years later Edinburgh saw also
the publication of Sir Robert Gordon's *Encouragement for such
as shall have intention to bee under-takers in the New plantation of*

---

[190] *Letters and Documents relating to the City of Glasgow*, ed. J. D. Marwick, 1894,
PT. II, Nos. lviii, lxi.
[191] Lesley, *Historie*, VOL. I, p. 16.
[192] These pamphlets are all reprinted in *Nova Scotia Charters*.

Cape Briton, now New Galloway. The year previous, Sir William
Alexander's *Encouragement to Colonies*, addressed specifically to
Scotsmen, had appeared in London. The inducements set out
were indeed attractive. All peoples, says Gordon of Lochinvar,
have sought to fill the earth with their own kind, "a pleasant
worke" which "Adam and Eve did first begine"; this urge was
both godly, in that it served in the propagation of the Gospel,
and loyal, in that it enhanced the dominion of the king.
Alexander was particularly eloquent on the material prospects.
Hitherto, he says, Scotland has had to export necessities to pay
for her imports, but if she would but adventure her men (of
which she had abundance), some cattle and some grain, she
could tap in Nova Scotia a great source of goods for commerce: fish, furs, pipe-staves, timber, potash, minerals, and—
he ends rather lamely—"other things that may be discovered
hereafter."

The story of the attempted colonisation of Nova Scotia
focuses attention on Sir William Alexander, the one Scotsman
of the time who fairly bears comparison with the Sidneys and
the Raleighs of Elizabethan England. He was, said Sir
Thomas Urquhart, "born a poet, and aimed to be a king. Had
he stopped there, it had been well: but the flame of his
honour must have some oyle wherewith to nourish it."[193] His
accomplishments and attainments constitute a catalogue in
themselves: courtier, statesman, adventurer, poet and play-
wright, knight, viscount, and, eventually, earl.[194] He was born
at Menstrie House, near Stirling (whence he took his title), of
a family which claimed descent from Somerled, Lord of the
Isles, down through a misty Highland genealogy with periodic
infusions of the blood royal. By the very early 1600's his verse
had established him among the galaxy of Jacobean poets; at
the Court of King James he advanced rapidly in office and
rank; in 1621 he received what was almost certainly the
greatest gift ever bestowed on a subject by a British sovereign.[195]

By this Charter of 1621 he acquired an immense territory

---

[193] *EKΣKYBAΛAYPON, or The Discovery of a most exquisite Jewel,* 1652, p. 208.
Reprinted in *The Works of Sir Thomas Urquhart of Cromarty, Knight,* Maitland Club,
1834, p. 266.

[194] C. Rogers, *Memorials of the Earl of Stirling,* 2 Vols, 1877; E. F. Slafter, *Sir
William Alexander and American Colonization,* Boston, Mass., 1873; T. H. MacGrail,
Sir William Alexander, First Earl of Stirling, 1940.

[195] *Register of the Great Seal,* VOL. VIII, pp. 72-3; *R.P.C.,* VOL. XII, pp. 570, 575.

in North America, which, if it had been developed and held, would at one stroke have elevated Scotland to the top rank of colonial powers. The very name was full of hope. Since, Sir William said, there already existed a New France, a New Spain, and a New England, this should be New Scotland. The territory selected for settlement, now called Nova Scotia, had been visited by the Cabots in 1497, but had not been seriously contemplated for European occupation until 1605, when a French expedition established a small number of posts which were held through the next decade in the face of extreme hardship and English hostility. By the early 1620's the territory was virtually vacant again, and the moment was highly opportune for a Scottish overseas venture. Since the late 1590's Scotland had enjoyed good harvests and relatively settled political conditions, resulting in the survival of more vigorous young men for whom outlets had to be found. The bulk of the estates in Ulster had by this time been taken up, and the King was discouraging the migration of Scotsmen to London and to the European armies.

Early in 1622 Sir William procured a ship in London and sent it to Kirkcudbright to be manned and victualled.[196] Despite a sudden rise in prices and the reluctance of artisans to join the expedition, all was ready by June; but the adventurers had a bad crossing and were forced to winter in Newfoundland. By the time the second ship sailed (March 1623) the original party had been broken up. Some had found employment with local fishermen; the minister and the smith, "for Spirituall and Temporall respects the most necessary members," were both dead. Accordingly the second party restricted its activities to a survey of the coasts of Nova Scotia, returning home with a favourable report.

This alone was obviously not enough to encourage further efforts, and fresh bait had to be laid. Both Sir William and Gordon of Lochinvar, the latter also interested in plantations in Nova Scotia, published eloquent appeals to their countrymen, while King James came to their aid with the scheme for the creation of Nova Scotia baronetcies.[197] Under the original

---

[196] This paragraph follows Alexander's own account in his *Encouragement to Colonies*.

[197] *A.P.S.*, VOL. V, p. 184; *Register of the Great Seal*, VOL. VIII, p. 288; Rogers, *Memorials of the Earl of Stirling*, VOL. I, pp. 71-4.

plan each baronet was to furnish Sir William with "sex sufficient men," adequately equipped and armed, together with "one thousand merkis Scottis money"; but this was quickly commuted into a single obligation of 3,000 merks (£150 sterling). A similar scheme had worked well for Ulster, but here the flow of "oyle" fell far short of expectations. "The canny Scot," Professor Andrews writes,[198] "was suspicious of even the existence of Sir William's transatlantic lordship"; family-proud lairds resented the precedence promised to the new baronets, and, inconsistently perhaps, offered in 1625 to bear the cost themselves should the settlement prove feasible. It says much for Sir William's determination that neither the jealous suspicion of his countrymen nor the overt hostility of the English could beat it down. Yet a further expedition, mustered in the spring of 1627 "with a joyful countenance and alacrity of mind," never left the shores of Britain. The final effort, prepared in the winter of 1628-9, would almost surely have been equally abortive but for a mutually advantageous arrangement with a group of English merchants, Jervas Kirke and others, who found that the wording of Sir William's patent stood in the path of their projected trade with Canada. Accordingly, in return for the right of access to the St Lawrence, the merchants shipped over a band of some seventy men and two women—Sir William's son accompanying them—and a settlement was at last achieved. The material results were slight. Apart from this initial settlement at Port Royal, no genuine colonisation seems to have been attempted. Those who had taken up Nova Scotia baronetcies, with a few exceptions, showed no anxiety to view their lands and many even sought exemption from their obligations. In fact the whole business of the baronetcies "quickly degenerated into a device for raising money by the sale of hereditary sinecure titles."[199]

At its peak, therefore, the first Scottish transatlantic colony was a disappointingly modest achievement, and recession came quickly. The French had never ceded their claim to the territory. They were kept out with some difficulty in the late 1620's and, about 1630, Sir William transferred almost all his

[198] C. M. Andrews, *The Colonial Period in American History*, Yale 1934, VOL. I, p. 316. The remainder of this paragraph is based on this work and on Insh, *Scottish Colonial Schemes*.

[199] *Nova Scotia Charters*, p. 24.

F

colonial rights to Claude de la Tour, a French Huguenot, preserving only Port Royal and the general overlordship of the British crown. There are suspicions that further "oyle" flowed during these transactions,[200] but in any event the end was near for under the Treaty of St Germain-en-Laye (1632) French sovereignty was restored. In preparation for the transfer, Alexander had been instructed to evacuate Port Royal "leaving the boundis altogether waist and unpeopled as it was at the tyme when your sone landed first to plant ther."[201]

Apart from this Nova Scotia episode, the history of the earliest Scottish trans-Atlantic ventures is obscure and fragmentary. That Scotsmen knew of the potentialities of Newfoundland is scarcely surprising since John Mason, its Governor in 1617, was employed in 1610-11 in policing the Western Isles (it is doubtful whether he ever got paid), and in 1620 his *Brieffe Discourse* was published in Scotland.[202] Similarly John Keymor drew attention to the valuable fisheries off Greenland,[203] and as we have seen the abortive Company organised by Sir James Cunningham embraced Greenland within the field of its authorised activities. The grant to Sir Robert Gordon of the geographically obscure "Insula Caroli" was even more inconclusive, for immediately after the grant Sir Robert, always a man of action, took to anti-Spanish privateering and died.[204]

Hume Brown believed that in these affairs "national ambition out-ran the national sufficiency."[205] We have considered already the strength of economic and social barriers in delaying the start of Scottish transoceanic expansion, and even in the more settled conditions of the 1620's the long ocean voyage to Nova Scotia still presented serious financial and psychological problems. It is, however, difficult to believe that national insufficiency, defined either in terms of economic resources or of national character, could alone have explained the poor performance and the miserable dénouement. The cost of establishing a few hundred settlers in Nova Scotia could not have been insuperable, for, as Alexander pointed out, all they

---

[200] *Nova Scotia Charters*, p. 99.   [201] *Op. cit.*, p. 114.
[202] *Op. cit.*, pp. 4-6; Insh, *Scottish Colonial Schemes*, Chapter I, *passim*.
[203] Keymor, "Policies of State," pp. 3, 22-4.
[204] *Register of the Great Seal*, VOL. VIII, pp. 344-5; Insh, *Scottish Colonial Schemes*, p. 100.
[205] Hume Brown, *History of Scotland*, VOL. II, p. 215.

needed was enough grain and cattle to establish themselves on their farms. Similarly the alarms and excursions of colonial frontier life were scarcely likely to deter a man whose forefathers had kept their daily watch on the Borders.

Basically, Scotland's failure in the colonial sphere is attributable to the anomaly of her diplomatic status after 1603. When she entered the race for colonial empire, claims to the unoccupied parts of the known world had already been staked by the leading West European powers. As a new claimant, Scotland could succeed only if she had either an independent foreign policy backed by appropriate arms, or, alternatively, the goodwill of a powerful friend. But after 1603 Scotland no longer had an independent foreign policy, she had not yet acquired the whole-hearted goodwill of England, and, in Nova Scotia, she fell foul of France, the one other nation which might have championed her ambitions.

III

OFFICIAL ACTION IN ECONOMIC AFFAIRS

POLICY-MAKING BODIES

For much of western Europe the sixteenth century was a period of political and administrative experiment. The related emergence of nation-states and strong monarchies involved the creation of machinery of government adequate to implement policies designed to serve the ends of national prestige and national expansion. Where central government was strong—as in the England of the Tudors or the Sweden of the Vasas—economic policy was characterised by a reasonable degree of coherence and continuity and by a dominant purpose.

A cursory view of the structure and history of Scottish institutions in this period will show how elusive these qualities must have been in Scotland. The natural diversities of interests between members of any nation were aggravated in Scotland by the broad gulf between Lowlander and Gael, and, within the zone of each, by powerful local or regional allegiances. The sharpest possible distinction existed between the largely self-contained and often isolated Highland community and the trading burgh of the east coast with its network of outside contacts. In such a society a positive economic policy could result only from central government decision backed by administrative machinery strong enough to command universal respect. But central government in Scotland was notoriously weak: the royal minorities and the succession of regencies; Mary's inability to distinguish between the private and public implications of her actions; the remoteness of the glens and the Isles; the intermittent border warfare; all these preserved and promoted a high degree of local independence and a low regard for royal authority.

The strength of sectional interests in Scotland was reflected in the variety and composition of her national representative bodies. Her Parliament consisted of a single chamber made up of the Estates of the Realm: the nobility, the small barons (or lairds), the burgesses and, at most relevant periods, the clergy.[1] The burgess members represented the royal burghs only, and were elected on a very narrow franchise; indeed it has been estimated that the entire burgh electorate was fewer than 4,000.[2] Shire representation, even after its reorganisation by the County Franchise Act of 1587,[3] was equally narrow and often incomplete. On most issues, certainly on those where economic interests were involved, the Estates retained a consciousness of individuality quite incompatible with the emergence of a genuinely national parliamentary spirit. Furthermore procedure within Parliament was so organised that all initiative lay in the hands of a steering committee, the Lords of the Articles, a body nominated by an ingenious method which ensured, after the Reformation, that it was little more than a tool of the monarch. The function of the rank and file member was restricted to the ratification of legislative proposals laid before him; his independence was such that the King could say with truth in 1607 that no member spoke save with the royal leave.[4] In short, until the eve of the Civil War, the Scots Parliament was in no true sense a national deliberative assembly and was quite incapable of formulating any independent legislative programme.

Throughout our period, therefore, Parliament, though theoretically representative, was in fact dumb. Alongside it there existed two other representative bodies, both more vocal. "After the Reformation," it has been said, "Parliament found a serious rival in the General Assembly of the Church, which, though not a democratic body, was more truly representative of national thought and feeling."[5] Looking at the span between the Reformation and the great upheaval of 1638 as a whole, we can see the hardening and enlarging of the claims

---

[1] R. S. Rait, *The Parliaments of Scotland*, 1924; and C. S. Terry, *The Scottish Parliament, its Constitution and Procedure, 1603-1707*, 1905, *passim*.

[2] Terry, *The Scottish Parliament*, p. 58.

[3] *A.P.S.*, VOL. III, p. 509; Rait, *The Parliaments of Scotland*, p. 206.

[4] *The Political Works of James I*, ed. C. H. McIlwain, Harvard 1918, p. 301.

[5] Rait, *History of Scotland*, 1929, p. 236.

of the Church in other than directly spiritual and disciplinary matters: a long-term movement, in other words, towards a theocratic state. But from the later 1590's to the end of James's reign the ministers were never safe enough in their own houses to launch any formidable assault on the temporal power. In an outburst of indignation Andrew Melville might tell James that of the "twa Kingdoms" in Scotland that of "James the Saxt" was subject to that of "Chryst Jesus,"[6] but the individual minister, isolated in his parish, pondered the fate of David Black whose outspoken sermons on royalty in 1596 resulted in his banishment from St Andrews to the remote Highlands.[7] Thenceforth James had so modified the structure of the Church and so subdued its chief spokesmen, that from about 1610 to the end of his reign the General Assembly itself lay heavily under royal influence. But whether free or servile, the Assembly never made any significant contribution to the shaping of a positive economic policy for Scotland. In so far as generalisation is possible, its attitude in this field would have to be defined as passive with a reactionary bias.

The Convention of Royal Burghs, the third of the national bodies, was, on the other hand, extensively, indeed sometimes almost exclusively, concerned with economic affairs.[8] The habit of consultation among the royal burghs, which began in Scotland before the Wars of Independence, had, by the later sixteenth century, produced the Convention, an institution of immense potentiality and unique in Europe. The Convention spoke as the voice of all the royal and free burghs; no royal nominee dominated its proceedings or dictated its agenda; it assembled where and when its members determined. It was capable of regulating burghal government and of settling inter-burghal disputes; it assessed the contribution of each burgh to national taxes; it could influence the composition of the Burgess Estate in Parliament. Nowhere was it more consistently active than in safeguarding the ancient trading privileges of its constituent members. Until the later part of the seventeenth century all overseas trade of any consequence was conducted under its auspices; it was competent to regulate the

[6] Melville, *Autobiography and Diary*, ed. Pitcairn, p. 370.
[7] *R.P.C.*, VOL. V, pp. 326, 334, 345.
[8] Pagan, *The Convention of the Royal Burghs of Scotland*.

relationships of merchants and factors and of skippers and crews; and by its management of the Scottish Staple at Veere its influence reached to the far end of Scotland's great traditional trading axis. Especially in times when Parliament seldom met—for instance in the early 1600's—it was often consulted by the King and his Council as an alternative mouthpiece of public opinion. But it belonged essentially to the old economic order, and we seek in vain for any substantial evidence of a positive contribution to the shaping of the new.

In the Scotland of our period the distinction between the legislative and executive arms of central government was so blurred that for all practical purposes the "Acts" of the Privy Council had the same force as the "Acts" of Parliament. The functioning and attitude of the Privy Council depended largely upon the strength of the monarchy. Under a weak monarch, or during a minority, the great lords of the Council could become the virtual dictators of the land, but under a strong or guileful ruler they became the effective instruments of royal policy. James was fully aware of this when he wrote his *Trew Law of Free Monarchies* in 1598. There were kings, he says, in Scotland before "any estates or rankes of men within the same, before any Parliaments were holden or lawes made," and therefore though no act of Parliament can be effective without the royal "Scepter," the king may make "daily statutes and ordinances . . . without any advice of Parliament or estates."[9]

Once he was safely established in London, his claim to the right of personal rule in Scotland became even more specific. "This I must say for Scotland, and I may trewly vaunt it; Here I sit and governe it with my Pen, I write and it is done, and by a Clearke of the Councill I governe Scotland now, which others could not doe by the sword." And again in 1609: "For six and thirtie yeares have I governed in Scotland personally."[10] Under the direction of a king so minded, the size of the Scottish Council was reduced until, as Professor Willson puts it, "the work of government was done by a handful of devoted and obedient officials who, like their English counterparts, awaited instructions and followed them closely."[11] So

[9] James I, *Political Works*, ed. McIlwain, p. 62.
[10] *Op. cit.*, pp. 301, 315.
[11] Willson, *King James VI and I*, p. 313; also Hume Brown, *History of Scotland*, VOL. II, p. 220.

in the last decades of his reign James exercised, through the compliant Scottish Council, all the effective functions of government in Scotland. By a skilful blending of guile and patronage he had contrived to establish a royal mastership which Scotland had known for no significant period since the death of James IV.

Down, however, to the end of the sixteenth century, the composition and balance of the main elements in Scottish central affairs, coupled with the instability of political life, had made for compromise, expediency, and indecision. In the Convention of Royal Burghs and in the General Assembly of the Church the country had two bulwarks of social and economic conservatism. Under their influence the national economic attitude was likely to be dominated by the medieval "love of goods"—what Heckscher calls "a policy of provision"[12]—and this attitude was likely to persist until some other organ of central government became sufficiently influential to impose an alternative. In short the movement in sixteenth-century Scotland in the direction of mercantilist economic policies was inevitably slow. It is, however, equally plain that by the turn of the century the King had so enlarged his influence over the whole machinery of government, from the Council and Parliament right down to local administration, that his ability to dictate economic policy was enormously enhanced.

THE CONTROL OF TRADE AND SHIPPING

In some sense all government action has economic implications. As we saw, for example, in Chapter II, the Scottish settlement of Church lands produced economic effects different from the parallel settlement in England, and, on an higher plane of action, Scottish foreign policy radically influenced the whole pattern of the nation's overseas trade. For our present purpose, however, we can conveniently concentrate on three relatively limited aspects of direct official intervention: the control of trade and shipping; the regulation of industry; the provision of coinage and control of prices. For each of these we shall attempt to analyse the intentions and assess the effectiveness of official action.

[12] E. Heckscher, "Mercantilism," in *Economic History Review*, henceforth cited as *Ec. H.R.*, VII (1936), p. 49.

The imposition of duties and bans on commodities passing to or from the country provides an obvious starting point. From the Middle Ages, overseas trade had been restricted to the royal burghs, which had exercised the right, generally authorised by their charters, to levy dues on commodities. These dues, "Holy Blood Silver" and the like, were in general neither onerous nor variable,[13] and consequently had relatively little effect on the volume or direction of trade. The royal Customs, on the other hand, had a very direct impact. Throughout the Middle Ages and right down to the 1590's, customs were levied almost exclusively on staple goods exported from the country, staple goods being best described by a fine exercise in circular definition as those on which customs were levied.[14] This concentration on export duties reflects two not wholly compatible theories, the one maintaining that an export tax would restrain the outflow of useful goods from the country, the other maintaining that by this concentration on exports the incidence of taxation—and hence the cost of running the country—was shifted onto the shoulders of the foreign customer. For most of the sixteenth century the administrative machinery of Scotland was weak; and especially in the frequent phases of political or military upheaval royal export duties were often not collected. In the early 1550's, for example, some of the Forth burghs were granted a remission because "portus vasti erant per invasionem veterum Anglie inimicorum,"[15] and the gap in the Exchequer Rolls from 1567 to 1570 implies another phase of administrative chaos. In any event, even in tranquil times, the yields were relatively small. In the reigns of James III and IV the annual total had been of the order of £3,000; in 1582, in spite of the depreciation in the value of money, the customs were let at an annual tack of not much over £4,000.[16]

The problem of adjusting national revenue to rising prices and rising expenditure was in no way peculiar to Scotland, but her political and administrative equipment for the task was inferior to that of most contemporary European nations. The expropriation of Church property gave some temporary flexi-

---

[13] E.g. the Gild Silver levies at Dundee—20d. on a last of herring, 5d. on a barrel of salmon, and 8d. on 100 deals; *Burgh Laws of Dundee*, p. 131.

[14] Davidson and Gray, *The Scottish Staple at Veere*, p. 340.

[15] *Exchequer Rolls*, VOL. XVIII, p. 227.   [16] *Op. cit.*, VOL. XXI, pp. lix, lx.

bility to the public revenue, but most abnormal items of expenditure—diplomatic embassies, royal weddings, and the like—had to be met by special subsidies. By the 1590's royal finance (which is the same as saying national finance) had fallen into desperate straits.[17] The King was regularly anticipating revenue: he was so badly in debt that "in payment of the dettis awand be his hienes" the "haill profeitt" of the Mint was assigned to Thomas Foulis, the Edinburgh goldsmith.[18] The Queen's jewels were in pawn[19]—which must have grieved her for she liked finery; the Mint and the Exchequer were in chaos.[20] Acting on the adage that desperate situations call for desperate remedies, James in 1596 harshly dismissed the Treasurer and other senior Exchequer officers and replaced them by eight members of his Queen's Council—the group popularly known as "The Octavians."[21] The new board held office for a year only, too short a period for any thorough-going recasting of public finances; but at least the appointment showed the King's determination to put his house in better order, and it is significant that thenceforth the whole system of revenue was much more effectively supervised.

The immediate outcome was the Act of 1597[22] under which, for the first time, Scotland had a general import tariff whereby goods entering the country became subject to a duty of a shilling in the pound. An official book of rates was immediately drawn up, but like most official price lists it was soon found to be defective and gave place to a much more elaborate schedule, issued under Royal Warrant in 1612.[23] This imposition of import duties was resisted by the Convention of Royal Burghs,[24] but the royal power was by now sufficiently strong to override opposition and to ensure reasonably effective collection. By comparison with earlier standards, yields were considerable. A little item such as 33 stones of powder brought in £13. 14s. 0d., a bigger item such as 33 lasts of "gaid" iron produced over

[17] *R.P.C.*, VOL. V, p. 117.
[18] Cochran-Patrick, *Coinage*, VOL. I, p. 191.
[19] Letter from James VI to the Lord Treasurer, quoted in *Analecta Scotica*, ed. Maidment, VOL. II, pp. 382-3.
[20] E.g. the Mint officials were all dismissed on 21 July 1597 and reinstated three weeks later; Cochran-Patrick, *Coinage*, VOL. I, p. 190.
[21] *R.P.C.*, VOL. V, pp. xli ff., 244; *Exchequer Rolls*, VOL. XXIII, pp. xxxvi ff.
[22] *A.P.S.*, VOL. III, p. 136.
[23] Reprinted in *Ledger of Andrew Halyburton*, ed. Innes, pp. cxii-cxvi, 279-341.
[24] *Convention Records*, VOL. II, pp. 19-21.

£260. Even excluding wine, the import duties at Dundee for the first sixteen months of the Act's operation yielded almost £2,580.[25] Thus notwithstanding certain exemptions in favour of private imports for barons and freeholders, the import duties proved immediately successful as a device for supplementing the existing sources of royal revenue.

So far the increase of revenue had been the foremost consideration, yet other motives can be detected in the confused background of current controversy. There is, for example, a hint in the Royal Warrant of 1612 that the official prices of certain essentials—pitch, hemp, lint, and the like—were deliberately underrated. This can only mean that, although the duty was nominally at a flat rate, some attempt was made to discriminate in favour of the industrial users of these imported raw materials. But the mixture, indeed often the incompatibility, of motives, comes out most clearly in the regulation of the export trade in raw wool and the import trade in cloth. Here the claims of influential groups ran directly counter to the royal interest in the collection of customs duties. As early as the 1570's the Convention of Royal Burghs began advancing the stock argument that poverty and unemployment among Scottish clothworkers called for the imposition of bans on the export of wool and the import of English cloth.[26] After 1581 the export of wool was, nominally, illegal,[27] but in spite of the continued protests of the Convention some continued to leave the country under royal licence. The exact extent of this quasi-legal evasion is difficult to determine, for in some periods—notably in the 1580's—the customs were farmed, and for others the surviving returns are incomplete. Where reasonable comparison is possible, it looks as if the level of wool exports in the 1590's was rather more than half as high as it had been forty years earlier.[28]

The conflict latent in this uneasy relationship between Crown and Convention was apparently suddenly resolved in 1597. Within a few months Parliament,[29] the Privy Council,[30]

[25] "Compota custumariorum de bonis importatis infra regum, A.D. 1599," in *Exchequer Rolls*, VOL. XXIII, p. 320.
[26] *Convention Records,* VOL. I, pp. 75, 76, 359, 464; Pagan, *The Convention of the Royal Burghs,* p. 154. [27] *A.P.S.,* VOL. III, p. 220.
[28] The Edinburgh returns, in *Exchequer Rolls,* VOLS. XVIII and XXIII *passim,* yield an average of 47 lasts a year for the early 1550's and 27 lasts a year for the later 1590's. [29] *A.P.S.,* VOL. IV, p. 135. [30] *R.P.C.,* VOL. V, p. 386.

and the Convention[31] all promulgated acts prohibiting both
the export of wool and the import of English cloth. But the
inevitable effect, a fall in revenue from the customs on wool,
led quickly to second thoughts and to a complete volte-face in
royal policy. The Privy Council, in spite of its own previous
action, in 1598 sternly condemned the Convention for its
"pretendit act" which bordered on usurpation of "the royal
power of his Majestie and his Estatis" and was harmful to "his
Heines in his custumes."[32] Accordingly the export of wool was
resumed: in 1611-14 the average annual value was over
£50,000,[33] and the sale of Scots wool to England's cloth-
making rivals was to be a sore point between the two countries
in the 1620's. In this matter at least it looks as if the Convention was prepared to make a stand on behalf of native
craftsmen, and as if the epithet "merchant-ridden" is un-
justified.

In other branches of trade the Crown was capable of justi-
fying its intervention by lofty arguments about the common
weal and the public interest, at times completely ignoring the
dynamic features in the country's economy. In the arguments
over the coal trade, the Crown and the mine-owners appear as
the principal disputants, with the Convention as an interested
but not very vocal third party. As Parliament was reminded
in 1609, there had been "divers acts," particularly that of 1563,
under which the export of certain types of coal, notably "great
coal," was banned.[34] In urging his Scottish Council to enforce
these statutes, James argued that restriction of export was
"agreeable to the generall benefeit of the commounwealth,"
and that those who sought to export put "the privat lucre" of
themselves and their friends before the common interest.[35]
This was an argument pitched on the moral plane of medieval
economics, and clearly ignored both the increasing capacity of
Scottish mining and the singular contribution of coal exports
to the nation's overseas purchasing power. The coal-owners,
politically an influential group, made two rejoinders.[36] They
said that mining involved the outlay of great capital and a long

[31] *Convention Records*, VOL. II, pp. 26-7.   [32] *R.P.C.*, VOL. V, p. 477.
[33] *Mar and Kellie Papers*, pp. 70-4.
[34] *A.P.S.*, VOL. II, p. 543, VOL. IV, p. 136; Nef, *Rise of the British Coal Industry*,
VOL. II, pp. 224 ff.
[35] *R.P.C.*, VOL. VIII, pp. 575-6.   [36] *Op. cit.*, VOL. VIII, pp. 568-9.

period of waiting for returns; no owner would face these without a reasonable degree of freedom in marketing. Secondly they maintained—through their mouthpieces on the Council —that by the export of coal a "greate deale of treasour . . . is yierlie broght within the cuntrey." In practice, the wealth and influence of men such as Samuel Johnston of Elphinstone who could lay out 20,000 merks on his coal works,[37] of John Dundas, or of Sir George Bruce, counted for more than the vestigial remains of a medieval theory, and the penalties threatened by the Convention in the 1590's for failure to enforce the ban on export were a gesture of despair.[38] Under licence or otherwise, the coal trade continued to expand.

The application of the doctrine of the common interest to trading in food preservatives and the basic foods was relatively easy. In the early 1570's, for example, a group of Acts of both Parliament and Council prescribed the conditions on which salt might be exported.[39] In brief they ruled that the needs of the native population were first to be met, and that export thereafter could be undertaken only for the homebringing of timber or coinable silver. The balance of Scotland's food supply, taking one year with another, was so finely poised that complete freedom of trade in grain and flesh seemed clearly contrary to the public interest; and as we saw in Chapter I, the pattern of harvests was closely mirrored in legislation and decrees. Suffice it here to observe that these fell into three related categories. In time of famine or threatened famine, the normal procedure was to ban exports either uncondition-ally or until the domestic markets were satisfied.[40] The domestic markets in turn were subject to price control and to prohibitions on hoarding and forestalling.[41] For the final stage, private consumption, a mass of Acts and proclamations existed:[42] sumptuary regulations in 1550 prescribing the maximum number of dishes permissible to each social stratum; the "political Lent" of 1562; the dietary prescribed for the staff and students of Glasgow University by a Royal Com-mission in 1602.

[37] Cochran-Patrick, *Mining in Scotland*, pp. xlviii-xlix.
[38] *Convention Records*, VOL. I, pp. 414, 445-6, 464.
[39] *A.P.S.*, VOL. III, p. 82; *R.P.C.*, VOL. II, p. 264.
[40] E.g. *R.P.C.*, VOL. I, p. 402.   [41] E.g. *op. cit.*, VOL. V, pp. 243-4.
[42] E.g. *op. cit.*, VOL. I, pp. 94-6, 200; VOL. VI, p. 452.

The attempts to control trading in semi-luxury wares disclose a jumble of economic and ethical motives. As we shall see in Chapter VI, price-fixing and royal pre-emption were well-established features of the wine trade; but as time passed the heavy and widespread drinking of wines gave rise to a puritanical demand for more effective and positive restriction. What, the Council said, had formerly been drunk in moderation to "manis comfort and preservatioun of his helth," had become, by excess, "the cutthrot of sa mony menis lyveis and robber of thair purseis."[43] It was argued that if the lieges insisted on wasting their substance the Crown might as well derive some passing benefit in the form of revenue. By 1610-11, therefore, the existing imports duties on wine were so far supplemented by local imposts that the total levies on wine amounted to almost £37 a tun.[44]

Tobacco gave rise to tremendous controversy. Lithgow, in his *Scotland's Welcome to King Charles*, loyally echoed the opinions of James VI:

> It spoyles their Memory, and blinds their sight,
> Dryes up the moisture of the Carnall wight.

But others, notably William Barclay of Aberdeen in his *Nepenthes, or The Vertues of Tabacco*,[45] held it to be "the princesse of physical plants" and a sedative or cure for almost every human ailment. The story of official intervention is recited in two Proclamations of 1622.[46] Heavy import duties had been nimbly circumvented by smugglers, and complete prohibition by "the shifts and subtiltyis of the importaris." Accordingly in 1617, as the King did "not resolve altogither to depryve his loving subjectis of the ordourlie seale and moderate use of tobacco," a compromise was attempted whereby import could be regulated to the financial benefit of the Crown, and to this end a monopoly of import was issued to the King's "auld servand," Captain William Murray. In view of the admissions of administrative failure, it is hardly surprising that no worth-

---

[43] *Op. cit.*, VOL. IX, p. 551.

[44] *Op. cit.*, VOL. IX, pp. 306-8; *Edinburgh Records*, VOL. VI, p. 57 and App. XIII, XV; *South Leith Records*, ed. D. Robertson, 1911, p. 12.

[45] W. Barclay, *Nepenthes, or The Vertues of Tabacco*, 1614, reprinted in *Miscellany of the Spalding Club*, VOL. I, 1841, pp. 261-9.

[46] *R.P.C.*, VOL. XIII, pp. 28, 102; VOL. X, p. 659.

while statistics of imports can be found: but it is evident from scattered references that the use of tobacco was widespread,[47] and the attempt to canalise the trade through Murray's agents produced a fresh crop of evasions. Accordingly, after another phase of vacillation, the Council in 1623 finally declared import to be legal, subject to payment of a royalty to the then owners of Murray's patent.[48]

So far, therefore, it cannot be said that Scotland had acquired either a distinctive or a decisive commercial policy. The one outstanding innovation, the general import duty of 1597, was, as we have seen, prompted mainly by consideration of revenue. In most other respects the policy towards both foreign and internal trade remained essentially medieval. By chance, rather than by intent, there were elements savouring of mercantilism. Thus the attempts to prevent the entry of English cloth and to restrain the export of wool are consistent with the formulation of a positive industrial policy, while the concern about food supplies is at least as consistent with mercantilist views on population as with the medieval love of goods.

In fact, any comprehensive policy was unlikely to emerge. Before about 1600, national poverty and the weakness of royal authority, coupled with the clash of interested parties, made for incoherence and expediency. It is true that after 1600, royal authority over Council and Parliament might have found expression in more positive and permanent measures, but commerce was not among the King's main interests. Perhaps there were limits even to the intellectual activity of a Solomon. It has been pointed out that James rarely attended Council meetings in London when commercial matters were under discussion;[49] he made no serious attempt to keep abreast of trade developments; he rarely even acquired the factual knowledge on which policy should have been based. In our examination of the timber trade we shall see that the King's proposal in 1608 to ban the export of Scottish timber compelled the Council to point out that none had in fact been exported within living memory.[50] His attempted interference with coal exports,

[47] *Burgh Laws of Dundee*, p. 152; *Aberdeen Council Letters*, ed. L. B. Taylor, 1942, p. xxii. [48] *R.P.C.*, VOL. XIII, pp. 189 ff.
[49] E. R. Turner, "The origin of the Cabinet Council," in *English Historical Review*, XXXVIII (1923), p. 188. [50] *R.P.C.*, VOL. VIII, p. 543.

clearly based on archaic notions of small-scale outcrop production, demonstrated his unfamiliarity with current Scottish
mining developments and significantly ceased after his visit in
1617 to the great mine at Culross. As we shall see presently,
his suggestions for limitations on the employment of alien
shipping reveal ignorance of the Scottish-Baltic carrying trade,
and seem to have proceeded from the assumption that what
was appropriate for England must also be appropriate for
Scotland. Because of his fondness for deducing policy from
first principles, his commercial proposals are invariably of
interest as intellectual exercises; and in some matters, notably
Anglo-Scottish trade relations, he was far ahead of popular
opinion. Yet the harsh truth is that in most commercial affairs
his interference was spasmodic and generally ill informed.

Control of trade was not, of course, limited to the creation
and application of commercial policies. In certain areas,
notably Holland and France, the conditions on which Scotsmen traded were frequently the subject of negotiation by the
Crown or the Convention of Royal Burghs. The Staple at
Veere was a classic example of continuous official economic
organisation,[51] and, especially after the Reformation, the
Convention displayed considerable activity in attempting to
preserve the old Scottish trading rights in France.[52] Nearer
home, the control of shipping lay within the accepted sphere of
official action. The objectives of this control can be considered
under two broad headings—the one covering matters of
discipline and safety, the other covering the attempted introduction of a mercantilist system of navigation laws.

Again, the background to the study lies principally in the
burgh records. From the later Middle Ages skippers and
shipowners had been subject to a mass of burghal rules about
loading, harbour conduct, sailing and so forth. As we see
elsewhere, there were both burghal and statutory restrictions
on winter sailings. Action at a higher level pursued two not
easily reconcilable policies: the employment of merchant
vessels for warlike purposes, and the suppression of hostile
piracy. Throughout our period letters of marque were periodically issued to skippers authorising them to engage in warlike

---

[51] See below, pp. 234-6.
[52] E.g. *Convention Records*, VOL. I, pp. 182, 211, 270-2 *et al.*

acts against specified enemies,[53] and on occasion merchant vessels were armed and put to sea as warships. After rehearsing how the King's father had been "horriblie murtherit" and his mother "raveist" by Bothwell, the Council in 1567 directed Sir William Murray and Sir William Kirkcaldy to requisition "and reg furth how many ships they sall think meet" to bring the perpetrator to justice.[54] In the event the Dundee ships employed missed their man, but had the consolation of rescuing a vessel and cargo piratically seized by Bothwell.[55] Similarly in the war scare of 1627 the *Grace* of Dysart was armed and put on patrol with eighty men aboard.[56] Especially in times of central governmental weakness, the Convention of Royal Burghs took the initiative in "purging of oure Soueranis watteris" of "pyrattis and wicked persounis." Thus after some negotiation Alan Lentron of St Andrews was commissioned to equip an anti-piracy vessel at the joint expense of the burghs;[57] Acts and action were directed against persons and burghs believed guilty of aiding or harbouring pirates;[58] and direct negotiations were at various times undertaken with foreign powers with a view to joint action.[59] In 1577, for example, the Convention sent Adam Fullarton to England to seek compensation for losses sustained by his countrymen at the hands of English pirates, and in London he found Elizabeth's Council very willing to consider measures for the prevention of further abuses.[60]

Any attempt to restrict Scottish trade to Scottish ships raised problems both of expediency and of long-term policy. As we shall see in our studies of overseas trade, while foreign vessels handled part of the carrying trade to and from Scotland, Scottish ships found some employment in similar trade elsewhere in European waters. No restriction was seriously contemplated until James issued from London one of his pontificial utterances on the proper conduct of Scottish affairs. "The very law of nature," he said, "teacheth every sort of corporation, kingdom or country, first to set their own vessels on work,

[53] E.g. the Letter of Marque issued to Thomas Ogilvy who appears to have abused the privilege; *R.P.C.*, VOL. IV, pp. 615, 627.
[54] *Op. cit.*, VOL. I, pp. 544-5.   [55] *Op. cit.*, p. 581.
[56] D. B. Morris, *The Stirling Merchant Gild and the Life of John Cowane*, 1919, Ch. XIX *passim*.
[57] *Convention Records*, VOL. I, pp. 27-8, 242.   [58] *Op. cit.*, pp. 197, 305.
[59] *Op. cit.*, pp. 44, 528.   [60] *Op. cit.*, pp. 50, 82, 116, 239, 298.

before they employ any stranger." To effect this, he proposed that a Proclamation of 1615, reviving the old English Navigation Laws, should be applied, *mutatis mutandis*, to Scotland.[61] The Scottish Council thereupon convened a joint conference of merchants and skippers at which, not unnaturally, a sharp difference of views emerged.[62] The skippers favoured restrictions on foreign vessels; the merchants advanced three counter-arguments. In brief they maintained that foreign charterers would, in retaliation, dispense with Scottish ships; that Scottish fish exports depended heavily on Dutch carriers; and that Scottish ships could not replace foreigners in the Baltic trades without loss of efficiency in deliveries and raising of freights. "After lang debait and contestatioun on ather syde," the Council in 1619 brought the conference "to this point, that with mutuall consent the restreante for all tradis, except the easterlyne [Baltic] trade, wes aggreit upoun"; and with abject apology for the reservation this finding was communicated to the King.

The exemption of the Baltic trade was akin to taking the Prince out of *Hamlet*, for the role of the pure "carrier" in other branches of Scotland's overseas trade was so small that even a rigid enforcement of the King's policy would have had comparatively little effect. In fact there is no perceptible change in the national pattern of the ships frequenting Scottish ports after 1619: Mrs Pagan's conclusion that the shipping regulations "soon fell into abeyance"[63] is scarcely surprising, for in no case could they have had much effect.

INDUSTRIAL POLICY

In the previous chapter we saw how any general expansion of the industrial life of Scotland depended upon the existence of such peaceful internal conditions as would create confidence and stimulate enterprise and capital accumulation. From the beginning of our period until about 1600, when James achieved real control, the royal administration cannot fairly be said to have provided this elementary basis for any significant period.

[61] *R.P.C.*, VOL. XI, p. 202.
[62] *Op. cit.*, VOL. XI, p. xli, VOL. XII, p. 107; *Convention Records*, VOL. I, pp. 66-7, 75-6, 88.
[63] Pagan, *Convention of the Royal Burghs*, p. 156.

The development of a positive industrial policy, which in any circumstances presupposes the elements of law and order, was further retarded by the rigidity of the existing industrial system and by the conservatism of the Convention of Royal Burghs. Mrs Pagan, the historian of that body, speaks of the "parochial character" of its interest in industry, and continues: "the burghs were more concerned in opposing patents obtained by individuals for the introduction of new processes than in trying to introduce or promote new industries themselves."[64] The attitude is well illustrated by discussions in 1616, when the Privy Council urged the Convention to develop wool cloth making, only to be told that though the burghs agreed that though this was both feasible and desirable, they "plainlie and flatlie refusit" to accept "ony burdyne in that mater."[65]

It would, however, be grossly unjust to the Convention to imply that its attitude towards industry was wholly negative. Its handling of complaints about the quality or quantity of goods was prompted by an anxiety to maintain standards and to do justice. Dunfermline, for example, brought complaints about the quantity of thread in reels of yarn made elsewhere;[66] Galloway "kerseys" were said to be "unloyall and insufficient";[67] plaiding was held to be badly made and packed.[68] The Convention was always ready to investigate such complaints, and, where appropriate, to make orders for redress. Similarly, and even more positively, it was prepared to co-operate with the Government in arranging for the immigration of alien craftsmen to demonstrate and teach new techniques of textile manufacture. The same kind of activity can be traced in the fisheries. To ensure uniformity in packing, an official barrel was defined and each town was instructed to stamp its barrels with a distinctive mark.[69] In 1611 a set of orders was issued for the better conduct of the herring fisheries of Dunbar,[70] including one to the effect that sand and not stones was to be used to ballast boats, because stones thrown overboard at sea were liable to kill or disperse the shoals of fish.

Furthermore the Convention assiduously promoted the

---

[64] *Op. cit.*, p. 213.   [65] *R.P.C.*, VOL. X, pp. 506-7.
[66] *Convention Records*, VOL. III, p. 14.
[67] *Op. cit.*, p. 136.   [68] *Op. cit.*, pp. 124, 130, 137.
[69] *R.P.C.*, VOL. X, pp. 578-9; *Convention Records*, VOL. III, pp. 11-12, 32, 42.
[70] *Convention Records*, VOL. II, pp. 426, 445; VOL. III, pp. 5, 19, 44-5.

standardisation of weights and measures, a by no means insignificant contribution to the process of knitting the economy
into a single whole.[71] In this endeavour the Convention, the
Council, and Parliament strove with but limited resources to
overcome the persistence of regional standards. Theoretically
the Four Burghs—Edinburgh, Lanark, Linlithgow, and
Stirling—were the custodians of the official measures, the ell
(linear), the pint (liquid), the stone (weight) and the firlot
(dry volume), but uniformity over either space or time existed
in little more than name. From 1552 onwards the Commissioners of Burghs in their periodic meetings pressed hard for
permanent uniform standards, and their recommendations
received statutory backing culminating in an Act of 1617[72]
which sought to establish "one just Measure and Weight
through all the pairtes of this kingdome." Respect for the law
was certainly higher than it had been and the administrative
system was enormously improved, yet such was the tenacity of
local standards that diversity continued, especially in grain
measures, down to the early nineteenth century.

The industrial policy of James VI and his subservient
Council and Parliaments hinged largely on the use of monopolies. The industrial impact of these was examined in
Chapter II; we are here concerned primarily with royal
motives and intentions. Financial considerations, which
featured so prominently in contemporary English monopoly
controversy, were certainly present in Scotland. When a
monopoly of certain mining rights was granted to Thomas
Foulis in 1593 it was admitted that the King was heavily in his
debt, and, the "royal fynance is being swa exhaustit and
sparpallit," could not repay in cash.[73] Similarly the salt patent
granted to Eustachius Roche openly professed to being "for the
advauncement and augmentatioun of his Heinis rentis and
revenews,"[74] and the Act confirming Roche's patent of lead-
mining in 1584 provided that 1,000 stones of melted lead
should be allocated annually to the Crown.[75] Though in many
instances the names and titles of the recipients hardly suggest
that technical or managerial experience was an essential

---

[71] This paragraph is based on J. M. Henderson, *Scottish Reckonings of Time,
Money, Weights and Measures*, Historical Association of Scotland, 1926.
[72] *A.P.S.*, VOL. IV, p. 409.   [73] *R.P.C.*, VOL. V, p. 117.
[74] *A.P.S.*, VOL. IV, p. 156.   [75] *Op. cit.*, VOL. III, p. 368.

qualification for the receipt of a patent, some attempt was normally made to justify each in terms of the public interest. Thus in the salt monopoly granted to Lady Burley in 1587 it was maintained that her new method would produce "salt upon salt" (purified salt), and that it would reduce the nation's dependence on supplies from overseas.[76] In response, no doubt, to the growing discontents about the granting and operating of monopolies, the patents issued in the later part of King James's reign were often accompanied both by an even fuller statement of the public interest and by provisions for price control. Lord Erskine's leather monopoly was established—ostensibly at any rate—in response to complaints from the cordiners about the inferior quality of home-tanned leather, and one of his duties was to induce the native tanners to accept instruction.[77] The operations of Hay in glass-making and of Udward in soap-making were both subject to some control of the prices of their products.[78] The formal justification of Murray's tobacco monopoly was partly that unless the trade were so canalised "men utherwayed serviceable" would be "allured" to the "licentious idleness" of dealing in tobacco,[79] and partly that the licensee intended "plantatioun . . . within the kingdome."[80]

The reign of King James ended with a remarkable quickening in the tempo of royal intervention in the industrial affairs of Scotland. In England, the Parliament of 1621 had insisted on the investigation into the working of monopolies which culminated in the great English statute of 1624, and, moved by this display of resolution among his southern subjects, James instructed his Scottish Council to establish a Commission for Grievances.[81] The royal letter refers specifically to the harm done in England and Ireland by the operation of certain private projects, and goes on: "we, preferring ever the common good before the respectis of privat persouns, intend that, if anie such disease hes happened there [i.e. in Scotland], our good subjectis may receive cure from our care." In pursuance of this missive, a Commission of thirteen Privy Councillors was established and met frequently from June 1623 to the end of the reign.[82] In fact its deliberations were by no means con-

---

[76] *Op. cit.*, p. 426. [77] *R.P.C.*, vol. xii, pp. 189-93.
[78] *Op. cit.*, vol. xiii, pp. 294-5. [79] *Op. cit.*, p. 102.
[80] *Op. cit.*, p. 191. [81] *Op. cit.*, pp. 219-21. [82] *Op. cit., passim.*

fined to the operations of monopolists; indeed it held that protests against Udward's soap monopoly and Mrs Murray's tobacco monopoly were *ultra vires* and should be handled by the parent Council.[83] On the vexed question of coal exports it very reasonably ruled that overseas sales should be allowed until the home market was big enough to give the mine-owners a reasonable return on their capital outlay.[84] On the equally vexed issue of the quality of Erskine's leather it staged in 1624 a competition between representatives of the traditional Scots method and the new English method to see which made the better job of tanning ten Highland cowhides.[85] Its record was not impressive in volume, but its few decisions were eminently sensible.

Its passing was ignominious: indeed after the accession of Charles I, according to the contemporary witness of Sir James Balfour, it "evanished in itselffe."[86] The facts are that Charles reconstituted the Commission, with powers so enlarged that, in the opinion of both contemporaries and later historians, it might well have become a Scottish version of the Court of Star Chamber. In this new form it met once amid considerable confusion, and then met no more.

In any event, the function of the Commission for Grievances had been investigation and recommendation rather than the independent formulation of positive industrial proposals. The simultaneous creation of another body, the Standing Commission on Manufactures, was potentially an altogether more important step. The proposal for its creation emerged indirectly from discussions on the best use of Scotland's raw materials, notably her wool. The gist of the matter is set out in Sir William Seyton's report to the Council,[87] in which he drew a sharp contrast between former generations when "the great troubles within this kingdome by incursionis and other mis-governaments" had "wounderfullie weakened" the stock of sheep, and his own time, when, "by his Hienes solid governament," wool production had so increased that there was a surplus. The English proposal that this surplus should go exclusively to England naturally prompted counter-proposals,

---

[83] *Op. cit.*, pp. 239-48.   [84] *Op. cit.*, pp. 570-1.   [85] *Op. cit.*, pp. 644-6.
[86] Balfour, *Annals*, VOL. II, p. 131; *R.P.C.*, 2nd ser., VOL. I, pp. liii, 263-5.
[87] *R.P.C.*, VOL. XIII, pp. 773-5.

in which the King participated, for the expansion of manufacturing within Scotland.[88]

The plan for a central body for industrial development met
with a hearty reception from the Scottish Council, which
promptly convened a meeting of representatives of the Estates
of the Realm, and, under an act of the Great Seal of 1623,
sixty-nine leading members were embodied in the Standing
Commission on Manufactures.[89] This might have been one
of the outstanding politico-economic innovations in European
history. Unlike the Commission for Grievances, it was no mere
committee of the Privy Council, for in constitution it was a
microcosm of Parliament and might have become a prototype
for industrial parliaments elsewhere. Its powers embraced the
whole field of industrial development: what new industries
were desirable, where they should be located, what structure
should be adopted, what regulations were needed about quality
and quantity of output, what skilled craftsmen were required,
and so on.

In the last two years of the reign of James VI, therefore,
Scotland was exceptionally well equipped for the formal
examination of economic problems. The Convention of Royal
Burghs remained as alert as ever, but initiative and inventive-
ness clearly lay rather in the creations of 1623. Unlike the
Convention, they were not the spokesmen of vested burghal
interests, and their detachment might have enabled them to
further that common weal of which the King spoke so often
with eloquence. What might have emerged in the way of
national industrial policy lies wholly in the realm of speculation,
for the machinery set up in 1623 needed the guidance of a
cunning master who, knowing the stomach of his countrymen,
would temper principle with expediency. After the succession
of Charles I guidance of this quality was no longer offered, and,
if it had been, Scotland was scarcely in the mood to accept it.

In the long view of history it seems that the greatest contribution by public authorities to economic growth has been by
indirect means: the establishment of order, the upholding of
contracts, the provision of means of communication, and the
like. In their attention to communications, the public authorities of Scotland served both administrative and economic needs.

[88] *Op. cit.*, pp. 70, 141.   [89] *Op. cit.*, pp. 235, 299-301.

Because of geographical hindrances and human interference, overland transport played a relatively small part; it was no accident that every town of any consequence was approachable either by sea or by river. Nevertheless the limitations of natural waterways were evident, notably in the absence of any direct east-west route, while the deep indentations in the coastline aggravated the problem of north-south overland movement.

With periodic prodding or help from the Convention and from Parliament, the burghs strove manfully to maintain their harbours and bridges in reasonable order. Sometimes, as at Aberdeen,[90] Kirkcaldy,[91] and Stonehaven,[92] harbour works could fairly be classed as developments; oftener, as at Dumbarton,[93] St Andrews[94] and Arbroath,[95] the burgh sought outside aid to combat the destructive forces of time and waves. In the building and repairing of bridges, economic and administrative interests fused into a common purpose: so the vital crossing over the Tay at Perth was "a work necessary for keeping the one half of the kingdom, with the other half thereof, in faith . . . and office towards us their kings."[96] Some were fortunate in inheriting substantial medieval bridges. At Glasgow the eight arches and twelve-foot roadway over the Clyde were to survive for centuries; at Aberdeen Bishop Elphinstone's fortune had gone into the building of a seven-span bridge over the Dee which his successor finished in 1527.[97] But by the middle of James VI's reign Stirling's medieval hump-backed bridge was so much in need of repair that in 1598 the Burgh Council was authorised to levy a custom for "beitting and repairing of the brig and calsay adiacent thairto,"[98] and the Council's accounts for the early 1600's show a regular revenue for this purpose.

Perth had the biggest problem, for in spite of its key position in communications—"the most centrical town in Scotland"[99]

[90] J. Milne, Aberdeen; Topographical, Antiquarian and Historical Papers, 1911, pp. 362 ff.   [91] Kirkcaldy Records, p. 151.
[92] Convention Records, VOL. II, pp. 113, 302, 351.
[93] Op. cit., VOL. I, pp. 134, 180; VOL. II, p. 160.
[94] Op. cit., VOL. I, pp. 293, 299; VOL. II, p. 79.
[95] Op. cit., VOL. I, pp. 329, 359; VOL. II, pp. 306, 320; G. Hay, History of Arbroath, 1876, pp. 317-8.   [96] New Statistical Account of Scotland, 1845, VOL. X, p. 99.
[97] H. Boece, Murthlacensium et Aberdonensium episcoporum vitae, ed. J. Moir, New Spalding Club, 1894, pp. 161, 181.
[98] Stirling Records, VOL. I, pp. 91, 132, 306.
[99] New Statistical Account of Scotland, VOL. X, p. 119.

it was later to be called—its bridge had always been ramshackle and exposed to exceptional hazards. Patched and restored at intervals throughout the Middle Ages, it was battered afresh by a succession of Tay floods in 1573, 1582, and 1589, temporarily repaired with timber, and then rebuilt by Mylne in masonry between 1599 and 1617.[100] Here was a task of national significance and financially beyond the capacity of one town. Edinburgh, apparently voluntarily, donated 500 merks in 1609,[101] and the next year the rebuilding was commended to the goodwill of Parliament and of all the burghs at the Convention.[102] In fact the money was wasted. Four years after their completion, the "spacious arches" were, as Mylne's lapidary epitaph had it, "demolish'd by a mighty spate." Popular opinion, reported by Calderwood, regarded the disaster as retribution for the episcopalian iniquities committed by the recent Assemblies and Parliament which had met in Perth.[103]

Bridges, harbours, and ferries were, as a rule, within the competence of the burghs and their Convention. Highways across the countryside were less adequately managed. Improvement here posed two related problems: how to create an administrative system which could raise the standard of roads to something better than the age-old drovers' and pedlars' ways so that travellers and traders could invoke the aid of the wheel to supplement the carrying capacity of the horse. Pointers had been given in Queen Mary's reign, partly by the highway legislation of 1555,[104] partly by the introduction of the first coach.[105] The coach came originally for royal use: a French model was imported for Queen Mary in 1561, and the Regent Morton—anxious no doubt to display the attributes of royalty —was using one in 1577. But real highway improvement had to await the creation of appropriate administrative machinery. This came after 1610 when James introduced into Scotland the system of road supervision by the Justices of the Peace which had already proved its worth in England; and within a decade

[100] T. H. Marshall, *History of Perth*, 1849, pp. 467-8.
[101] *Edinburgh Records*, VOL. VI, pp. 52-3.
[102] *A.P.S.*, VOL. IV, p. 451; *Convention Records*, VOL. II, pp. 299, 320.
[103] Calderwood, *History of the Kirk of Scotland*, VOL. IV, p. 377; Marshall, *History of Perth*, p. 461.   [104] *A.P.S.*, VOL. II, p. 498.
[105] D. G. Moir, "The roads of Scotland," in *Scottish Geographical Magazine*, LXXIII (1957), pp. 101-10.

the "statute labour roads" of later Scottish history were coming into existence.[106]

CURRENCY, USURY, AND PRICE CONTROL

The provision of a medium of exchange was, by the sixteenth century, an accepted attribute of Scottish sovereignty and a profitable service rendered by the ruler to the people. For most of that century the economy of Scotland laboured under currency arrangements which, at best were inadequate and at worst were chaotic. It must, of course, be recognised that this was a period when the great influx to Europe of American silver had destroyed the traditional ratio between silver and gold, and when every European country was faced with the recurrent problem of readjustment to prevent the drain of one or other of its precious metals. Furthermore, even if the implications of the new situation were understood, Scotland's administrative organisation was normally incapable of applying any consistent policy and her rulers were constantly beset by the temptation to stretch their limited resources.

In Scotland, as in most countries in the sixteenth and seventeenth centuries, the domestic coinage furnished only a part of the circulating media, for in the great commercial centres of the Continent hundreds of different coins were in daily use and a fair assortment made its way to Scotland. In Aberdeen in 1590 the precious metal alone ranged widely from Portuguese ducats valued at over £37 each to the silver half-mark pieces worth 7s.,[107] and David Wedderburne's repeated references to money prove that the same variety circulated in Dundee.[108] From the fourteenth century onwards the Scots Parliament and Council had repeatedly defined and re-defined—in Scottish terminology—the value of the various foreign coins in the country.[109] Sometimes *ad hoc* valuations were necessary, as in 1551 when the value of the sou, which had been issued as pay to the French soldiers serving in Scotland, was fixed at 6d. Scots.[110] National policy was in-

---

[106] Moir, *loc. cit.*, A.P.S., VOL. IV, p. 536.
[107] Kennedy, *Annals of Aberdeen*, p. 185. There is similar evidence for Stirling in *Stirling Records*, VOL. I, pp. 74-5.
[108] *Wedderburne Compt Buik*, pp. xxxvii-xxxviii.
[109] Summarised in Cochran-Patrick, *Coinage*, VOL. I, pp. xci-xcv.
[110] *Op. cit.*, VOL. I, p. 75.

creasingly shaped to compel merchants to bring foreign money into the country as part of the proceeds of overseas sales, and William Fairlie in 1582 would have met with complete official approval when he instructed his factor in Flanders to send home "9 merks 2 unce weight Spanish ryal" to pay his debts in Scotland.[111] It has been suggested that, as an additional inducement, foreign coin in Scotland was deliberately over-valued,[112] though this must have been a two-edged weapon as it would also tempt merchants to smuggle domestic coin out of the country in order to purchase the over-valued foreign currency abroad. At all events the activities of merchants as purveyors of foreign coin could be a sore trial to the authorities. In the late 1560's, for example, there was a spate of "fals cuyne," especially of "hardheidis" from Flanders, "to the heuy dampnage and skaith of the haill liegis."[113] A series of exe-cutions—Andrew Murray of Perth, and Patrick Ramsay and Robert Jacke of Dundee—for importing hardheads, and the public display of the culprits' "heidis, armis and leggis" in their native towns,[114] apparently failed to stop the traffic, for three years later (in 1570) the Convention of Royal Burghs was still pressing for action.[115]

The prevalence of foreign, and the drain of domestic coin, continued into the next century. Lithgow's jingling verse:

> There are no moneyes going, nor golden collours,
> Save Dutch and Holland, Saxone, Austrian dollours

was no mere flight of fancy, for its sense is borne out by the very frequent discussions in the Privy Council and among the Mint officials,[116] and by the way in which purely domestic transactions were at times conducted in foreign currency. When the Kirk Session of South Leith bargained with William Smyth to repair the parish clock for 22 rex dollars it showed a fine disregard of the nationality of coins.[117]

---

[111] *R.P.C.*, VOL. III, p. 558.

[112] T. Ruddiman, *An Introduction to Mr James Anderson's Diplomata Scotiae*, 1773 edn., p. 156.

[113] *A.P.S.*, VOL. III, p. 30; *R.P.C.*, VOL. I, p. 510.

[114] Balfour, *Annals*, VOL. I, p. 342; "Diarey of Robert Birrel, Burges of Edin-burgh," in J. G. Dalyell, *Fragments of Scottish History*, 1798, p. 14.

[115] *Convention Records*, VOL. I, p. 22.

[116] Cochran-Patrick, *Coinage*, VOL. I, pp. 239-40, 287-93.

[117] *South Leith Records*, p. 27.

This everyday use of foreign coin, especially by financial innocents, inevitably created confusion and provided scope for fraud. Many people had no accurate knowledge of either the metallic or the official value of the coin, and simply assessed it by its size and superficial appearance. From this point of view the domestic coinage of Scotland was little better. A bag of Scottish coins in the 1590's could have included gold lions and half lions, ryalls and half ryalls, lion nobles, thistle nobles, bonnet pieces and hat pieces, silver testoons, thistle dollars and groats, to say nothing of a great ballast of copper of low denomination. For at least one period, in the early 1570's, rival mints operated in Edinburgh and Dalkeith;[118] but the chief cause of confusion arose from the fact that the coins bore no fixed face value as we understand the term today. Nicholas Briot, in a communication to the Privy Council in 1626, put the matter in a nutshell: "The most common marks of soueranety," he wrote, "is the right of forging and stamping coynes, and it lyes in the princes power to impose such value as he please."[119]

The distinction, therefore, has to be drawn between the actual metallic coin and what it was made to represent in accounting: the difference between "real" and "imaginary" money. In Scotland the distinction was unusually sharp, for the accounting terms—pounds, shillings, merks, and so on—bore little terminological resemblance to the coins of the realm. This in itself would have been tolerable if the relationship between real and accounting money had remained constant, but rulers soon learned that the simplest means of monetary manipulation was to adjust—either by enhancing or calling down—the accounting equivalent of the coin.[120] This practice, attractive because it involved no recoinage, was used with bewildering frequency in the later decades of the sixteenth century. So, to give one instance from dozens, the current value of the lion noble was arbitrarily raised in 1588 from £3. 15s. 0d. to £4.[121] As David Moysie noted, these changes

---

[118] Cochran-Patrick, *Coinage*, VOL. I, p. cxlvi.

[119] *Op. cit.*, pp. 53-4. The implications of this kind of currency manipulation are considered in B. E. Supple, "Currency and commerce in the seventeenth century," in *Ec. H.R.*, x (1957).

[120] It is possible that the "calling down" of the Dalkeith money in 1575 was a cause of Morton's unpopularity; Cochran-Patrick, *Coinage*, VOL. I, p. cxlvii.

[121] *Op. cit.*, p. clvi.

in the value of money were much "mislykit be the commone pepill."[122]

When Thomas Ruddiman analysed the causes of the depreciation of the old Scottish currency, he rightly gave first place to the "necessities and poverty of princes."[123] Coinage was a profitable business, but it required bullion; bullion was almost always scarce in Scotland, and therefore the rulers succumbed to the temptation to make their bullion stretch further with each new issue of coins. The usual process is all too familiar. By reducing the quantity of precious metal, or by using metal of lower fineness, they debased the coinage and then—as Gresham observed—the poorer money tended to drive the better out of circulation, either into hoards or into the goldsmiths' crucibles. As a further complication, knowledgeable traders refused to accept payment in the new debased coin at its face value. After much experience of these reactions, the Scottish rulers' normal practice was to enhance the official value of the surviving old issues so that the ratio between the accounting and the metal value of both old and new was approximately the same.

Arbitrary changes in official value, variations in thickness and weight, disparity between official value and metal value, the prevalence of clipping and forgery, similarity in appearance between different coins, inscriptions in unknown tongues: all these brought confusion to the guileless and profit to the guileful. Can it be wondered that payment in kind and barter arrangements persisted so strongly in sixteenth- and seventeenth-century Scotland?

The combination of debasement and enhancement, widening the gap between the metal value of the coin and the accounting value assigned to it, resulted in the well-known fall in the exchange rate between Scotland and England. So long as the English coinage was suffering debasement, as it was to about 1560, the late fifteenth-century ratio of about 4 to 1 remained fairly steady; but once the great Elizabethan recoinage was complete and English money became more stabilised, the relative value of the Scottish began to fall rapidly.[124] In 1571

[122] Moysie, *Memoirs of the Affairs of Scotland, 1577-1603*, p. 10.
[123] Ruddiman, *An Introduction to Mr James Anderson's Diplomata Scotiae*, p. 154.
[124] Craig, *De unione*, pp. 291-3.

John Lesley, Bishop of Ross, noted in London that Michael Gilbert (a goldsmith) had offered "to ressave fra me here, and give in Edinbrucht, v li. vi s. for every pound sterueling, bot I wold have had v li. x s."[125] This was sound financial sense, for the value of the Scots pound in London was falling fast, and the fall continued apparently unabated until 1603 when the ratio was down to 12 to 1.[126] As we shall see in Chapter VII, the stabilisation of that ratio was one of the solid economic by-products of the Union of the Crowns.

Down to that point, the handling of monetary affairs by the Scottish authorities had been at best inept, and at worst vicious. How far were their actions determined in ignorance of the consequences, and how far were they the result of sheer force of circumstances? In most fields of thought Scotland was in intimate contact with the Continent, and there is no reason to think that the current European controversies on money and prices passed unobserved in Scotland. The evidence is to the contrary. Among the Hopetoun Papers, a major original source on Scottish monetary affairs, is one entitled "Touching Money," in which, in the economic jargon of 1564, the writer presents a well-reasoned analysis of the money-price relationship.[127] When Napier of Merchiston, General of the Scottish Mint, went to London in 1604 to confer about the possibility of a common Anglo-Scottish coinage, "he carried hes bussines with a grate deall of dexteritey and skille . . . to the grate amazement of the Englishe."[128] Similarly the disputations among the Mint officials and royal advisers of the early seventeenth century, notably John Acheson and Nicholas Briot,[129] would not disgrace an economics seminar in a modern Scottish university.

In any environment, a double-standard currency presents acute problems to its managers when the relationship between the market values of gold and silver is fluid. In the Scotland of the sixteenth century these problems would have taxed the financial acumen of a Gresham and the statecraft of a Cecil;

---

[125] "Diary of John Lesley," in *Miscellany of the Bannatyne Club*, VOL. III, p. 131.

[126] Cochran-Patrick, *Coinage*, VOL. I, p. lxxvi.

[127] Printed *op. cit.*, pp. 90-2.

[128] Balfour, *Annals*, VOL. II, p. 2.

[129] Briot, a native of Lorraine, is yet another instance of the employment of Continental skill in Scotland; Cochran-Patrick, *Coinage*, VOL. I, p. xci; VOL. II, pp. 45, 52.

and the one Scot who might have grappled with them, Maitland of Lethington, died in 1573, still in the prime of life, a
political prisoner under sentence of execution in the old
Tolbooth at Leith. During the reign of Mary, and during most
of the subsequent regencies, at the very moment when the
English were setting their monetary house in order, the Scots
were still pursuing a poverty-stricken opportunist existence.
Furthermore effective currency management, especially in a
time of rapidly changing world prices, calls for a more effective
system of public administration than Scotland possessed at any
time before about 1600. Finally Scotland's bullion shortage
was chronic. We saw in Chapter II that domestic production
of the precious metals was never very great, indeed the Scottish
output of gold at least seems to have fallen off at the very time
when widening economic activities called for a greater supply
of money. From the fifteenth century merchants had, theoretically, been required to bring in specified amounts of "burnt
silver" against each consignment of goods exported,[130] but
again the application of the law fell far short of its intention.
The interest displayed by kings and officials, from James IV
and Damian in 1500 to Napier of Merchiston in 1600, in the
production of gold by alchemical methods, involved substantial
expenditure on whisky and other unlikely substances, but
yielded no gold.[131] In an emergency, as in 1553, plate could be
taken to the Mint and melted,[132] but there were obvious limits
to that source. Secretly or openly, coin passed in and out of the
land as it suited the private interests of merchants; but the
overall balance of payments was not sufficiently favourable
over any significant period to stimulate a lasting net inflow of
bullion large enough to furnish the country with an adequate
domestic coinage.

In the attitude of her official bodies towards usury, Scotland
was moving roughly in step with her Protestant neighbours
around the North Sea. This was a matter on which both
Church and State professed themselves competent to pronounce.
In so far as the Church followed Calvin, its attitude should
have been one of conditional approval. Calvin, refusing to

[130] E.g. *A.P.S.*, VOL. II, pp. 23, 106.
[131] Their efforts are summarised in E. J. Holmyard, *Alchemy*, pp. 214-7.
[132] Cochran-Patrick, *Coinage*, VOL. I, p. 75.

base his judgment on a narrow reading of any single scriptural text, held that usury was permissible subject to seven rigid safeguards devised to protect both debtor and society. "As a man of the world," writes H. M. Robertson, "he recognised the necessity for some payment to be made for the use of capital in many commercial transactions."[133] In practice the activities of the petty usurer in Scotland could rouse the wrath of the local Kirk Session—as when Katherine Neische, accused before the Session at St Andrews, "comperit and purgest hirself"[134]—but with a few exceptions it would be hard to maintain that the Church seriously interfered with the business man's use of his money.

The breakdown of the whole-hearted ban on usury was, in part, a reflexion of the increasingly secular approach to economic affairs. "The preachers," wrote Thomas Wilson in his *Discourse on Usury* in 1572, "crie out continually against all usurers . . . in all their sermons; and yet what availes it? Nothing at al."[135] From the thirteenth century the Schoolmen had fractured the rigid law by ingenious circumventions such as the doctrine of *titulus morae*, whereby a penalty for delayed repayment could be justified. Three centuries later Scotsmen were employing this device: thus David Wedderburne, the Dundee merchant, recorded in March 1596 that he had "lent James Kyd . . . x lib in Inglis money to be payit this day 8 dayis under the pane of dubling thairof."[136] Similarly a form of interest in kind, apparently prevalent in the later sixteenth century, is described by Estienne Perlin and Fynes Moryson. In Edinburgh, they said, "a man who is possessed of an hundred golden or sun crowns, will lend them to a merchant, for which the merchant will maintain him for a whole year in his house, and at his table, and at the end of the year will return him his money."[137]

Whether the Churches liked it or not, the strictly ethical approach to usury was yielding before the necessities and the empirical ingenuity of the business world, and realists were

---

[133] H. M. Robertson, *Aspects of the Rise of Economic Individualism*, p. 117.
[134] *Register of the Kirk Session of St Andrews*, ed. D. H. Fleming, Scottish History Society, vol. I, 1889, p. 309.
[135] *A Discourse upon Usury by Thomas Wilson*, ed. R. H. Tawney, 1925, p. 181.
[136] *Wedderburne Compt Buik*, p. 68.
[137] Quoted in Hume Brown, *Early Travellers*, pp. 77, 81.

willing to legislate accordingly. "It is better," concludes Bacon in his essay on usury, "to mitigate it by declaration, than to suffer it to rage by connivance."[138] As the sixteenth century drew to its close, the debate in Scotland was no longer about usury as such but rather about the permissible maximum, and 10 per cent—which at least possessed the merit of mathematical simplicity—became the accepted boundary stone between the legitimate and the immoral. The Act of the Scottish Parliament of 1587[139] formalised the official lay attitude: "It is not lesum [lawful] to take ane greater rent for the 100 pundes nor ten pundes or five bolles victual." Once this Act was passed, lending at or below the legal maximum became respectable, even for the public authorities themselves. Within three years the King disposed of the tocher brought to him by Anne of Denmark by lending it to his chief burghs, each loan bearing interest at 10 per cent.[140] Similarly in Dundee, where the spokesmen of the Church could never be called taciturn, the Guildry in 1603 openly instructed their Collector to "borrow fra ony persone fiftie merkis for ane terme, and to pay L ss for the profeit thairof"—the equivalent of about 7 per cent interest.[141]

This Dundee offer bore signs of the borrower's eternal optimism, for all the evidence points to a market rate above the statutory maximum. In 1591 the Dean of Gild at Ayr paid 12 per cent on a loan "due to Lokhert,"[142] and in the following twenty years excess rates raged by connivance. Then in 1610-11, when the Government awoke to the situation, a wave of consternation broke over the Scottish burghs. The Convention appointed four Commissioners (Lokhert of Ayr, who obviously had inside knowledge, being one) to proceed to the King and plead for a discharge from the "penall act" against the taking of more than "ten of the hunder."[143] The burgesses of Edinburgh, against whom Burleigh had assumed the potentially profitable role of informer, were especially perturbed. In August 1612 their Council made the seemingly

---

[138] *The Works of Francis Bacon*, edd. J. Spedding, R. L. Ellis, and D. D. Heath, 7 vols, 1857, VOL. VI, p. 477.   [139] *A.P.S.*, VOL. III, p. 451.
[140] A. Montgomerie, "King James VI's Tocher Gude," in *S.H.R.*, XXXVII, (1958), p. 13.
[141] *Burgh Laws of Dundee*, p. 147.
[142] *Ayr Burgh Accounts*, ed. G. S. Pryde, p. 173.
[143] *Convention Records*, VOL. II, p. 325.

improper suggestion—which nevertheless was accepted—that, in return for exemption from prosecution, they would cancel the debts owed to the "gude toun" by the King; and, clearly as part of the same bargain, in October of the same year they discharged a debt of 4,000 merks owed by Lord Burleigh himself.[144]

As the wheels of government investigation turned, it became evident that the extent of infringement had been too great for the ordinary processes of the law. A powerful Commission, representative of the Church, the landowners, the law, and the Crown officers, was accordingly appointed to report on those "poenall Laws which have heirtofoir beine left in sik deswetude . . . as micht have induced the subjects to expect impunitie of contraveining the same."[145] Its report, embodied in an Act of 1612,[146] tendered the advice that pardon should be extended to all who, before Martinmas 1611, had taken not more than 12 per cent. All others were to suffer as the laws prescribed; and during the course of 1612 some 350 "ockerers"—including some parish ministers—were rounded up for prosecution.[147] In short, the vital distinction was clearly preserved: what the Act of 1597 called "exorbitante profite . . . taken for the lene of money"[148] was condemned by the laws of God and of the realm, but any rate of 10 per cent or below was legal if not wholly morally commendable. The sin lay not in cutting the flesh, but in exceeding the allotted pound.

According to Hume Brown, the burgesses in Scotland in the time of Queen Mary were more concerned over prices than over religion.[149] In a sense the antithesis is defective, for attitudes to buying and selling were still to some extent conditioned by the legacy of medieval theological economics. The prescription and enforcement of price and marketing regulations rested by the mid-sixteenth century in lay hands, primarily in those of the burghs, with periodic strengthening by Acts of Parliament or of the Privy Council. Under this network of regulation, markets were anything but free. Competitive bidding was strongly discouraged, especially in dealings in the basic foodstuffs. Thus the Aberdeen Burgh Council in 1555,

---

[144] *Edinburgh Records*, VOL. VI, pp. 74, 87, 89.   [145] *Op. cit.*, VOL. VI, App. XVII.
[146] *A.P.S.*, VOL. IV, p. 473.   [147] *R.P.C.*, VOL. VI, pp. 20-2; VOL. IX, p. lxiv.
[148] *A.P.S.*, VOL. IV, p. 119.
[149] Hume Brown, *Scotland in the Time of Queen Mary*, p. 160.

with the consent of the local baxter (baker) craft, ruled "that nane of the saidis baxteris by quhit [wheat] attour his nychbouris heyd; that is to say, where his nychbour hes bene to make ony buying of quhyt, and bidden ony money thairfor, that his nychtbour bid na mair nor is offerit."[150] Similarly the multitude of burghal ordinances against forestallers and regraters reflected a profound mistrust of the middleman, who seemingly profited by handling materials without adding anything to their real worth. The persistence of this essentially medieval attitude is demonstrated in an Act of the Scots Parliament of 1592 which forebade forestalling;[151] by a local regulation of the baxter trade in St Andrews in 1595 against the pre-emption of wheat;[152] and by an order of the Dundee Head Court in 1598 against those "couperes and regratores" who bought fish before the vessels had been "dewly entered."[153] In view of what we already know of the family, it comes as no surprise to find an Udward in conflict with the Edinburgh Council in the 1590's over breaches of local market regulations.[154] This was Robert, son of a Dean of Gild, "indweller in Leyth," and not for nothing "callit Robin Huid." Preventive measures abounded: thus the common practice of restricting hours of sale to simplify supervision is illustrated by the Kirkcaldy ruling of 1587 that "na maill maker opin his sakis to sell maill quhill twa efternon";[155] and the Dundee ban of 1582 on trading in "mirk [dark] houses and quiet lofts"[156] was clearly aimed against shady transactions.

The prescription of prices was, therefore, the second line of official action in market control. Reasonably enough, price-fixing was most generally and regularly applied to three groups of commodities: the essential foods, notably grain, meal, malt, and bread; the essential lighting materials, notably tallow and candles; and the staple beverages, notably ale, beer, and wine. Outside this range, where demand was generally less rigid and definition certainly more complex, various methods of control were employed. Some burghs issued standard annual price schedules: thus Edinburgh in 1553 defined the prices of "wyld

[150] *Aberdeen Council Register*, VOL. I, p. 290.
[151] *A.P.S.*, VOL. III, p. 577.
[152] *The Baxter Books of St Andrews*, ed. J. H. Macadam, 1903, p. 53.
[153] *Burgh Laws of Dundee*, p. 51.   [154] *Edinburgh Records*, VOL. V, *passim*.
[155] *Kirkcaldy Records*, pp. 117-8.   [156] *Burgh Laws of Dundee*, p. 43.

mete and tame foullis";[157] at Aberdeen in 1584 grievous complaints against local weavers were answered by an official schedule of maximum prices for "tartane" and other fabrics;[158] and at Inverness the Burgh Court often fixed the prices of shoes for gentlemen, women, servants, and children,[159] those for children—in flat disregard of nature—varying simply with the age of the child. Alternatively a burgh might control a market by *ad hoc* price fixing, as in 1583 when the Edinburgh baillies were authorised to assign prices to butter, cheese, fish, and poultry each market day.[160] Finally, and more commonly, the burgh might adopt the traditional gild practice of supervising quality. A typical burgh order runs: "It is statut and ordanit that the deacon of the flesheors crafts sall appoynt two masters of yr craft who sall be sworn to appryse all skaithes of all flesh in the land mercat."[161]

Price-fixing, if it were to be both realistic and socially just, had somehow to avoid being swept headlong by the tide of market conditions, and yet display enough flexibility to maintain a reasonable flow of trade. The degree of responsiveness to short-term fluctuations in supply is most easily illustrated by the commonest application of price-fixing—the "assize" of bread. In theory adjustments were effected by altering the weight of a standard-price loaf; but over a long period the deterioration in the value of Scots money was such that the standard price itself had to be increased. While in the days of James V twopenny loaves had been general, by 1600 the typical Scots burgh legislated in terms of either the sixpenny or the twelvepenny loaf.[162] Nevertheless in the short run price variations were effected by alterations in weight. In normal times the weight was fixed in late October or November after the ingathering of the current harvest, and in towns where the records are reasonably complete the impact of every major variation in the domestic harvest can be traced either in changes in bread prices or in disputes between the town and the bakers.

Local control of prices, whether exercised by the burgh

[157] *Edinburgh Records*, VOL. II, pp. 184-5.
[158] *Aberdeen Council Register*, VOL. II, p. 55.
[159] *Inverness Records*, pp. 26, 35, 46.
[160] *Edinburgh Records*, VOL. IV, p. 298.
[161] *Burgh Laws of Dundee*, p. 30.
[162] The change can be traced through the entries in *Edinburgh Records*, VOLS. II-V *passim*.

council, by the sheriff-depute, or by a Barony Court like that of Urie,[163] though in some measure a comment on central administrative impotence, was both reasonable and desirable because of the strongly regional character of most commodity markets. Thus Buchan and the Moray coastlands were sufficiently remote from central Scotland to have a semi-independent price life. In 1549, and again in very different harvest conditions in 1596, the women of Aberdeen got roughly 50 per cent more bread for their money than those in Edinburgh, while in 1562 they got rather less.[164] In the more compact group of central and southern burghs, the effect of transport costs—considerable even over short distances—was strengthened by the refusal of the burghs to open their markets to all sellers. In 1569 twelve Scots pennies would secure 48 oz. of wheaten bread in Kirkcaldy, 60 oz. in Edinburgh, and 64 oz. in Selkirk; and despite the broad tendency towards a more integrated economic life, these local variations are still traceable into the seventeenth century.

Short-term adjustments, made in the light of easily comprehensible market conditions, were well within the competence of local councils and courts. They cannot so readily have grasped the logic of the long upward heave in prices—the historians' "Price Revolution"—which, stemming from the Iberian empires, drew nourishment through adventitious roots in the soil of every European land. In the long term the prices that the Scotsman paid in his own currency were subject to two kinds of upward pressure. In what he paid for his imports he experienced the effects of the general change in European price levels, and this rising cost of imports accelerated the upward trend in his domestic prices which, in turn, arose from political uncertainties, instability of domestic production, and inept currency management.

Burghal assessed prices, notably those of Edinburgh, Glasgow, Stirling, Kirkcaldy, and Lanark, survive in sufficient quantity to provide a reasonable view of the Scottish price

---

[163] *The Court Book of the Barony of Urie in Kincardineshire*, ed. D. G. Barron, Scottish History Society, VOL. XII, 1892, p. 181.

[164] Save where otherwise indicated, the burghal prices in the following paragraphs are extracted from the records of the burghs concerned. I am indebted to Mr James Mason for providing me with extracts from the unpublished Selkirk records.

revolution. The prime deduction from them is that, between the mid-sixteenth century and the death of James VI, the price of Scottish domestic produce increased at least fourfold in terms of the domestic currency. But the rate of increase was far from uniform. Down to the 1570's it was at least tolerable, in fact there were isolated years around 1570 when prices were as favourable to the consumer as they had been twenty years earlier. Thus in 1569 ale was the same price in Edinburgh and Lanark as it had been in 1556 and 1560, and candles, which had been 11*d*, a pound in Stirling in 1554, had not risen to much over 1*s*. by the early 1570's.

It is indeed abundantly clear, both from the assessed prices and from the isolated records of market transactions, that much of the upsurge of Scottish prices took place in the last quarter of the sixteenth century. In most burghs, tallow, which had remained narrowly below £1 a tron stone until the early 1580's, leaped to £1. 10*s*. 0*d*. by the late '80's and to £2 or more by 1600. The Edinburgh tippler, in a good year in the late 1570's, could still drink his fill of ale at 4*s*. a gallon; in a bad year, such as 1596, he would have to pay nearly 12*s*., and in any subsequent year either good or bad a minimum of 8*s*. Even though she made do with the inferior "hard wick" variety, his wife's candles cost just twice as much in 1600 as in 1580. Similarly in three decades the price of the best wheaten bread trebled; good harvests were to come, but the cheap loaf was lost to all save memory. But by about 1600 the upward rush was slackening, so that, for the last twenty-five years of James VI's reign, the overall rise was everywhere slight and, for some commodities, negligible.[165]

The study of prices thus confirms the contention that, in the closing decades of the sixteenth century, the Scottish economy passed through a critical and turbulent phase. The impact of the harvest failures in the 1570's, 1580's and 1590's, coupled often with political disorders, was felt in every sector of society. Operating on a primarily rural economy, where rising population was matched neither by expanding agricultural production nor by significant industrial growth, each food shortage drove the prices of grain and grain products to a peak from which the

---

[165] See especially *Stirling Records*, where a very complete series from about 1600 is available.

subsequent recession was never more than partial. This stepping-up process was aggravated by that enhancement and debasement of the coinage to which, as we have seen, the Scottish rulers resorted with reckless frequency.

The effect of this currency depreciation—a matter quite outside the control of the burghs—can be seen in sharp outline in the movement of wine prices. At La Rochelle, which can be taken as representative of the districts from which much of the wine was procured, the price in terms of French currency rose exactly threefold between 1557-65 and 1617-25.[166] Over the same period the prices paid for "chapel" wine at Eton and Winchester rose three to fourfold.[167] The contrast in Scotland is striking. In the middle years of the sixteenth century French wines were retailed at a penny or so either side of 1s. 3d. a pint;[168] by the late 1580's nothing recognisable as wine was to be had in Scotland for less than 5s. to 5s. 6d. a pint;[169] by 1608-9 Aberdeen's retail price was 10s.[170] and Ayr's 10s. to 13s.[171] Some small part of the increase may have been occasioned by higher transport costs, and by the end of the period the import duty on wine (effectively £32. 8s. 0d. a tun) and the special imposts granted to certain of the burghs certainly forced up the price within the country.[172] But when all allowance is made for these the fact remains that the cost of wine to Scotsmen in terms of their own money rose between 1550 and 1625 something like sixfold. In other words the rise, in terms of the domestic currencies, was twice as great in Scotland as in France or England.

It will be evident, therefore, that when the bailies gathered in solemn conclave in the Tolbooth or Town House to assess their prices, they were subject to a formidable conjunction of economic pressures which aggravated their basic task of providing justice to both consumer and supplier. This objective was inevitably hardest to achieve in the pricing of manufactured goods, where various components entered into the final cost. The crude method of varying the price of a manu-

---

[166] E. Trocmé and M. Delafosse, *Le Commerce rochelais à la fin du moyen âge,* Paris 1952, pp. 178-80.
[167] W. Beveridge, *Prices and Wages in England,* 1939, pp. 85-8, 114.
[168] *Ayr Burgh Records,* p. 100.   [169] *Op. cit.,* p. 171.
[170] Kennedy, *Annals of Aberdeen,* p. 191.   [171] *Ayr Burgh Records,* p. 240.
[172] *Edinburgh Records,* VOL. VI, Apps. XIII and XXIX.

factured article in direct relationship to that of its principal raw material constituent had the merit of simplicity and can be traced all over the country. It was employed at Inverness where the price of aquavitae officially fluctuated with that of grain, and the price of shoes with that of leather; and, as late as 1624, at Edinburgh where the Council issued a table of hypothetical wheat prices and bread weights in which the relationship is an exact inverse ratio.[173]

The achievement of social justice clearly demanded a more sophisticated method of price determination, and an examination of the relationships between the prices of tallow and candles, and of wheat and bread, enables us to test—in a rough fashion—the extent to which the price-fixing bodies in practice considered other cost components. Candle-making, pursued in every burgh, was an essential but obnoxious trade. "Vyle, filthie and contagious savoures"[174] arose from the heating of the tallow which, with either "hard" or "rag" wick, constituted the only material constituent of the finished candle. Between 1562 and 1592 the price of tallow in Edinburgh rather more than doubled, but the margin per pound to the candle-maker (to cover the cost of wick, fuel, and labour) rose only from $3\frac{3}{4}d.$ to $6d.$ On the other hand at Stirling between 1599 and 1625 not only did the broad trend favour the candlemaker, but in years when tallow was cheap the price of candles was often maintained at what was probably regarded as the "usual" level. A tentative conclusion is that in the phase of rapidly mounting prices (down say to 1600) the burgh authorities tried to protect the consumer; but thereafter, when prices steadied and the whole economy became more buoyant, they were willing to allow a rather more generous margin to the producer.

Tables published in 1638 by John Penkethman in his *Artachthos* (a treatise on baking) show that, in the typical year, milling and baking absorbed about a quarter of the final cost of the loaf. Though relatively small, these elements in the baker's costs were certainly not inflexible. Thus an agreement between the Baxter craft of St Andrews and their ovenmen in 1596 clearly envisages annual wage adjustment;[175] the millers,

[173] *Op. cit.*, App. XXXIV.   [174] *Op. cit.*, VOL. V, p. 83.
[175] *The Baxter Books of St Andrews*, p. 58.

commonly remunerated by a share of the grain they ground, had, according to scandalous tradition, their own devices for keeping abreast with prices; and even if he used only heather and brushwood, the baker's fuel bill could scarcely fail to rise. But these costs would be unlikely to move with the rapidity of wheat prices, and consequently if the price of bread were related solely to that of wheat and the demand for bread remained stable, the bakers would gain from sudden upward movements and lose from downward.

Bitter disputes at Dundee in the 1560's and again in the 1580's—when the bakers virtually went on strike—provide further illustration of the price-fixer's resistance to sharp upward movements, a resistance so obstinate that in 1561 the Dundee bakers were driven to seek redress from the Court of Session.[176] Yet once again, when the major price rise was over, compromise and a more or less conventional price triumphed. Thus at Stirling between 1600 and 1625, while the price of wheat ranged from £6 to £12 the boll, the weight of the twelve-penny loaf neither rose above 16 oz. nor fell below 12 oz. Official action, in short, ensured that the price of bread was relatively more stable than the price of wheat, but in so far as any long term trend is visible from the Stirling prices it seems that the Council allowed the margin between the cost of the wheat and the value of the bread baked from it to widen slightly as the years passed.

The effect of these permitted price changes on the material well-being of the urban populations defies exact analysis. We cannot, for example, even guess how far the housewife economised by buying "the second sort of quheitt breid, alias callit four breid," or even "the third sort . . . commounlie callit the masloche breid,"[177] so as to get a third or two-thirds more bulk for her shilling. Alternatively she may have persuaded her family that rye bread was more nutritious and better for the teeth. If the Edinburgh Council's ruling of 1606 was typical, rye bread was only about one-third the price of the best wheaten.[178] The fact, as we saw in Chapter II, that money wages over the whole period lagged appreciably behind prices,

[176] *Burgh Laws of Dundee*, p. 336; Maxwell, *History of Old Dundee*, pp. 94-8.
[177] The editorial notes in *The Baxter Books of St Andrews* are a mine of information on varieties of bread.
[178] *Edinburgh Records*, VOL. VI, p. 25.

suggests that, given equal regularity of work, the average wage-earning labourer's household experienced some deterioration in its standards of comfort and diet. On the other hand the greater social stability and the industrial expansion in the last three decades of James's reign made for wider and steadier employment, and, simultaneously, the run of better harvests from the late 1590's to the early 1620's removed the threat of actual starvation.

That prices and price-fixing agitated the minds of townsmen needs no further demonstration. Instability, both of commodity prices and of the official value of the current coins, helps to explain the persistence, even in the bigger towns, of business dealings based on barter or near-barter exchange. So late as 1614 Wedderburne "payit to a Glenesk man xxvii meill a half for twa stane 3 quarteris quhyt wol";[179] several times he took payment in kind for services rendered to clients, and in 1596 he agreed with "Niniane Copen and Margaret Jak his spous . . . be thair faythfull promes besyd the mercat croce" to accept in payment of feu duty "a knag of vinacre and can oyle doly" (olive oil) each time Copen returned from Bordeaux.[180]

Furthermore, to envisage the extent of official price-fixing in its true perspective, we must remember that outside the burghs—in other words among perhaps five-sixths of the population—transactions of a barter character were normal. "In Halyburton's time, and, I may say, for two centuries afterwards," wrote Cosmo Innes, "the Scotch laird estimated his income in bolls of meal and malt; and the surplus, after maintaining his family and a large following of dependants, was turned to account in Leith and Aberdeen."[181] The prevalence in the countryside of payments in kind for rent and even for labour was not, however, any bulwark against the impact of rising prices. The adjustment of the rents of the burgh-owned lands around Inverness illustrates the extent of exposure.[182] There, at least from the 1550's, rents were paid either in victual or in the money equivalent according to the "fiars' price (the official price of grain) struck annually at

179 *Wedderburne Compt Buik*, p. 41.
180 *Op. cit.*, pp. 41, 45.
181 "Rental of the Lordship of Huntly, 1600," in *Miscellany of the Spalding Club*, VOL. IV, 1849.
182 *Inverness Records*, p. lxxxiii.

Martinmas either by the sheriff-depute or by representatives of county and burgh jointly.[183] All the evidence indicates that, with the passing of time, some such form of commutation tended to spread, so that changing values made themselves felt throughout the entire range of rural relationships. At the lowest level, the small working tenant was pressed for more rent: "the malis and fermes of the grond that i laubyr is hychtit to sic ane price, that it is fors to me and wyf and bayrns to drink wattir"—so in the *Complaynt of Scotlande*[184] the tiller of the soil bewailed his lot. At the peak of the social pyramid, the great nobles and Churchmen and the Crown resorted to the feuing of land, not as a means of rural improvement, but because—as Parliament had long before advised the King—it was "to the grett proffitt of his croun swa the samin be maid in augmentatiounn of his rentale."[185] Alike in the burghs, where regulation may have mitigated its impact, and in the countryside where strength was the arbiter, the price revolution was relentlessly pervasive.

[183] D. Murray, "Scottish local records," in *S.H.R.*, xxiv (1927), p. 100.
[184] *The Complaynt of Scotlande*, ed. J. A. H. Murray, Early English Text Society, 1872, p. 122.
[185] *A.P.S.*, vol. ii, p. 49. A further Act of 1508 had extended the invitation to spiritual and temporal lords, *A.P.S.*, vol. ii, p. 244.

IV

TRADERS AND TRADING METHODS

The structure and inter-relationships of the institutions through which Scottish trade was conducted are familiar from a number of specialist studies published over the past century. From these it is clear that to a remarkable extent the leading families in the coastal royal burghs constituted close-knit corporations of mercantile interest. At home they controlled the domestic affairs of their towns; through the Convention of Royal Burghs they exerted a co-operative authority in economic matters comparable to that of a parliament; by their share in the conduct of the Staple at Veere they kept a jealous watch over the far end of Scotland's most stable trading axis. Put briefly, the overseas trade of Scotland was in large measure a monopoly of the royal burghs; the overseas trade of each burgh was a monopoly of the members of its own Gild Merchant (or Gildry); the members of the Gild Merchant were invariably linked to each other by ties of blood, marriage, or commerce. The merchant class thus emerges as something like a state within a state, a compact body jealous of its privileges and watchful against possible intrusion upon them by craftsmen or strangers.

It is not the intention here to retread this familiar ground, but rather to penetrate—so far as the limited material allows— into the home and booth of the merchant, with an eye to his furnishings and dress, his literature and the contents of his treasure-chest, and with an ear to his dealings with his fellows. The emergence of these merchant families as recognisable units and as members of a highly self-conscious group is the clearest evidence of middle-class development in the Scotland of our period, but to see this development in true perspective it is useful first to consider the size and distribution of the burghs in which it took place.

In the middle years of the sixteenth century some thirty-five burghs boasted the cherished prefix "royal" which alone conveyed the full range of burghal privilege; but among this thirty-five were several which, by the test of population or built-up area, would today rank only as villages. The total burgh share of national taxation was never more than one-sixth, and the dominance of Edinburgh in burghal life is demonstrated by the fact that, of every £100 raised by the burghs, its contribution was in the region of £28.[1] Of its population no precise figures are available: probably Hume Brown's estimate of 30,000 for the time of Queen Mary is not far off the mark.[2] By the test of tax contributions, Dundee and Aberdeen came second and third, paying about £11 and £9 per cent respectively, and housed populations which, by 1600, were probably of the order of 7,000 or 8,000.[3] The old capital, Perth, came fourth with an estimated population in the late sixteenth century of 5,000 or 5,500;[4] its high position resulting partly from historical momentum, partly from its concentration of crafts, but mainly from its ideal location as an inland trading centre. By 1591 a west coast port, Glasgow, for the first time rose to the fifth place hitherto occupied by St Andrews. After the setback of the Reformation Glasgow recovered quickly, and though its population in 1581 was not much over 2,300[5] and its percentage contribution in 1585 only £3. 10s. 0d., all the significant trends were decisively upward.

This ascent by Glasgow was, so far, the only real sign of burghal vitality in the west. In 1591 Ayr occupied the tenth position in the burgh tax list and Dumfries the twelfth, much the same as in 1535. In the centre of the country Stirling remained relatively stable in about the eighteenth place, its qualities and potentialities as an inland trading point never fully exploited. Inland towns with no direct access to foreign trade were, in general, humbly placed on the burgh list. In

[1] The relevant burgh tax rolls are in *Convention Records*, VOL. I, pp. 47, 73, 173, 246, 253, 365, 451, 519, 522, 526, 530; VOL. II, pp. 10, 488.

[2] Hume Brown, *Scotland in the Time of Queen Mary*, p. 52.

[3] Kennedy, *Annals of Aberdeen*, pp. 186-7; E. Bain, *Merchant and Craft Guilds*, 1887, p. 86; S. G. E. Lythe, *Life and Labour in Dundee from the Reformation to the Civil War*, Abertay Historical Society, 1958, p. 5.

[4] Marshall, *History of Perth*, p. 486; *Statistical Account of Scotland*, VOL. XVIII, p. 524.

[5] A. MacGeorge, *Old Glasgow*, 1888, p. 144.

the Borders proper, burghal growth had been retarded by invasion and feud, and was recognisable only in Jedburgh and Selkirk, both far down on the list. In the north the relative prominence of Brechin and Elgin was primarily a legacy of their former high ecclesiastical status. Dunfermline, for all its royal connexions, paid only 16s. to every £100 raised by the burghs in 1591, and when the "quholl bodey of the toune" was destroyed by fire in 1624 it contained only 120 tenements and 287 families.[6] Cupar occupied a strong local position in the centre of Fife, but the real vitality in the county lay along the golden fringe—the string of ports from St Andrews round into the Firth of Forth, which, from about 1580 to the Civil War, occupied a remarkably prominent place in the external trade of the nation.

The coastal burghs of Fife were outstanding but not unique, for the same vitality was displayed by almost every east-facing Scottish burgh from Inverness down to Dunbar. The combined contributions of Inverness and Montrose in 1591 were almost equal to Glasgow's, and Arbroath, with a population in the early 1600's of perhaps 1,400,[7] paid as much as Dumbarton or Renfrew. There were little burghs up and down the east coast, each containing 1,000 or fewer people, handling so considerable a volume of foreign trade that almost every able-bodied male inhabitant must have been in some way associated with the sea and the goods that passed upon it.

The study of the towns in which the Scots merchants conducted their affairs thus involves drastic modification of many modern concepts of Scottish town life. The Scottish burgh of 1600 was a very small place when tested by population, and an even smaller place when tested by area. Around a focal point—the palace at Linlithgow, the cathedral at Elgin, the harbour at Dundee—lay a labyrinth of close-packed tenements and twisting vennels, an insanitary cluster of wood, stone, and humanity. Yet precisely because the burghs were socially and geographically so compact, the merchant families were able to exercise the greater dominance over civic affairs. Whether we look at the burgess rolls, the lists of provosts and deans of gild, the inscriptions on tombstones, or the gildry and shipping records, the same names occur. In Dundee, for example the

---

[6] Balfour, *Annals*, VOL. II, p. 99.   [7] Hay, *History of Arbroath*, p. 148.

Wedderburne family predominated in every sphere: in the Reformed Church, in town government, in the law, in property owning and in trade;[8] and around them were grouped the Goldmans, the Findlaysons, the Clayhills and half a dozen others, linked into a compact circle by matrimonial and economic ties.

In the face of grave obstacles they attempted to enforce civic rule and orderly government, a task anything but easy when noblemen carried their feuds into the streets of towns, when fire and plague spread panic, and when famine, strong drink, and religion were equally likely to produce street brawling. To the service of their towns, and of the Convention of Royal Burghs, they devoted time and effort, and, as when Bailie MacMorran was shot in 1595 by a rebellious pupil at Edinburgh High School, life itself.[9] Benefactions, such as those in Edinburgh to the Town's College, can be cited in their favour,[10] and for all the brawling and the pestilence, daily life in their towns was more regular and secure than in the rural countryside. On the other hand their essentially acquisitive instincts were not likely to pass unchallenged in an age when moralists still exalted the doctrine of the common good. They behave, wrote James VI in his advice to his son, as if "the whole common-weale" were "ordayned for making them up."[11] The King was echoing a theme which runs strongly through contemporary Scottish poetry: thus Dunbar on the merchants of Edinburgh,

> Singular profit so dois you blind,
> The common profit gois behind.

The prominence of these merchant families was symbolised by their houses. By the later part of the reign of James VI the construction of upper middle-class town houses was gradually beginning to change; indeed some of the traditional timber-fronted houses in Edinburgh were deliberately demolished for fuel during the seige of 1572,[12] and a great deal of excellent

---

[8] *Wedderburne Compt Buik*, pp. xlvii-lxxii.
[9] *Edinburgh Records*, VOL. V, p. 138.
[10] See above, p. 33.
[11] *The Basilikon Doron of King James VI*, ed. J. Craigie, Scottish Text Society, 1944, VOL. I, p. 89.
[12] R. Chambers, *Ancient Domestic Architecture of Edinburgh*, 1859, p. 11.

new building was undertaken in the two following generations. The visible relics are most abundant in the Old Town where, to cite one famous example, in about 1620 Thomas Gladstone acquired an existing house in the Lawnmarket[13] and added a piazza and Italianate painted ceilings to produce the building which—beautifully restored in the 1930's—survives as Gladstone's Land. Whether it retained the old-fashioned wood and plaster front, or whether it had the up-to-date stone façade, the typical merchant house advertised the substance of its occupant. In such houses the great Edinburgh merchants, the Mac-Morrans, the Udwards, the Heriots, the Fowlers, and the Clarks, could without shame entertain royalty and nobility.[14] And though the house was often the hub of business activity, its contents proved that the merchant was neither mean nor uncultured. There is clear proof of this in the *Compt Buik* of David Wedderburne, which is full of references to literature: indeed one entry alone details the loan of thirty-four volumes in various languages ranging from a Hebrew Bible to *Dr Faustus* and from Drake's *Voyages* to "tua gryt buikis of Law."[15] Travel abroad and the presence of foreigners—especially Frenchmen—in Scotland gave the merchant a reasonable fluency in European languages; but the dead languages must have been acquired the hard way at the hands of the local schoolmasters. A boy who survived the prescribed five-year course at Edinburgh High School in the early 1600's would work up from Dunbar's *Rudiments* and Despauter's *Grammar* until in the "hie classe" he was fit to do battle with "Cicero his orationes or de Oratore . . . Salust, Plautus, Horace, Juvenal, Persius," and to undergo instruction in "the greek grammar, Hesiod or Theognis."[16]

Nor does the concept of a cold-blooded materialist square with the evidence of interest in the supernatural and attachment to astrology and superstition. If Wedderburne was typical, the merchant of his time must often have consulted the almanack for fear of stumbling on days of ill omen. Wedder-

[13] *Edinburgh Records*, VOL. VI, p. 299.
[14] J. Warrack, *Domestic Life in Scotland, 1488-1600*, 1920, pp. 65 ff.; R. Chambers, *Edinburgh Merchants and Merchandise*, henceforth cited as *Edinburgh Merchants*, 1859, pp. 5-7.
[15] For the contents of Wedderburne's library see *Wedderburne Compt Buik*, pp. xxii-xxxi.
[16] *Edinburgh Records*, VOL. VI, p. 121.

burne's calendar contained forty-seven such evil days against only twenty-six invariably favourable ones—"the quhilk wes revelit to ye gude patriache Joseph quhen he servit Kyng Pharow in Egypt be the angell of God."[17] His "buik of prophesie" circulated a good deal among his acquaintances, and in 1607 he lent to Alexander Clayhills a book of necromancy of which the very title was scaring—*Of Ghosts and Spirites Walking by Night, and of Strange Noyses, Crackes and sundrie Forewarnynges.*[18]

In formal religion, almost of necessity, the merchant adhered to the Reformed Church, though he might have episcopalian leanings. Wedged among the rulings issued in 1568 by the Dundee Head Court (a merchant-dominated body) about hucksters, cadgers, butter, and candles is a vigorously-worded ban on "argument and disput agains the good Trew religion," especially argument whereby "Papistrie with the detestable superstutions yrof" was defended.[19] But adherence to the New Kirk was not carried to the point of interference with commercial enterprise. So in 1582 the Convention of Royal Burghs heard that Scottish traders resorting to France and Flanders had daily commercial intercourse with "ignorant and conjurit papists"; and to check this the Convention ruled that a fine of £40 should be imposed on any Scotsman who henceforth dealt with a trader "nocht of the trew religion."[20] Neither moral suasion nor the threat of a fine seems to have been very effective, for eight years later the Privy Council was receiving complaints that Scottish skippers and traders were carrying wine from Bordeaux to St Valery and other towns held by French Catholics and consequently hostile to the aims of the Protestant Henri de Navarre.[21] The little we know of the activities of individual merchants illustrates their rejection of religious scruples. John MacMorran of Edinburgh, "the richest merchant in his tyme" according to Calderwood, was "not gracious to the common people, becaus he carried victuall to Spaine, notwithstanding he was often admonished by the ministers to refraine";[22] but the ministers had more success with Robert Gourlay whom they forced into repentance

[17] *Wedderburne Compt Buik*, pp. 3-4.   [18] *Op. cit.*, p. 87.
[19] *Burgh Laws of Dundee*, p. 35.
[20] *Convention Records*, VOL. I, pp. 402, 485.   [21] *R.P.C.*, VOL. IV, p. 526.
[22] Calderwood, *History of the Kirk of Scotland*, VOL. V, p. 382.

in St Giles' for having exported grain in time of domestic shortage.[23]

The recognition of common interests among members of the mercantile groups is reflected in the mutual insurance arrangements which they created for themselves in most seaports. Thus at Dundee in 1570 the Gildry, "considering the estaite present of the common weill of the merchandis, how thair is no common guid . . . and how thair can be no common guid except thaire be fordell geare [stock in hand] to the help theairof,"[24] instructed their Dean to levy specified duties on certain merchant goods passing through the port. The fact that within six years this had become "the pennies of the hailie silver"[25] suggests that it was, in fact, parallel to the pre-Reformation levy of Holy Blood Silver for the maintenance of an altar in the parish church which, after 1560, had been devoted to the sustentation of the ministry. Similarly in Kirkcaldy in 1591 forty-six members of the mercantile community foregathered and, with "the great zeale, favor and luve they beir to thair God," made the like provision for a levy, called the Prime Gilt, for the support of such of their members as fell into poverty and necessity, "waistouris and drunkardis exceptit."[26]

The exception symbolised something more than mere prudery, for the social compactness of the merchant families, their relatively high standard of living, and their decisive voice in burghal affairs, bred a consciousness of class and an emphasis on what Tudor England knew as "port." In a sense the wealthier Scottish merchant was seeking to express Renaissance standards which, diluted no doubt, were seeping into Scotland by way of France and the Low Countries. To the individual it meant the possession and appreciation of silverware, jewellery, pictures, and solid furniture. Wedderburne was proud of his family heirlooms: the bedstead "of aik [oak] with my father and motheris armes thairon"; the copy of "Metamorphosis Ovidii in Laten with the pictouris bund in ane swynis skyn of werry braw binding sumtyme apertening to Robert Wedderburn my uncle"; and the two "payntit brodis" (painted tapestries) which Thomas Young was commissioned to bring from

[23] Chambers, *Edinburgh Merchants*, p. 6; Calderwood, *op. cit.*, VOL. III, p. 328.
[24] *Burgh Laws of Dundee*, p. 113.
[25] *Op. cit.*, p. 117.
[26] *Kirkcaldy Records*, pp. 127-9.

Flanders in 1598 were among the several additions which Wedderburne made to the family's domestic treasures.[27]

To the official bodies concerned with merchant affairs, this consciousness of class meant an emphasis on a standard of dress and behaviour by which the merchant and his wife might be distinguished from the craftsman and the country folk. There were many backsliders. At Dundee in 1590 the Gildry was greatly concerned about the way in which certain local merchants publicly displayed eggs, kail, onions, fruit, and "uthers ye lyke hockstrie form of trade";[28] and at Edinburgh an applicant for admission to the Gildry was required to undertake that his wife and servants would not appear in the streets in their aprons "as common cooks and servants uses to do."[29] In every self-respecting burgh the wearing of the plaid —the cloth of the common people—was banned for merchants and their womenfolk. Aberdeen in 1580 went the whole way in banning it for all women "except thai be harlottis and suspect personis,"[30] and a group of Aberdonians was sharply rebuked in 1611 for having journeyed south to Dundee and Edinburgh wearing "plaidis and blew bonnatis . . . as giff they were land-wart men . . . and not merchantis."[31] As the burghal authorities failed to control the dress of men, it is not surprising that they failed even more completely with women. When King James was contemplating a return visit to Scotland in 1608 he requested the Convention of Royal Burghs to have the towns cleaned up against his arrival.[32] This was within their competence; but to be asked also to consult upon "ane decent, handsome and complie sorte of habite, apparrell, and heid attyre" to replace the cloaks and plaid which the women normally wore, called for qualifications which not even the Convention possessed. Despite the edicts of burghs and the requests of the King, women persisted in the wearing of the plaid, so that, twenty years later, Lithgow could still ask

> Should Woemen weare
> Their Winding-sheets alyve, wrapt up I sweare
> From head to foote in Plads?

[27] *Wedderburne Compt Buik*, pp. 54, 168, 111.   [28] *Burgh Laws of Dundee*, p. 129.
[29] J. D. Marwick, *Edinburgh Gilds and Crafts*, 1909, p. 151.
[30] *Analecta Scotica*, VOL. II, p. 327.
[31] Ibid. At Dundee they might wear "black bonnatis," but were not allowed to push wheelbarrows: *Burgh Laws of Dundee*, p. 125.
[32] *Convention Records*, VOL. II, pp. 252-3.

When the merchant went abroad, the maintenance of a suitable standard of dress and behaviour became all the more important, for by the individual the nation would be judged. Regulation in these matters was set out in detail in the Conservator's book for the guidance of Scottish merchants at Veere, providing, for example, that "none seil in merchandise except he be honestly abuillzied [clad] like an honest merchant."[33]

Prosperous groups throughout history have always aimed at social advancement for themselves and their offspring. In his *Historie of Scotland*, published in 1578, Lesley praises those merchants who have had their sons so well educated in the "liberal sciences that eftirward they ar sik [such] instruments in the commoune weil that thair labour is bath to the gret Joy and honour of thair parents";[34] and he goes on to specify their services in the Church, at the law and in the army. Land-owning was an alternative road to social advancement. The burgess, particularly of a small town, can scarcely have been the innocent abroad in the country that Henryson portrays in his Town Mouse, for essentially rural interests easily penetrated the town boundaries. In his typical long narrow garden a townsman such as Thomas Gray of Inverness might cultivate "four beddis young plantis, four beddis ingyeonis, ane persell bed, sindrie herbis, sic as gentiane, roismarie and laurie";[35] his cows would pass daily to the meadows along the Cow Gait; and from these beginnings his scope might broaden into farming proper. Wedderburne at Dundee often noted transactions about ploughing, buying "muk," and the like;[36] and for a prosperous merchant the step from farming to landowning was short and easy. With some, such as John Cowane of Stirling, loans to local lairds possibly paved the way.[37] At all events we find the Clayhills acquiring lands at Baldovie and Inver-gowrie,[38] John Sinclair buying the estate of Stevenston, and George Baillie buying land at Jerviswood and later the estate of Mellerstain in Berwickshire.[39] Similar intrusions of merchant capital into landowning can be traced in the hinterland of

[33] Quoted in J. Yair, *An Account of the Scotch Trade in the Netherlands*, 1776, p. 100.
[34] Lesley, *History*, VOL. I, p. 116.
[35] *Inverness Records*, p. 261.
[36] *Wedderburne Compt Buik*, e.g. p. 73.
[37] Morris, *The Stirling Merchant Gild and the Life of John Cowane*, pp. 206-7.
[38] *Wedderburne Compt Buik*, p. 97.
[39] Chambers, *Edinburgh Merchants*, pp. 9-10.

almost every substantial trading centre.[40] And though, as we have seen, the merchant class was normally endogamous, the establishment of landed connexions by marriage was not un-known. Male members sometimes married above their station: Dunbar had a case in mind when writing his *Twa Mariit Wemen and the Wedo* where the widow recounts how, despite the gulf

betwixt his bastard blood and my noble birth

she had married a "merchant mighty of gudis" whose credulity and generosity had subsequently served as a comforting back-ground to her continuing love-affairs.

As even in the great mercantile operations of the Dutch the specialist merchant was so far unknown,[41] in the smaller trading world of the Scots extensive division of labour could hardly be expected. In Wedderburne's *Compt Buik* the entries about farming operations, rents, and leases stand cheek by jowl with entries about dealings in cloth, flax, fish and wine, copper and iron. Similarly from the Dundee Shipping Lists we can trace Robert Clayhills's imports which included peas, "French Wares," timber, lint, pitch, iron, rye, and salt.[42] The typical merchant was prepared to trade wherever the ships of his port might go, whether it be to the Baltic, the Low Countries, England, Ireland, France, or Spain. The records of James Bell's overseas trading from Glasgow are confined to his dealings with Holland, but the range of goods is enormous, from ribbons to figs and from tobacco to kirk stools.[43] Perhaps because overseas trade was essentially seasonal, the merchant had time to engage in domestic trade, both overland and coastal. Wedderburne shipped meal from Dundee to St Andrews and Leith, and had innumerable small dealings in lint with the goodwives of Angus.[44] To collect material for commerce the merchants travelled to inland and northern fairs—we find them for example at Turiff Fair in 1611 trying to pass off base continental coin in exchange for cloth offered by the local people.[45] William Rollock, who appears in the

---

[40] D. Mathew, *Scotland under Charles I*, 1955, p. 125.
[41] Christensen, *Dutch Trade to the Baltic about 1600*, p. 188.
[42] E.g. Dundee Shipping Lists, pp. 237, 244, 247, 252.
[43] James Bell's Notebook, henceforth cited as Bell Notebook, Glasgow University Library MS BE 7-f. 14.
[44] *Wedderburne Compt Buik*, e.g. p. 81. [45] *R.P.C.*, VOL. IX, p. 259.

Dundee Shipping Lists as an importer of goods from Bordeaux,[46] appears also in the Breadalbane Household Book as a supplier of "Sweit meattis and spyceis" to the Highland nobility.[47] The same is true of retailing. The evil men who looted the booth of Alexander Johnsone in Inverness took a remarkable assortment of goods—bonnets, nutmeg, arrow-heads, "gros silk buttonis," pepper, "Inglisch garteris"—all of which would add to the gaiety of life in the raiders' homes in Glenelg.[48] All the available evidence points to the conclusion that the Scottish trader, at home or abroad, possessed a certain expertness in markets and commercial practice; in no other sense can he fairly be called a specialist.

As in most primitive trading communities, the ownership of goods led often to the ownership of means of conveyance. Nothing like a distinct shipowning group can be identified. Individual ownership of vessels by merchants was not unknown, and, by the seventeenth century at least, the skipper-owner was fairly common in mercantile circles. The innumerable instances of apparently shared ownership may be ambiguous, for sometimes the sharing related to a particular arrangement for the use of the vessel on a single trip rather than to the permanent ownership of the vessel as such. None the less the latter form of ownership did prevail widely, with the capital value of the ship split up into all sorts of fractions down to twenty-sixths, with merchants generally prominent among the shareholders. Thus the *Grace* of Dysart was owned by her master (David Robertson of Dysart), an Edinburgh merchant (Andrew Ainslie) and a Stirling merchant (John Cowane).[49] Cowane also owned a part of the *Gift of God* of St Monance and of the *George* of Queensferry. In 1595 Wedderburne bought an eighth share of the *Thomas* with her new sails and tackle, and three years later he wrote of "my half quarter of the crear to Norroway presently bound God willing."[50]

An extension of this pooling of resources to other mercantile activities might have been expected in a society where capital

[46] Dundee Shipping Lists, pp. 213, 214.
[47] Household Book of Breadalbane, printed in *The Black Book of Taymouth*, p. 301.
[48] *The Book of Dunvegan*, ed. R. C. MacLeod, p. 116.
[49] Cowane's shipowning ventures are described in Morris, *The Stirling Merchant Gild and the Life of John Cowane*, Ch. XIX *passim*.
[50] *Wedderburne Compt Buik*, pp. 53, 70.

was scarce, yet the joint-stock trading company, then becoming so fashionable in Holland and England, remained virtually unknown in Scottish practice. No single explanation is wholly satisfactory. It has been argued that the control exercised by the Convention of Royal Burghs and by the Staple organisation at Veere fulfilled at least some of the functions of the organised company.[51] The joint-stock company was of particular value to traders adventuring into new and distant markets where risks were high; throughout our period Scotsmen made little attempt to go beyond the traditional North Sea and Baltic routes where, as we shall see later, familiarity and personal contacts kept risks relatively low. Furthermore, the very compactness of the Scottish trading communities facilitated local *ad hoc* arrangements among traders; indeed the most striking feature of the surviving cargo lists is the way in which a small cargo would often belong to a score or more of traders. It was only as the seventeenth century went on, and Scotsmen became more enterprising in commerce, that more permanent collective trading associations were found necessary.

Writing in the hey-day of Free Trade, Robert Chambers said that the merchants of the sixteenth century were thwarted by the "false political economy" of that time.[52] How widespread and how effective was public control? In the interests of the domestic population, exports, especially of foodstuffs, were periodically banned, and from the 1590's imports became subject to duties and to that closer control always associated with nascent mercantilism.[53] From well before our period the Crown had imposed revenue duties on the staple exports, those commodities in which the royal burghs had a trading monopoly. But customs duties were never prohibitive, and official bans were made to be by-passed by licence. One gets the impression that the merchant was less thwarted by "false political economy" than a simple reading of the statutes and proclamations might suggest, and that, in his day-to-day activities, he was more affected by local burgh regulations. The interests of the burgh were focused firstly on the collection of local dues: thus the collection of the Holy Blood Silver at Dundee prompted the compilation of the now invaluable Shipping Lists which

---

[51] Pagan, *The Convention of the Royal Burghs of Scotland*, pp. 150-1.
[52] Chambers, *Edinburgh Merchants*, p. 20.   [53] See above, p. 82.

survive from 1580 to 1588 and then in almost unbroken series from 1612 onwards. Secondly the burgh sought to maintain discipline in and around the harbour—a matter of great importance when harbours were small and when the landward approaches were often limited to a few narrow wynds. Thirdly in every major burgh there existed a series of regulations designed to preserve the monopoly of the burgh itself and to maintain a code of commercial morality within it. A random selection of burgh regulations of the 1550's and 1560's will illustrate the nature of these aims: no freeman to act as factor for an unfreeman; no charter-party to be valid unless ratified by the Dean of Gild; weights and measures to be tested by the Dean four times a year; no ship to sail on a Sunday. In a compact community these must have been hard to evade.

To recreate any picture of commercial procedure in the time of Queen Mary and King James VI we must first abandon many modern conceptions. By any modern standard the scale of operations was minute: indeed in the records of our period, as in the Ledger of Andrew Halyburton a century earlier, a great many of the overseas trading transactions are of a scale which suggests personal rather than commercial purchasing. Perhaps this personal characteristic, even more than the difference in scale, most sharply differentiates the trading of our period from that of the nineteenth and twentieth centuries. As we shall demonstrate later, a strong element of quasi-barter persisted in Scottish overseas trade, with the result that a merchant either had to accompany his goods or put them in the hands of a trusted friend or factor. A merchant ship, therefore, would often carry a group of merchants: in one instance thirteen sailed together with their cargo from Leith.[54] But obviously the average merchant, with his other numerous affairs at home, could not afford the several weeks involved in a round trip to Danzig or Bordeaux merely to sell a few hundred skins or a few score yards of cloth, and consequently he had to rely on an agent who accompanied the cargo and undertook factorial duties for him and other merchants. The factor might be a trusted confidant. Thus in 1593 Wedderburne sent goods in the care of his uncle by marriage, Peter Imbrie, "to be sauld

[54] D. Robertson and M. Wood, *Castle and Town. Chapters in the History of the Royal Burgh of Edinburgh*, 1928, p. 280.

quhair he makis mercat . . . and war it on sic profitable waring as he dois to himself";[55] and he also asked Imbrie to keep an eye on the skipper, Alexander Rankin, who had some of Wedderburne's linen to sell. Alternatively, the charge to the factor could be set about with conditions and detailed instructions. Two years earlier than the case just quoted, Wedderburne had sent a last of herring with Peter Mann "to be sauld quhair he happenis to mak mercat." If the market were in France then Mann was either to put the money on loan or bring it home in "myln rays of gold" (Portuguese milreis), but if in England then he was either to effect a loan or to buy linen hats with velvet trimmings, two lengths of fustian "of trym cullouris" and as much dyestuff as the balance might purchase.[56]

Because of its importance, the function of factor was subject to regulation by the gild merchant. Thus: "It is devysed and ordained yat no merchand mak any facter for him or give his commission of merchandise . . . but to an qualified merchand, and sick as is admitted by ye deane of gild";[57] "It is agreed . . . that no merchand presume to mak any mariner or skipper his factor to his geare . . . in respect ye great skaith of making yer mariners and skippers factoris who have no perfection nor knowledge to doe ye same."[58] Though this last rule had the assent of eighty-five Dundee merchants in 1580 it was not well observed in the following decades, for Wedderburne frequently employed skippers as factors for his goods, though it is significant that he generally gave them very specific instructions so that their true factorial function was restricted.

For the most part, however, the merchants employed the skipper simply to convey their goods from port to port under contractual terms set out in the charter party. This instrument was drawn up at the beginning of every voyage whether the ship was to carry cargo or whether it was to convey a royal ambassador. Its completion often marked the sort of haggling to which Peter Young refers in one of his letters to Sir Patrick Waus, Ambassador-designate to Denmark: "The skipper was at me again to see gif we wald giue the 1800 merkis. I stude still at the 1000 merkis . . . I shall not pass the 1200 quhill I see

[55] *Wedderburne Compt Buik*, p. 79.   [56] *Op. cit.*, p. 140.
[57] *Burgh Laws of Dundee*, p. 118.   [58] *Op. cit.*, p. 121.

quhat shipping thair is.''[59] The normal charter party for a trading voyage set out, under the approval of the Dean of Gild, the financial arrangements with each merchant concerned, the destination and intermediate calls, and the terms on which the factors of the charterers should travel on board. Substantially similar documents were drawn in foreign ports regarding sailings to Scotland.[60]

We have seen that merchants featured largely as shipowners. To what extent did they use their own ships? In the entries of salt imports from La Rochelle and of timber from Norway, the cargo is often described as "pertaining to ye awneris of ye said schip";[61] but in other branches of trade the evidence is less conclusive. Thus Alexander Duncan, part-owner of the *Eagle*, carried his own goods in her from London to Scotland in August 1588, but when she arrived again in the following January from Flanders there were no goods for Duncan aboard her.[62] The impression is that where a uniform cargo awaited collection, and the owners had a ship, they would whenever possible employ her for that purpose; but where—as in the import trade from Holland—the cargoes were invariably assorted, it was a matter of convenience whether or not a merchant's goods were carried in his own ship.

A closely related question is the extent to which ships concentrated on the trade of their home port. From the generally fragmentary port books it looks as if the trade of an old-established major port was handled mainly by its own vessels or by those of near neighbours. This was certainly true at Dundee where, in the Shipping Lists, entry after entry records "ane schip" or "ane bark" of Dundee. The home ports of ships recorded as departures from Leith in 1627-8 can be summarised thus:[63]

Leith	19
Local Forth and S. Fife	36
Foreign	18
Unspecified	7

[59] Sir P. Waus, *Correspondence*, ed. Agnew, VOL. II, p. 383.
[60] E.g. Trocmé and Delafosse, *Le Commerce rochelais*, pp. 18-19.
[61] E.g. Dundee Shipping Lists, p. 243.
[62] Dundee Shipping Lists, pp. 217, 219.
[63] Derived from "The Entress of Ships, Guidis, and Geir transportit at the port of Leith," MS in General Register House.

By contrast, Glasgow's trade in April and May of 1597—
admittedly a very small sample—was handled by six local ships
and four from remote Scottish ports, two of them from Pittenweem (Fife) and one each from Aberdeen and Dundee;[64] but
the general impression is that normally in this period Glasgow
drew on Dumbarton for shipping reinforcements. The arrival
at Fraserburgh in 1572 of Peter Waus of Inverness in his
Dutch ship,[65] inviting local merchants to participate in a
round trip to Norway, symbolises both the geographical complexity of mercantile activities and the dependence of some of
the small ports on outsiders. From disputes determined in the
Burgh Court at Inverness we get the same impression of the
role of outsiders: how, for example, in the early 1570's, John
Berne of Perth was bargaining with local merchants at Inverness to send salmon to Dundee for reshipment to France.[66]

The geographical distribution of Scottish shipping was
determined to some extent by such combinations of coastal and
overseas activity. The facts about genuine coastal shipping are
distressingly elusive, yet consideration of the physical structure
of the country, the consequent difficulties of overland transport,
and the coastal or riparian location of most towns, demands
the conclusion that it must have been considerable. We know
that coal was shipped northwards from the Forth and Fife and
slates were taken back to Edinburgh;[67] we know that Perth
men took salt to Inverness in "crears";[68] we know that there was
considerable traffic between the Clyde and the Western
Isles;[69] but how much of Scotland's mercantile energies and
shipping tonnage was thus absorbed remains completely
indeterminable.

By most contemporary standards the ships employed in
Scottish trading, and the cargoes they carried, were alike
small—though mere size was no guarantee of fame, for did not
Drake sail out of Plymouth Sound in 1577 in a flagship of only
120 tons and with two accompanying sloops of only 50 and 30
tons apiece? Though their recording was seldom very explicit, the Scottish port clerks occasionally distinguished

[64] *Glasgow Records*, p. 187.   [65] *Inverness Records*, pp. 222-3.   [66] *Op. cit.*, p. 219.
[67] Nef, *Rise of the British Coal Industry*, VOL. I, pp. 91-2; *Edinburgh Records*, VOL.
IV, p. 406.
[68] *Inverness Records*, p. 175.
[69] *R.P.C.*, VOL. II, pp. 470-1; VOL. III, p. 125; VOL. IV, p. 535.

between kinds of ship: thus we encounter "ane crear," a low-built smack of 30 or 40 tons; "a pink," a vessel distinguished by its very narrow stern; "ane hoy," the Scotticised version of the Dutch "heu," a single-decker rigged as a sloop;[70] and very occasionally "ane flieboat." The appearance of a flyboat must have stimulated keen interest among the pier-side experts in a Scottish port, for its prototype, the fluitschip—or "flute" as the English called it—was a recent Dutch innovation. It was an ideal merchantman for North Sea trading, an essentially utility vessel of high cargo capacity, cheap both to build and maintain, and easy to operate.[71]

Apart from a few specialised branches, to which we shall return in their appropriate connexions, the bulk of Scotland's overseas trade was handled by Scottish-owned ships. How far they were Scottish-built is quite another matter. The assumption that, whenever funds allowed, the Scots would buy ready-made ships from lands where the technique of building was highly advanced or where costs were low, is supported by a few pieces of direct evidence. Captain David Murray, "being in the toun of Bruges, bocht a schip of fiftie tun callit the *Mellingell*," and had her sent to Banff in 1581.[72] David Wedderburne bought a ship in Norway,[73] and in 1622 John Wood and six other merchants got a certificate from the Edinburgh Burgh Council testifying that the *Archeangell* "bocht be theme in Ambsterdame" was indeed their property and that the country from which it came was "frie of pest."[74] On the other hand, native shipbuilding was high on the list of mercantilist priorities, and a nation which had built so famous a ship as the *Great Michael*[75] was unlikely to abandon its shipyards or to forget its skill. From the *Protocol Book* of Mark Carruthers[76] it is clear that ships were sometimes built at Dumfries. The "tymber holff" at Leith was a recognised shipyard: in December 1609, for example, Edward Macmath, merchant of

---

[70] Most of these terms are discussed in A. Clark, *History of the Shipmaster Society of Aberdeen*, 1911, pp. 11-12.
[71] V. Barbour, "Dutch and English shipping in the seventeenth century," in *Ec. H.R.*, II (1930), pp. 279-80.
[72] *Annals of Banff*, ed. W. Cramond, New Spalding Club, 1893, p. 211.
[73] *Wedderburne Compt Buik*, p. 101.
[74] *Edinburgh Records*, VOL. VI, p. 231.   [75] See below, p. 149.
[76] *Protocol Book of Mark Carruthers, 1531-61*, ed. R. C. Reid, Scottish Record Society, 1956, p. 56.

Edinburgh, was licensed to build a ship there "in the plaice alreddy appoyntet to him," and sixteen months later the Town Council despatched a small delegation to witness the launch and to see that the site was properly restored.[77] Whether bought or home-built, the typical Scots merchant ship would look small as it lay among the Dutchmen and the Hansards in the harbourage at Danzig or off the salines in the Bay of Biscay.[78]

Because of the assortment of goods and the vague statements of quantities it is often impossible even to estimate the size of cargoes in modern terms—what, for example, is one to make of "two dousone of gryitt peces of aik"?—but where the cargo was uniform we can make a reasonable guess. Thus an average cargo of Swedish iron imported in a Scots ship might run to 60 or 80 tons, and a wine ship from Bordeaux or Spain might have ten to fifteen thousand gallons aboard.[79] Outward cargoes, notably those of skins and hides, were bulky but light, and a substantial tonnage of stone or other ballast must have been carried to ensure a reasonably smooth crossing of the North Sea. Small as the activities appear, they strained the harbour and quayside accommodation of most Scots ports. At Aberdeen, for example, the bigger ships still had to lie out from the quays to await unloading by "cabars" (lighters), though harbour improvements were afoot both there and elsewhere. The outstanding feat, the removal of the great boulder called Craig Maitland from the mouth of the Dee, was accomplished in 1610 by David Anderson with—so tradition says— the aid of a fleet of empty casks lashed to the boulder at low tide.[80]

The rate of turn-round was slowed by these primitive harbour facilities, by the repairs and refitting often required by ship and rigging, and by the seasonal congestion which characterised all north-west European trade. Annual totals of arrivals and departures—for example the 80 odd at Leith in the 1550's and '60's[81]—disguise the extent to which activity

[77] *Edinburgh Records*, VOL. VI, p. 57, 73.
[78] Lythe, in *Dundee Economic Essays*, ed. Eastham, p. 65.
[79] Calculated from cargo lists in the Dundee Shipping Lists.
[80] Milne, *Aberdeen: topographical, antiquarian and historical papers*, pp. 362 ff.; and Clark, *History of the Shipmaster Society of Aberdeen*, p. 13.
[81] Robertson and Wood, *Castle and Town*, p. 279.

was concentrated between about May and November. The fifteenth-century statutes of the Scots Parliament,[82] banning sailings between Michaelmas and Candlemas, simply gave formal expression to the natural reluctance of mariners to undertake winter voyages, particularly in northern waters. The cry of Sir Patrick Spens

> O wha is this has done this deed
> And tauld the king o' me,
> To send us out, at this time o' year,
> To sail upon the sea?

was no more than any experienced skipper would have said at the prospect of a winter crossing to Norway. Partly because of less violent weather, partly because of the nature of the wine trade, sailings to the south were rather more evenly spread through the year; but the overall activity of a Scots port displayed two well-defined phases: a slack winter, followed by the "tyme of thrang" when, to speed up handling, "na ship lay too hir braid syde to load or liver . . . but hir forship or hir starne."[83]

The comparatively slack winter season and the slow turn-round at all seasons meant that the average mariner spent appreciably less time at sea than the typical merchant seaman of today, and it is not surprising that both skippers and crews found time to do some trading on their own account. Yet because the skippers' skill was specialised, they naturally developed a group self-consciousness which found expression in the establishment of Shipmaster Societies such as that founded at Aberdeen in 1578 by a group of twenty-four skippers and mariners.[84] While charts and navigational aids were slowly being improved, the skipper's "haven-finding" skill came mainly from experience and familiarity, and we find many instances of a skipper commanding the same ship for long periods and concentrating heavily on one or two routes. We can trace some seventeen trips made by the flyboat, *Hope for Grace*, between foreign and Scottish ports in the period 1612 to 1620. All but two of these were from Biscay or Spain, and the skipper was always William Kinnereis or his brother

---

[82] *A.P.S.*, vol. II, p. 87.
[83] *Burgh Laws of Dundee*, p. 21.
[84] Clark, *History of the Shipmaster Society of Aberdeen*, pp. 2 ff.

Andrew.[85] Between 1602 and 1612 George Balcanquell in the
Bruce of Kirkcaldy operated regularly between Scotland and
Boston (Lincs.), varying the monotony of the routine by an
occasional trip to the Baltic on charter to English merchants.[86]
In 1611 and 1612 he took six cargoes from Scotland to Boston,
and between April and July 1611 he did the round trip between
Boston and the Baltic with cargo for Matthew Foxley, a Boston
merchant. A particularly energetic skipper like Robert
Halyburton seems to have operated on the Scandinavian route
in summer and the Biscay in autumn or winter. His recorded
arrivals at Dundee in 1616-18 display this pattern:[87]

April	1616	in the	*Thomas*	from	Bordeaux
Sept.	1616	,,	,,	,,	the Baltic
Jan.	1617	,,	,,	,,	Bordeaux
Sept.	1617	,,	*George*	,,	Norway
Jan.	1618	,,	*Swan*	,,	La Rochelle
Aug.	1618	,,	*Patience*	,,	Norway

Three round trips a year seems to have been about the maximum, either two to Biscay and one to the Baltic, two to Norway
and one to France, or some other similar combination. No case
has been found of a skipper making more than one trip a year
into the Baltic proper. Greater activity could hardly be
expected when we recall the speed of the sailing ships, the
partiality of skippers for sailing in company, the delays over
customs at places like Elsinore, the problem of finding "mercat"
for the cargo, the infuriatingly slow handling of ship and cargo
at ports, and, quite often, time-wasting disputes over damage
sustained by cargo when hides had been saturated by sea-water
or wine casks had been tapped by unruly mariners.
   The practice of sharing in ship-owning and consigning goods
in small quantities reflects the relatively high risk of physical
loss which faced the overseas merchant. Despite the familiarity
of masters with their own waters and despite the avoidance of
bad weather sailing, losses by shipwreck were considerable. It
is perhaps significant that in spite of the coastal dwellers' well-
known propensity to loot vessels stranded on the shore, the
mariner's hand could reach out to help the fellow mariner in

[85] Dundee Shipping Lists for years cited.
[86] *The Port Books of Boston,* henceforth cited as *Boston Port Books,* ed. R. M. K.
Hinton, Lincoln Record Society, 1956, *passim.*
[87] Dundee Shipping Lists for years cited.

distress—even though he were a foreigner. Lesley describes how a Russian ambassador, bound for England and wrecked on the north-east Scottish coast, was succoured and sent on his way, and the "puir schipbrokkin Spayngyerts" from the Armada were fed and clothed wherever they landed in Scotland.[88] These disasters were common, and the tale of loss of ships and cargo told by the Forth shipowners in support of a proposal to light May Island could have applied to most of the unlit promontories.[89]

Piracy was the second main cause of physical loss. It was an old-established occupation of the less reputable seamen, and it acquired a veneer of respectability in the frequent wars of the sixteenth century when official seizure was barely distinguishable from sheer piracy of wholesale dimensions. Thus according to Holinshed's *Chronicle*, the burgesses of Edinburgh lost nearly thirty ships with their merchandise when the marriage negotiations with England broke down in 1547.[90] The records of the period, from the Privy Council's Register to the popular ballads, are packed with the sinful deeds of the reivers, and the experience of the Lass of Lochroyan was all too typical for peace of mind at sea:

> She hadna sail'd but twenty leagues,
> But twenty leagues and three,
> When she met wi' a rank reiver
> And a' his companie.

One of the few women shipowners of whom we have knowledge, Agnes Cowty of Dundee, had two of her vessels raided by English pirates in the Channel in 1582, involving loss of cargo and life on a scale big enough to warrant an approach to Walsingham himself.[91] Four years later a group of Edinburgh shippers complained that their salmon in ships en route for Dieppe had been looted by English and Flushing pirates.[92] The tale of alleged Scottish losses could be extended for pages, and, it must be added, an equally formidable indictment could

[88] Lesley, *History*, VOL. II, p. 367; *Edinburgh Records*, VOL. IV, p. 528.
[89] *R.P.C.*, 2nd ser., VOL. VI, pp. 59, 562-79.
[90] R. Holinshed, *Chronicles of England, Scotland and Ireland*, 1807 edn., VOL. III, p. 884.
[91] F. E. Dyer, "A woman shipowner," in *The Mariner's Mirror*, XXXVI, 2 (1950); *Calendar of State Papers relating to Scotland preserved in H.M. Public Record Office*, ed. M. J. Thorpe, 1858, VOL. I, p. 441.
[92] *Edinburgh Records*, VOL. IV, p. 466.

be drawn up against the Scots from English and Continental records. For safety, skippers sailed in convoy, but there were always stray vessels and the reivers were often bold enough to come well inshore:

> The reivers they stole Fair Annie
> As she walked by the sea,

and, in 1596, with more strictly commercial motives, they stole a Danzig ship out of Burntisland harbour, though retribution was to overtake them at Aberdeen at the hands of John Justice, the aptly-named local executioner.[93]

Flagrant piracy persisted strongly into the seventeenth century, and the North Africans were not the only offenders. Remoteness from the heart of government combined with geographical convenience to make the south-west coasts of Ireland an ideal setting for pirate haunts. So, in 1608, the Mayor of Cork was able to send to the burgesses of Kirkcaldy a detailed account of how one of their ships, the *Hert*, had been "spoilyeitt of hir best anker and tow with hir furniture wittal," and how the pirates had looted her cargo of wheat, tallow, fish, and yarn.[94] The depredations of a single pirate company, based on Long Island (off the south-west corner of County Cork), are vividly rehearsed in the indictment of Captains Randell and Parkins and twenty-eight others before the Admiralty Court in Edinburgh in 1610.[95] From Long Island, "ane plaice of resort of all pirates and opin Roberis," they had swept the seas, south, west, and north, in a great arc from Gibraltar to Norway. In the course of a year they had intercepted and seized or robbed a dozen or more ships, their prey including "ane puir fischar man and his bot," a Frenchman homeward bound from Newfoundland, a "carvall of Yermouth" on which they stole money from two falconers going to Norway to buy hawks, and a bark of Caithness off Zetland laden with cloth. Landing at Kirkwall, the "wicket crew" roistered around the town, behaving "maist barberouslie and beistlie," being "evir and at all tymes drukin and fechtand," until three of them in their "mad and drukin humoris"

---

[93] "Accounts of the Burgh of Aberdeen, 1596-7," printed in *Miscellany of the Spalding Club*, VOL. V, 1852, pp. 64-5.   [94] *Kirkcaldy Records*, p. 320.
[95] *Edinburgh Records*, VOL. VI, p. 63 and App. XVI; R. Pitcairn, *Criminal Trials in Scotland*, 1833, VOL. III, p. 102.

K

violently entered a ship of the Earl of Orkney in the harbourage at Kirkwall. At this point the forces of law and order at last moved into action. Under instructions from the Privy Council, Edinburgh victualled and armed three Leith ships which sailed with all haste for Orkney; a month later the "pyrat schip" and her crew had been brought to Leith; justice took its course in the Admiralty Court, and thirty corpses (twenty-seven according to Calderwood)[96] swung from a gibbet within the "sie fluid and mark thairoff" on the shore of the Firth of Forth.

Loss from piracy and by tempest and other acts of God lay beyond the control of the individual trader, but he could at least keep his commercial risks within bounds by concentrating his activities on a few markets familiar either to himself or to his trusted associates. The absence of any means of communication faster than the sailing ship meant that the trader approached his foreign market in ignorance of current conditions there. In consequence factors were often authorised to sell wheresoever they "happnit to mak mercat," and the experience of John Spens, whose herring was shipped in 1566 from Crail to Dieppe and then back to Hull before a buyer could be found, cannot have been unique.[97] Yet though the phrase "wild adventure" was sometimes used, the element of "adventure" was generally so slight that it is difficult to believe that serious loss often occurred through ignorance of market conditions. The goods handled by the typical Scots trader, especially on the export side of his business, were not subject to rapid deterioration, and, barring widespread war, there were generally alternative markets only a few days' sailing apart.

Furthermore the trader must have derived enormous confidence from the knowledge that in nearly all his traditional markets there existed groups either of compatriots or of sympathisers. At Veere the Scots were organised in their officially recognised Staple, the factors there were under the eye of the Conservator,[98] and there were Scottish mercenaries in the neighbouring Low Countries continuously from 1572.[99] Of France it has been said that "there were very few Scotsmen

[96] Calderwood, *History of the Kirk of Scotland,* VOL. VII., p. 118.
[97] Maxwell, *History of Old Dundee,* p. 583.
[98] Davidson and Gray, *The Scottish Staple at Veere,* PT. III, Ch. III *passim.*
[99] *Papers Illustrating the History of the Scots Brigade in the Netherlands 1572-1772,* ed. J. Ferguson, Scottish History Society, VOL. I, 1899.

who did not look with friendship to one element or other in the country . . . this applied equally to Calvinist and Catholic";[100] and this summary of the Scots' relations with the French can be illustrated from the history of the ports of Normandy where Scottish arrivals quickly became fully integrated with the native population.[101] Before 1603 contacts with England lacked this personal character; thereafter the number and influence of Scots increased, especially in London where the burghs for a time maintained their own resident agent and where, by the 1620's, David Murehead was the commercial representative of William Dick of Edinburgh.[102] In the Baltic and Scandinavian lands throughout our period Scotsmen were ubiquitous as soldiers, pedlars, merchants, and craftsmen. The first town council of Gothenburg was virtually monopolised by Dutchmen and Scots;[103] there were enough Scottish Protestants in Danzig in 1587 to justify a special message from the General Assembly;[104] there was a Scottish gild at Königsberg; Sweden raised troops in Scotland;[105] there were Scots residents in Elsinore and Copenhagen[106]—the instances could be multiplied indefinitely and confirm the impression that the interests of Scottish traders were in most places guarded by relatives or at least by fellow-countrymen.

By the second quarter of the seventeenth century Scotland was beginning to align her mercantile practices to those of the more sophisticated trading nations. By the early 1630's the great Edinburgh merchant, William Dick, had so regularised his financial contacts with Paris that the young Montrose, on his tour of France in 1633-4, could draw bills on Edinburgh through Dick's Parisian factor,[107] and about the same time Dick was also negotiating bills of exchange with Holland.[108] But down to this time the trading techniques of Scottish merchants had retained so elementary a character that they must have appeared archaic to men of Antwerp or London.

[100] Mathew, *Scotland Under Charles I*, p. 206.
[101] Mollat, *Le Commerce maritime normand*, p. 508.
[102] *Edinburgh Records*, VOL. VI, p. 295.
[103] E. F. Heckscher, *An Economic History of Sweden*, Harvard 1954, p. 107.
[104] On the Scots in Danzig and the East Baltic see below, pp. 156-7.
[105] For one example see T. Mitchell, *The Scottish Expedition to Norway in 1612*, Christiana 1886.
[106] E.g. Richard Wedderburne; *Wedderburne Compt Buik*, p. 14.
[107] J. Buchan, *Montrose*, 1937 edn., p. 25.
[108] Chambers, *Edinburgh Merchants*, pp. 14-15.

Put simply, the normal basis of Scottish commercial exchange had been either goods for goods or specie for goods. Straight barter—at least in foreign trade—had certainly disappeared by Queen Mary's reign except on the remoter fringes of the commercial world; what persisted was a quasi-barter into which money entered either as a measure of value, a link between transactions, or as a final makeweight in adjusting balances. We consider elsewhere the particular application of these methods in Baltic trading; for our present purpose it suffices to cite one of the many instances in which David Wedderburne sent parcels of goods abroad with instructions that the "free money" (i.e. the money realised) should be converted at once into other goods. In 1598 he sent "with James Neilsone maryner in the schip callit the Robert quhairof William Christie in Master under God, of myn markit with this by mark D W, Sex elnis small lyning, 24 ellis small lyning clayth (and several other items). . . . To be sauld in Bordeaux or in Ingland and the fre money to be warit on fyn Burdeaux Wynis half clarit half quhyt, and to be schippit with himself in the same schip."[109] Thus a high velocity of circulation was maintained and a small quantity of cash was made to go a long way.

The merchant needed to be of tough fibre, for he operated within a cross-fire of conflicting ideals. The Church embodied the old doctrine of "plenty"; the Government—because of its monetary problems—thought in terms of a favourable balance and an inflow of precious metal and coin; the merchant himself sought primarily to exchange his exports for goods which he might resell at a profit at home. The remarkably wide international circulation of national coins indicates that no one view continuously triumphed and that trade made its own laws. The historians of La Rochelle, where the Scots did extensive business, emphasise this aspect of commerce: "La forme de change le plus ancienne est le change manuel, l'échange d'une monnaie contre une autre. Le grand variété de monnaies circulant à La Rochelle l'avait très tôt rendu nécessaire. Il conservait encore son importance vers 1600."[110] Money, in short, was carried to and fro either as the whole or

109 *Wedderburne Compt Buik*, p. 72.
110 Trocmé and Delafosse, *Le Commerce rochelais*, p. 57.

part proceeds of sales or as the means of effecting spot purchases. In spite of much legislation to the contrary,[111] Scottish
merchants such as Wedderburne carried assorted coin out of
the country on their trading voyages, or sent it in the hands of
skippers or factors. When a group of merchants was officially
asked in 1622 whether overseas trade could be conducted
without the export of money, the answer was that in some
branches it would be impossible, and everywhere it would be
difficult.[112] Nobody seriously challenged the opinion.

We shall consider later the factors bearing on the balance in
these different branches of overseas trade and the effect of
unfavourable balances on Scotland's domestic economy. What
is relevant to our present theme is that the day-to-day practice
of a Scottish trader in the time of King James VI was not
substantially different from that of Andrew Halyburton in the
time of James IV.

[111] *A.P.S.*, VOL. II, pp. 336, 538; VOL. III, p. 108.
[112] Cochran-Patrick, *Coinage*, VOL. I, p. 272.

V

TRADE WITH SCANDINAVIA
AND THE BALTIC

The Norwegian Timber Trade

Though his precise identity is uncertain, it can only have been
a cynical Englishman who wrote in 1617 that if Christ had been
betrayed in Scotland ("as doubtless he should, had he come
as a stranger"), Judas would sooner have found the grace of
repentance than a tree on which to hang himself.[1] But other
less prejudiced observers, Aeneas Sylvius[2] and the like, were
equally emphatic about the general absence of standing
timber in the parts of Scotland they visited, and their accounts
are not easy to reconcile with the persistent traditions of great
forested areas. Some confusion has unquestionably arisen over
the interpretation of the word "foresta," which refers not
necessarily to woodland, but more certainly to hunting ground
or even waste, in somewhat the same sense as "deer forest" is
used today. Furthermore it must be remembered that, for
excellent reasons, the early travellers in general refrained from
penetrating very deeply into the inner recesses of the country,
so that what Fynes Moryson had to say of Fife[3] may not have
applied to the landward parts of Perthshire or Inverness-shire.

Whilst this whole problem of the history of natural vegetation in Scotland needs further specialised investigation,[4] it is
clear that in the sixteenth century—notwithstanding the

---

[1] Hume Brown, *Early Travellers*, p. 97. For a discussion on the writer's identity
see Mitchell, *List of Travels and Tours in Scotland, 1296-1900*, pp. 44-5.

[2] Aeneas Sylvius visited Scotland in the 1430's and later became Pope Pius II.
His account of the country is reprinted in *Concilia Scotiae*, ed. J. Robertson, Bannatyne Club, 1866, VOL. I, pp. xci-xcii, and in translation in Hume Brown, *Early
Travellers*, pp. 24-9. He saw coal for the first time in Scotland, and found the
women remarkably free with their kisses.

[3] See below, p. 145.

[4] For an account of the problems involved, see H. Fairhurst, "The natural
vegetation of Scotland," in *Scottish Geographical Magazine*, LV (1939), pp. 208-11.

travellers' accounts—some genuinely forested areas survived. A few burghs had their own local plantations: at Inverness in 1586 John Neilson was charged with taking "tuaye horse laidis of greyne young saplyne" from the burgh's woods,[5] and Stirling regularly drew revenue from timber cut out of Murray's Wood.[6] On a larger scale, parts of Ettrick were still woodland, and, according to Taylor's *Pennyles Pilgrimage* of 1618, the Earldom of Mar contained enough great trees to provide masts for the entire world's shipping for forty years. Taylor, it should be added, having penetrated the interior, had just enjoyed the lavish hospitality of the Earl—"venison . . . fresh salmon . . . capons . . . good ale . . . with most potent Aqua-vitae"—and it is therefore conceivable that his report was based on hazy impression rather than on sober statistics.[7]

It is, however, indisputable that the great waterway of Loch Ness provided a channel down which logs and cut timber could be conveyed at little expense from Glengarry and Glenmoriston and from the lands of The Chisholm and Fraser of Aberchalder. At Inverness, to which this timber came, local merchants such as James Kerr[8] regularly dealt—and argued—with the great proprietors of the inland glens from whom they bought whole trees, rails, cabers, stakes, wands, and oak bark, and in 1575 the aid of the Privy Council was invoked to restrain Hugh Fraser of Lovat from impeding the Glengarry men in their timber trade down the Loch.[9]

In this facility for drawing on a timber-bearing hinterland, Inverness was unique among the leading Scottish burghs. The country's chief timber users were the burghs of the Lowlands; the trees about which we have certain knowledge were remote and inland, and, to quote again from Taylor, "so farre from any passage of water, and withall in such rockie mountaines, that no way to convey them is possible, either with boate, horse, or cart." In short, the condition of Scotland's internal timber supply in 1576 was not radically different from what it was in 1776 when, as Adam Smith pointed out, for lack of transport facilities good trees fell and rotted on the spot where they had grown.[10]

[5] *Inverness Records*, p. 307. [6] *Stirling Records*, pp. 107, 306.
[7] The *Pennyles Pilgrimage*, 1618. See Hume Brown, *Early Travellers*, pp. 104-31.
[8] *Inverness Records*, pp. 141, 145. [9] *Op. cit.*, pp. lxxiv, 142, 206.
[10] A. Smith, *The Wealth of Nations*, ed. E. Cannan, 1930, VOL. I, p. 164.

Though the effective domestic supply was small, domestic demand was great, for timber played a major part in the life of the nation. It was the principal fuel of the urban communities. The east coast towns were, in general, devoid of any considerable local peat supplies; in their industries the use of coal was severely limited both by technical considerations and by prejudice; in the home prejudice was even stronger, for the house-proud wife believed that its fumes ruined her cherished hangings and encouraged the breeding of bed-bugs.[11] Constructional work came very high in the scale of timber consumption. From time to time the burghal authorities had to patch or reconstruct their piers and harbours with stones and great beams: in 1555, for example, the Edinburgh magistrates sent two agents to Norway to buy timber for harbour works at Newhaven.[12] Notwithstanding a trend in the bigger towns towards stone and slate, domestic building was still predominantly a matter of timber and thatch. Burgess houses of consequence commonly incorporated a galleried or balconied timber front with expanses of plaster facing, though less ambitious frontages, as Brereton noted even in Edinburgh in 1636, were simply "faced with boards."[13] Interiors were full of wood—the massive beams and ship-like framework in Huntly House (c. 1570) almost overwhelm the modern visitor—for roof principals were left exposed in unashamed strength, and ceilings and walls were often lined with fir boards[14] or—as in Queen Mary's apartments at Holyrood—with oak panelling. From the constant references in the Inverness Court Book[15] to couples, gale-forks, cabers, stakes, and wattling-wands it is plain that the typical small town house was wood-framed, wattled and thatched.

The predominance of these materials, often with generous coatings of pitch and tar, explains the frequency of major fires which in turn cleared the ground for rebuilding. The conflagration at Haddington in 1598,[16] started, so tradition says, by laundry catching alight, was followed by comparable

---

[11] A belief which persisted into the eighteenth century; see M. Plant, *Domestic Life in Scotland in the Eighteenth Century*, 1952, p. 218.

[12] *Edinburgh Records*, VOL. III, p. 211.

[13] Brereton, *Travels*, p. 100.

[14] Chambers, *Ancient Domestic Architecture of Edinburgh*, p. 2.

[15] *Inverness Records*, e.g. pp. lxxiv, 142.

[16] *Convention Records*, VOL. II, pp. 33-4.

disasters in 1599 at Irvine and Dumfries;[17] Peebles suffered "ane grate fyre" in 1604;[18] twenty years later the whole body of the town of Dunfermline went up in flames.[19] Fire was the nightly dread, and the Haddington town-crier's voice echoed the sentiments of all responsible citizens:

> I warn ye a' keep weel your fire!
> For oftentimes a little spark
> Brings mony hands to meikle wark.

Unlike houses, ships could be imported ready-made, but the timber requirements of shipwrights, either for building or repairing, were none the less considerable. By our period their chief glory, the huge but unmanageable *Great Michael*, lay rotting in Brest harbour; but according to Lindsay of Pitscottie the effect of her building was still apparent in the countryside. He says, and his knowledge was first-hand for he lived near Cupar, that she was "of so great stature, and took so much timber that, except Falkland, she wasted all the woods in Fife which were oakland, besides all timber that was gotten out of Norway."[20] His picture of deforestation is confirmed by Fynes Moryson who, in 1598, wrote of Fife that "the trees are so rare, as I remember not to have seen one wood."[21] Compared with those of the builders and shipwrights, the timber requirements of other craftsmen were individually modest, though in the aggregate their effect was considerable. The cooper craft provides an outstanding example. The wood barrels made by the coopers in almost every town were the standard containers for fish, fruit, onions and other vegetables, water and oil, and almost every conceivable form of dry goods and small wares. All told the coopers used good quality staves on a scale far exceeding the productive capacity of Scottish woodlands.

From the time of James II the Council and Parliament had endeavoured to stimulate domestic timber production, partly by a policy of positive afforestation, partly by regulations for better woodland management.[22] In response to these measures

---

[17] *Op. cit.*, VOL. II, pp. 53, 56. [18] *Op. cit.*, VOL. II, p. 183.
[19] Balfour, *Annals*, VOL. II, p. 99. The burghs naturally attempted to enforce the use of slates instead of thatch for roofing; e.g. *Edinburgh Records*, VOL. VI, App. xxxvi.
[20] Robert Lindesay of Pitscottie, *The History and Cronicles of Scotland*, ed. A. J. G. Mackay, Scottish Text Society, VOL. I, 1899, p. 257.
[21] Moryson, *Itinerary*, PT. III, BK. iii, p. 154.
[22] E.g. *A.P.S.*, VOL. II, pp. 242-3; *R.P.C.*, VOL. I, p. 279.

and to the rising price of timber, planting and woodland utilisation had received considerable attention on Crown and certain of the Church lands, and, by the end of our period at least, some private proprietors were beginning woodland development on their own estates. In the early 1600's such landowners as William, Earl of Gowrie, his kinsman Duncan Campbell of Glenorchy ("Black Duncan of the Cowl"), and the Earl of Lauderdale were becoming active in rearing and planting forest trees.[23] In spite of these efforts, however, a gap remained between domestic supply and domestic demand. Its width is revealed in the verbal exchanges between King James and the Scottish Council in 1608 when the former proposed the imposition of a ban on the export of timber from Scotland. As a polite way of telling him to base his proposals on facts, the Council replied: "It is notour, and we doubt not bot your Majestie understandis sufficiently, that in no tyme . . . within the memorie of man thair hes bene ony tymmer transported furth of this kingdome the haill cuntrey being almost naked and mony yeiris ago spoled of all the tymmer within the same, so that now thair is no such a quantitie thairin as may serve the hundreth pairt of the necessair uses of the same, wherby your maiesties subiectis hes bene constrayned . . . to mak their provision . . . from foreyne pairtis."[24]

In this context "foreyne pairtis" meant Norway, and, to a lesser extent, Sweden and the south-east Baltic. As we shall see later, ports such as Danzig and Riga sent smallish consignments of the relatively valuable wainscot and "knapholt," but Scotland's bulk timber imports came from Norway. The dominance of Norway can be plainly illustrated from the shipping records of Dundee where, from 1580 to the end of our period, roughly one cargo out of every three came from Norway and almost invariably consisted of timber.[25] Behind this Norway-Scotland trade lay a powerful non-economic community of interests. There were close racial affinities between the peoples of the two lands. Traditionally the Western Isles and the Orkneys were more intimately linked to the royal house of Norway than to that of Scotland. Memories of royal contacts, from the fatal crossing of the Maid of Norway in 1290

[23] C. Innes, *Sketches of Early Scotch History*, 1861, pp. 345-7, 519.
[24] *R.P.C.*, VOL. VIII, p. 543.   [25] Dundee Shipping Lists, 1580-1625, *passim*.

to the marriage of King James at Upsloe in 1589, merge in the "Ballad of Sir Patrick Spens":

> To Noroway, to Noroway,
> To Noroway o'er the faem,
> The King's daughter o' Noroway,
> 'Tis thou must bring her hame.

In both countries geographical and economic conditions facilitated the expansion of this sea-borne timber trade. For a timber user in Edinburgh or Aberdeen it was certainly simpler and probably cheaper to arrange direct shipment from a Norwegian port, for the alternative involved a devious cross-country haul from a forest in a remote glen. During the winter freeze, great stocks of timber were accumulated at the ports of south-west Norway from Larvik and Christiansand round to Bergen. The crossing from Scotland, given reasonable weather, took only about four days; there were no hostile waters to penetrate; there were no delays or complications such as those which skippers encountered on entry to the Baltic; the cargo was easy to handle and not liable to damage in transit. Hence it is hardly surprising that from the spring to the late autumn a substantial part of Scotland's merchant tonnage, supplemented by some Dutch and some Norwegian, was engaged in this movement of timber. Official approbation made self-interest a virtue. Thus the statute of 1573, which banned the export of salt from Scotland, made specific exception in favour of merchants trading with Norway,[26] and five years later the Convention of Royal Burghs recommended that no impediment be placed in the way of salt and cloth sales to Norway for "hamebringing of tymmer."[27]

Scotland was prepared to buy: Norway was anxious and equipped to sell. Though in this period Norway was, as Dr Derry says, "a nation in eclipse," and in spite of her political subjugation by Denmark, her economy was undergoing a radical transformation. After two centuries the Hanse grip was weakening, even in Bergen, where, because of the tenacious quality of its occupants, the Hanse depot was locally known as the "Lice Wharf." In place of the Hanse a cosmopolitan mercantile community was created by Dutch, Danish, Scottish, and native merchants, under whose influence Norway's ex-

---

[26] *A.P.S.*, VOL. III, p. 82. [27] *Convention Records*, VOL. I, p. 76.

ternal trade acquired a greater degree of geographical flexibility. Equally important was the change in the composition
of her exports, hitherto dominated by dried fish. In the
sixteenth century, because the price of fish rose less rapidly
than that of their principal imports, the Norwegians were
embarrassed by an adverse trend in their terms of trade.[28] To
counteract this unfavourable trend they stepped up the felling,
preparing, and exporting of timber for which demand was
brisk and prices buoyant. As so often happens, technique
responded to economic necessity, and by the latter part of the
century the adoption in Norway of the comparatively new
water-driven saw-mill enabled the country's production of
squared timber to outstrip the old limits imposed by the hand-
saw and the axe.[29]

Apart from such obvious words as "deallis" and "sparris,"
the terminology of the sixteenth-century Scottish timber trade
would be unfamiliar to a modern merchant, though some of
the terms are certainly self-explanatory.[30] The "crukit tymmer"
would be for roof principals or for ship framework; "500
arrow shaftis" needs no comment; "burnewood" emphasises
the role of wood as fuel in this period; "trein naillis" were
wood pegs used as dowels in carpentry or for hanging slates;
while "pype stavis" and "fathoill wode, quhairof the grite
pypis are maid" requires no explanation save to say that
"pypis" were barrels. Some etymologists hold that "scowis"
were the offcuts of logs, but Jamieson's *Dictionary* calls them
wattles for thatching. "Steyngis"—the word appears unend-
ingly in the cargo lists—were poles; "knapholt"—with numerous variant spellings—which also came from the east Baltic,
was planking or staves, at all events cut and squared wood.
"Wainscot," which came predominantly from Danzig, was
better quality planking. Guicciardini says that the "waghes-
cot" he saw in Antwerp was "truly beautiful, variegated like
walnut,"[31] and in 1573 it was used at Haddington for the

---

[28] These economic problems of sixteenth-century Norway are discussed in
J. A. Gade, *The Hanseatic Control of Norwegian Commerce*, Leiden 1951, pp. 48, 115,
122.
[29] T. K. Derry, *A Short History of Norway*, 1957, p. 91.
[30] In interpreting these contemporary trade terms I have used Jamieson's
Dictionary of the Scottish Language (1912 edn.); the glossary to *Convention Records*,
VOL. VI; and, where all else failed, my imagination.
[31] Quoted in *Tudor Economic Documents*, VOL. III, pp. 149 ff.

church door.[32] "Garronis" is vague: the Haddington Common Good records have an entry for payment for "ane dusin garronis to be skaffetis" which might mean "for scaffolding."[33] What it all amounted to in cubic feet nobody can say, for what is the modern quantitative equivalent of "200 tymer, ane dussone aik, 5,000 steings," or of "ane hunder bittis of aik"?[34]

Timber of these kinds was the mainstay of Norway's export trade to Scotland, and though small amounts of tar, tallow, and butter were bought from time to time, the only other significant payment made to Norwegians was for the purchase or use of ships. Thus in 1603 James Kineris acknowledged the receipt from David Wedderburne of a hundred merks to buy for him in Norway a share in a vessel,[35] and a few years earlier two citizens of Trondhjem began proceedings against two of Leith for non-payment of the agreed price of the *Falcon*.[36] Occasionally Norwegian ships carried timber to Scotland: in 1613, for example, Knaud Fredericksone brought over "his schip callit ye fortoun of upslo" with a cargo of "steynis" and "deallis" belonging to himself.[37] Not surprisingly, however, Scotsmen preferred to employ their own ships and crews, especially in the timber trade where freight charges represented a very high proportion of the value of the cargo at its Scottish destination. The delivery of a cargo of timber by a foreigner, even if his rates were attractive, might double the charge on Scottish resources.[38]

THE EXPANSION OF TRADE WITH SWEDEN

Though the sudden emergence of Sweden as a major force in European military affairs has long been a stock theme in political history, the extent to which her activities were based on economic development has only recently become plain to British scholars. Both Professor Roberts and the late Eli Heckscher, whose works have illuminated this relationship for readers in English, agree that the cost of Sweden's growing military commitments was met by increasing her production

---

[32] "Haddington Records: Books of the Common Good," ed. H. M. Paton, in *Transactions of the East Lothian Antiquarian Society*, VII (1958), p. 46.
[33] *Op. cit.*, p. 58.
[34] Dundee Shipping Lists, p. 227.   [35] *Wedderburne Compt Buik*, p. 101.
[36] *R.P.C.*, VOL. IV, p. 79.   [37] Dundee Shipping Lists, p. 238.
[38] This was certainly true in the seventeenth century. See R. Davis, "Merchant shipping in the seventeenth century," in *Ec. H.R.*, IX (1956), p. 59.

and export of metals, especially iron and copper.[39] "Without copper," Heckscher wrote, "presumably Sweden's part in the Thirty Years War would not have been feasible." The extent to which metals dominated Sweden's external economic relationships in the time of Gustavus Adolphus is most sharply illustrated by the fact that in 1613 copper and iron together represented (by value) over 82 per cent of the country's total exports. Copper was a state monopoly, and though output at the peak was not more than about 3,000 tons a year, the skilful operations of merchants like Louis de Geer[40] enabled the Swedes to control European markets until the oriental copper of the Dutch East India Company appeared as a serious competitor in the late 1620's.[41]

Though the reputation of Swedish iron went back into the Middle Ages, the iron industry also underwent great technical change and great quantitative expansion in the sixteenth century. By about 1500 the blast furnace was replacing older smelting devices,[42] and the resulting pig iron, cut into "osmundar" or blocks, soon acquired a high reputation with West European iron-workers because of its uniformly high quality. Soon afterwards—about the reign of Gustavus Vasa—the process of refining into malleable iron was also revolutionised, so that about 1550 Swedish bar iron—"gad" or "gaid" iron to Scotsmen—was beginning to appear in the country's exports.[43] From the point of view of employment in Sweden, the production of bar iron was obviously desirable, and as time went on the Swedes discriminated against the export of osmund and ultimately in the early seventeenth century banned it completely.[44]

As in Norway, these economic changes were accompanied by the gradual erosion of Hanse privileges; yet though economic policy was decisively shaped by the Swedish monarchs, the

---

[39] M. Roberts, *Gustavus Adolphus*, VOL. II, 1958; E. F. Heckscher, *An Economic History of Sweden*, Harvard 1954 (a summary of his *Sveriges ekonomiska historia fran Gustav Vasa*, Stockholm 1935-6).   [40] Roberts, *Gustavus Adolphus*, pp. 111-7.

[41] Astrid Friis, in her review of Heckscher's *Sveriges ekonomiska historia* in *Ec. H.R.*, VIII (1938), p. 196.

[42] E. F. Heckscher, "Sweden in Modern History," in *Ec. H.R.*, IV (1932), p. 12; Roberts, *Gustavus Adolphus*, VOL. II, p. 104.

[43] The same process was employed in Scotland; see *The Perth Hammermen Book, 1518-68*, ed. C. A. Hunt, 1889, p. 102.

[44] Roberts, *Gustavus Adolphus*, VOL. II, p. 105. The ban was not fully enforced until 1636.

place of the Hanse was not immediately occupied by native merchants. It is certain that the main initial replacement was by the Dutch, and Heckscher believed that they were accompanied by a fairly strong Scots contingent, though—as Professor Roberts has pointed out—it is possible that the Dutch expression "schots koopman" referred to any small trader and not specifically to a Scotsman.[45] But while it is true that no Scot in Sweden remotely approached the wealth and influence of the Dutchman Louis de Geer, there were few activities in which the Scots had no part.[46] In the later sixteenth century many Scottish soldiers of fortune turned to civilian occupations in Sweden and joined the ranks of the rural traders—the "landsköp"—who challenged the trading privileges of the townsmen. In the decades about 1600 Blasius Dundee was engaged in trade and finance in Stockholm on a significant scale, and Jacob Robertson of Struan had an apothecary's shop there and sold medicines to the Court of Gustavus Adolphus. When Gothenburg was refounded in 1619 (the earlier foundation of 1607 having been destroyed during the War of Kalmar) Scotland was represented on its town council, and among its early inhabitants were Stewarts and Spaldings, Carnegies, Sinclairs and Lindsays, Ogilvies and Kinnairds.

Personal links thus fortified the economic convenience of trade between Sweden and Scotland at a time when Gustavus Adolphus was deliberately abandoning the isolationism of his predecessors. The pattern of trade reflected broadly the character of Sweden's economic evolution: it began relatively late, it blossomed fast, it was based—on the Swedish side—on metals. In the Sound Toll Registers there are virtually no references to the passage of ships bound for Scotland from Swedish ports before about 1570. In confirmation of this, the earliest surviving Shipping Lists at Dundee, for the 1580's, show twenty-nine arrivals at Dundee from Baltic ports, but only one of them from Sweden. By the last ten years of King James's reign, however, the pattern had changed decisively. At the Sound, something like 15 per cent of the Scottish ships

---

[45] *Op. cit.*, p. 41. I am also indebted to Professor Roberts for advice on these topics in private correspondence.

[46] What follows here is drawn from T. A. Fischer, *The Scots in Sweden*, 1907; G. A. Sinclair, "The Scottish trader in Sweden," in *S.H.R.*, xxv (1928); and O. Donner, *Scottish Families in Sweden and Finland*, Helsingfors 1884.

passing West had been freighted at Swedish ports; and for the same period over a quarter of the Baltic arrivals at Dundee were from Sweden, nearly all in fact from Stockholm.[47]

The composition of these rapidly increased imports from Sweden was simple. Occasionally a cargo of timber or a part-cargo of tar arrived. Comparatively little copper came in ingots or sheets; presumably Scottish demand was small and in any case the Swedes preferred to sell in bulk to their major Continental customers.[48] Copper kettles came more regularly. No doubt many of them became the treasured and well-polished possessions of Scots housewives, but copper vessels also called "kettles" were used by dyers in the textile trades and by the gold refiners on Crawford Muir.[49] At best these were minor items for by any test Sweden's export trade to Scotland was dominated by iron. Scotland had long been an iron importer, largely from the Baltic, and there are indications that the part-cargoes brought from Hanse ports were Swedish in origin. In 1596, for example, David Wedderburne sent to Lübeck half a last of herring, four old rose nobles and a "prince" dollar, the proceeds to be spent either on peas or on "Suadins gad iron and oismontis equaly."[50] After about 1600 doubt disperses. Iron was coming to Scotland in full shiploads, direct from Sweden. The typical cargo consisted at first of both pig and bar ("oismontis and gaid" in the Scottish Customs Books) but as time passed the Swedish discrimination against osmund became effective and by the 1620's and 1630's malleable bar had become the standard form of Swedish iron available to the hammermen of Scotland.

The sequence of development needs little elaboration. Under the pressure of State needs, Swedish metal production underwent technical improvement and quantitative expansion. The high quality bar iron which, in consequence, the Swedes could export in bulk, was one of the raw materials for the industrial growth which was taking place in Scotland between the Union of the Crowns and the Civil Wars.

---

[47] Calculated from *Sound Toll Registers* and Dundee Shipping Lists for the relevant periods.

[48] Another suggestion communicated to me by Professor Roberts.

[49] *The Records of a Scottish Cloth Manufactury*, ed. W. R. Scott, Scottish History Society, VOL. XLVI, 1905, p. xxi; *Accounts of the Lord Treasurer*, VOL. X, p. 223.

[50] *Wedderburne Compt Buik*, p. 71.

Imports from the South Baltic[51]

In the Middle Ages and later, much of the trade of central and eastern Europe followed a series of river valleys, from the Elbe in the west to the Vistula in the east, with the result that north-west Germany, Denmark, and the south coast of the Baltic generally acquired a commercial importance out of all proportion to their local material resources. By the early part of our period the grip which the Hanse had exerted over this commercial fringe was weakening. Within the League itself serious disloyalties became apparent as both eastern and western members found their interests increasingly incompatible with those of Lübeck in the centre.[52] The individual towns lost little if anything of their commercial importance; the difference was that the trade of the Baltic was becoming more accessible to outsiders.

The great response to this opportunity came from Holland.[53] Between 1574 and 1640 there is only one year—1587—when the Dutch proportion of the vessels entering the Baltic fell below 50 per cent.[54] For the whole period their average was nearly 70 per cent. By comparison the Scottish share of ships was little more than 3 per cent, and as there is good reason to think that the usual Scottish ship was appreciably smaller than the usual Dutchman,[55] the Scottish share of tonnage was most likely not over 2 per cent. Valuable as these flat averages are in enabling us to see Scottish trade in perspective, they conceal some important periodic fluctuations and of course give no indication of the role of this relatively small traffic in the economic life of Scotland herself.

The Sound Toll Registers, despite known and surmised errors, constitute the most continuous and detailed record for the study of Scottish overseas trade before the Civil War. They distinguish, in ship movements into the Baltic, between Scottish ships and ships from Scotland. Of the thirty to sixty Scottish

[51] I have not repeated all the details or statistics from my "Scottish Trade with the Baltic, 1550-1650," in *Dundee Economic Essays*, ed. Eastham.

[52] Gade, *The Hanseatic Control of Norwegian Commerce*, pp. 109-10; C. E. Hill, *The Danish Sound and the Command of the Baltic*, Duke University Press, N. Carolina, 1926, p. 41.

[53] A. E. Christensen, *Dutch Trade to the Baltic about 1600, passim.*

[54] *Op. cit.*, pp. 84-6.

[55] The fullest examination of the relative sizes of ships is in W. Vogel, *Zur Grosse der europäischen Handelsflotten*, Hamburg 1915.

L

ships which, in years of normal conditions, appeared off the Customs House at Elsinore, it was unusual for more than four or five to have sailed from a foreign port. In years of abnormal activity the proportion was generally higher. Thus in 1576, of the 67 Scots ships entering the Baltic, 10 had sailed from the Netherlands, 4 from France, and 3 from other countries. In 1578, of a total of 104, 13 were from France, 6 from the Netherlands and 2 from Norway. Of the 124 Scots vessels in the peak year, 1587, 12 were from France and 4 from other countries. In these years of great activity a high proportion of the Scottish vessels always sailed to the Baltic in ballast and returned with cargoes of grain. This coincidence of great numbers, empty ships, sailings from foreign ports and return cargoes of grain, admits of two interpretations. One—perhaps the likeliest—is that when the Scotsmen urgently needed food they bore their exports to any available market, collected payment if possible in bullion and sailed with the utmost expedition direct to the Baltic grain ports. Alternatively these Scots skippers arriving at Elsinore from Dutch or French ports may have been working for foreign charterers. In any case the behaviour of Scottish shipping in these exceptional years does not seriously affect the conclusion that normally a simple pattern of bilateral trading existed between Scotland and the Baltic.

In the Privy Council's discussions on commercial topics in the early 1600's, the employment of alien vessels in the Eastland trade featured prominently.[56] Some merchants maintained that foreigners were better equipped for the handling of timber, pitch, and tar, and offered more attractive rates than the Scots. The Sound Registers indicate that, once year-by-year fluctuations have been eliminated, roughly one ship in every three in the normal Baltic-Scotland trade was a foreigner. Of these by far the greatest number belonged to the old Hanse towns, especially Stralsund—"Trailsound" as the port officers generally entered it. Dutchmen were less common than their prominence in the North Sea might have suggested, though their share, especially in the carrying of Scottish coal, was certainly increasing after about 1600. Other nationalities were exceptional: Englishmen were rare before 1600; Frenchmen always rare; Swedes so rare till the early seventeenth

[56] *R.P.C.*, VOL. XI, pp. 202-3.

century that "The Mercurius, a ship of Sweden," lying at Leith in 1602, must have been a local curiosity.[57]

The vessels of Scottish nationality passing east through the Sound can be classified under port of domicile ("hjemsted" in the Sound Registers): those passing west can be similarly grouped under port of departure ("afgangshavn"); and from this a reasonably clear impression of the contributions of the various Scottish and Baltic ports emerges. In busy and slack years alike, roughly half of the Scots vessels sailing to the Baltic belonged either to Leith or Dundee. Aberdeen, a port traditionally strongly associated with the Eastland trade, rarely sent in our period more than six ships a year. Perhaps there is truth in the story that Eastland traders had deserted Aberdeen because of the dishonest payments tendered to them by Aberdonians.[58] Taken as a group the East Fife and Firth of Forth ports were strongly represented, especially St Andrews and Dysart in the earlier decades, and Anstruther, Kirkcaldy, Burntisland, Pittenweem, Queensferry and Bo'ness in the later. Montrose was generally represented, and in some years a ship or two made the long voyage from Ayr.

Within the Baltic, the geographical pattern of Scottish shipping routes was simple, for the main focus was always "the classical market of the Baltic"[59] dominated by Danzig, Königsberg and Riga. In the early decades of our study, up to 75 per cent of the Scots ships leaving the Baltic had been freighted at Danzig. As time passed this fraction fell to below half,[60] while the share of Königsberg ("Queinsbrig" to Scotsmen) rose from an eighth to over a quarter. Departures from the ports of north Germany remained small and constant, but, especially after the 1590's, more and more Scottish ships loaded in Sweden and Denmark.

As elsewhere, this penetration by Scotsmen into the commercial life of the south Baltic was accompanied—and no doubt accelerated—by the establishment of personal contacts.[61] In view of the control which the Danes exercised over the

---

[57] *Op. cit.*, VOL. VI, p. 752.
[58] Grant, *Social Development*, p. 340.
[59] Christensen, *Dutch Trade to the Baltic*, p. 289.
[60] Danzig's share of total Baltic trade fell similarly; Christensen, *loc. cit.*
[61] T. A. Fischer, *The Scots in Germany*, 1902, and *The Scots in East and West Prussia*, 1903; *Papers relating to the Scots in Poland*, ed. A. F. Steuart, Scottish History Society, VOL. LIX, 1915.

Sound, good relations with them were of supreme importance to any seafaring nation. The ambassadorial mission of Sir Patrick Waus, the resulting marriage between James and Anne of Denmark, James's mediation between Gustavus Adolphus and Christian IV, all helped to create a favourable atmosphere for more mundane Scottish activities. So in 1619, when an aged Scottish merchant fell foul of the customs officers at Elsinore and there was every likelihood that "his gray hairis" would "with greif, sorrow and wracke, go to the grave in Denmark," his friends petitioned the King to intercede for the old man with his royal relative in Denmark.[62]

From Denmark to Lithuania, Scotsmen were common both as travellers and residents. David Cunningham of Aberdeen was at "Copinhann within ye realme of denmark" in 1591, and Andrew Robertson, also of Aberdeen, died there the following year.[63] Richard Wedderburne seems to have lived permanently at Elsinore, for in 1587 the Scottish ambassador spent a night in his house there, and three years later Wedderburne sent timber to repair the church in Dundee.[64] Somewhat later, a "Mr Balfour" and a "Mr Sinclair" were shipbuilders in Copenhagen under Danish royal patronage.[65] Further east, in north Germany and Poland, there were thousands of Scotsmen in various military and civil occupations. While Lithgow's familiar figure of 30,000 Scottish families in this area[66] has that suspicious rotundity which characterises so many early demographical statistics, it is none the less plain that Scotsmen had a big part in the trading life. When Lithgow visited Poland in 1616 he received a cordial welcome in Cracow from "diverse Scotish Merchants . . . especially the two brothers Dicksones, men of singular note of honesty and Wealth"; and in his journeys between Cracow, Warsaw, and Lublin he encountered an "abundance of gallant, rich Merchants, my Countrey-men, who were all very kind to me."[67] There is similar evidence from the Baltic ports. Year by year Scotsmen were admitted

---

[62] *R.P.C.*, VOL. XI, p. 521. The letter is printed in full in Hume Brown, *Scotland before 1700*, pp. 277-8.

[63] "Testimonialis Grantit be ye Bailies [of Aberdeen], 1589-1603," ed. L. B. Taylor, in *Miscellany of the Third Spalding Club*, VOL. II, 1940, pp. 27, 69.

[64] *The Correspondence of Sir Patrick Vaus*, VOL. II, p. 396; Council Minutes of Dundee, VOL. II, p. 52, MS in Dundee City Archives.

[65] Mathew, *Scotland Under Charles I*, p. 278.

[66] Lithgow, *Totall Discourse*, p. 422.   [67] *Op. cit.*, pp. 420-1.

as burgesses in Danzig, forming their own church community and leaving their imprint on street-names. There were Scottish merchant groups in Königsberg and Elbing, while in Memel a local proverb, "with a Scotsman or a priest never go to law," commemorated their acumen.[68]

The sea voyage from Scotland to the east Baltic was long and often hazardous. Vessels might become involved in one of the numerous wars among the Baltic powers; the Danes might prove difficult at Elsinore; storm, shipwreck, and piracy were ever present threats; any serious delay might mean an ice-bound winter in an alien port. That skippers and merchants were prepared to face these risks is in itself proof of the importance of Baltic wares to the economy of Scotland. Normally these wares came to Scotland in mixed cargoes, but it is easy to distinguish the two main categories: food and industrial raw materials. As we saw in the first chapter, Scotland's domestic food supply was nicely poised and, in years of crop deficiency, urgent recourse had to be made to foreign suppliers. In such times Scotsmen joined the queues of West European vessels in the ports of the south-east Baltic, the northern outlets for the great farming hinterland of Poland and East Prussia. Its agricultural productivity impressed every British visitor, and Lithgow's claim that it was "the Girnell [granary] of Westerne Europe for all sorts of graine"[69] is completely substantiated by modern historical research.[70] In lean years, such as 1563, 1574-5, 1595-7, and 1622-3, every available ship in Scotland must have been diverted to the Baltic for grain, which, in this context, normally meant rye, though wheat, flour, oats, peas, and malt were shipped from time to time. By contrast there were years when Scotsmen brought no grain whatever from the Baltic, and apart from 1621-3 shipments in the first three decades of the seventeenth century were almost invariably very low.[71]

Among the industrial raw materials the textile fibres, flax and hemp, demand first attention.[72] In occasional years the

---

[68] Fischer, *The Scots in East and West Prussia, passim.*

[69] Lithgow, *Totall Discourse,* p. 422.

[70] E.g. Christensen, *Dutch Trade to the Baltic,* pp. 361, 415; *Cambridge Economic History of Europe,* VOL. II, edd. M. Postan and E. E. Rich, 1941, p. 121.

[71] See above, p. 32.

[72] These statements of the volume and fluctuations of trade are all based on *Sound Toll Registers.*

relative quantities were about equal, but generally flax considerably predominated. The overall total tended to fall, decade by decade, from the early 1560's to the early 1620's with some exceptionally low years in 1613-20, but a tremendous revival began in the early 1620's and was sustained until the general collapse of the Scottish economy during the Civil War. Potash—"aiss" as Scotsmen wrote it—was produced extensively in the Baltic forests and was used in soap-making and similar alkali-using processes, and, especially in association with woad, in cloth-dyeing.[73] Somewhat surprisingly the quantity brought from the Baltic by Scotsmen in the 1620's was only a fifth of what it had been two generations earlier. As the Scottish cloth industry had expanded meanwhile, one can only assume that the dyers were using some other mordant, possibly alum; and it is likely that the Scottish soap- and glassmakers were deriving at least part of their alkaline raw material from local kelp.[74]

In the supply of timber to Scotland the east Baltic played a secondary but nonetheless important role. Though this timber came to Scotland in relatively small quantities—generally as part-cargoes—its value was relatively high, for the main items were either knapholt or the even costlier wainscot. In the supply of pitch and tar the Baltic lands as a whole had, so far, something approaching a monopoly. The widespread use of these materials by all manner of craftsmen from shipwrights to shepherds ensured a stability of overall demand, and apart from a dip in the years about 1620 shipments were remarkably steady. Especially before the expansion of direct trade with Sweden, Scotsmen bought metals in the south-east Baltic: iron, copper, pewter, lead, and shot. The movement of lead in and out of Scotland defies complete explanation. As we saw in Chapter II, lead ore was mined and exported on a substantial scale. References to the export of lead appear with ominous frequency in the years just after 1560: there were protracted proceedings before the Burgh Court at Inverness about shipments to Hamburg by Lewyr Smyth,[75] and some of the lead

---

[73] E. Carus-Wilson, "The raw materials of the mediaeval wool industry," in *Cambridge Economic History of Europe*, VOL. II, p. 376.

[74] The issue in 1622 of a patent for kelp-burning seems to support this contention; *R.P.C.*, VOL. XII, p. 771.

[75] *Inverness Records*, pp. lxxxi, 102.

certainly came from the Friars' Church; some saw the hand of God when a cargo of lead stripped from the cathedrals at Elgin and Aberdeen sank en route for Holland;[76] what was described as "lead" was still leaving Scotland in quantity in the 1580's.[77] Twenty years later the loot was evidently exhausted, for when the people of Aberdeen had to repair their church roof they bought sheet lead in Danzig.[78]

Finally we can only resort, with the Scots port officers of the time, to the comprehensive heading "otheris Danskyne waris." In the mixed cargoes which were characteristic of the east Baltic—Scotland trade, these other Danzig goods included such things as "cradillis" or "kists" of glass; gunpowder, of which 200 stones were bought for the armoury at Edinburgh Castle in 1619;[79] ships' tackle; soap, tow, saltpetre; wax, sometimes in bulk, sometimes as "a gryt roll of wax candell" such as Wedderburne purchased from Königsberg in 1616.[80] The common characteristic was strict utility: there were no frivolities in the Baltic trade.

EXPORTS AND OTHER PAYMENTS

The extension of the Sound Tolls in the mid-sixteenth century to include an *ad valorem* levy on cargoes involved the compilation of a record of goods as well as ships. In spite of a few gaps and certain suspected distortions, this record, from 1562 onwards, provides the raw material for a quantitative analysis of that branch of Scotland's export trade which flowed down the Kattegat to the Sound en route for the Baltic ports. The main components of this branch may be simply listed: skins, salt, fish, cloth, leather, and coal. Apart from such odd items as the two "woffin beds" which Wedderburne sent to Stockholm in 1623,[81] the minor items in Scotland's exports to the Baltic lands cannot have filled more than a dozen or twenty barrels a year. In our examination of these major components, skins demand priority, for it was here that Scotland made her greatest relative contribution to Baltic imports. In a typical

---

[76] *R.P.C.*, VOL. I, p. 609; J. Jamieson, *Bell the Cat, or Who Destroyed the Scottish Abbeys*, 1902, p. 275.
[77] Balcarres Papers, printed in *Analecta Scotica*, VOL. I, pp. 91-4.
[78] *Aberdeen Council Letters*, ed. Taylor, p. xxi.
[79] Fischer, *The Scots in Germany*, p. 29.
[80] *Wedderburne Compt Buik*, p. 88.
[81] *Op. cit.*, p. 84.

year in the 1560's and 1570's about a million skins and hides passed eastward through the Sound. Of these, on the average, a quarter came from Scotland. In the decades around 1600 the Scottish contribution fell to an annual average of some 120,000, only to revive again in the 1620's to well over the quarter-million mark. If we bear in mind that Scotland was also sending skins and hides to the Low Countries and to France, we can begin to form some impression of the extent to which her external economic relationships hinged on the products of her pastoral farmers and her huntsmen.

The Baltic lands were great buyers of salt. Almost all of it was carried to them by Dutchmen, whose convoys moved annually from the salines of the Bay of Biscay, and in comparison their purchases from Scotland were highly marginal. None the less the trend was generally upward. From very modest beginnings, shipments from Scotland had a minor peak in 1576-8 when both French producers and Dutch shippers were suffering from political upheavals. As in other commodities something of a slump occurred in the early 1600's—in salt it came between 1609 and 1619—but the ensuing recovery was so brisk that for the 1620's generally Scotland was providing the Baltic lands with about 3 per cent of their imported salt.

The shipment of Scottish coal was stimulated by the levying of export duties on English coal, and, for a short period at least, Scotland occupied an apparently monopolistic position. Coal from Scotland appears hardly at all in the Sound Registers until 1611, and then, for three years, direct shipments from Scotland represented about two-thirds of all the coal entering the Baltic. Significantly, much of this was carried in Dutch vessels, and though direct shipments fell off again after 1613, it is probable that substantial amounts of Scottish coal continued to enter the Baltic in Dutch vessels but via Dutch ports.[82]

In the supply of fish, especially of herring, the Dutch were equally well entrenched, and again there is no means of telling what proportion of the fish they carried to the Baltic had originated in Scottish waters. In direct shipment of herring in the latter half of King James's reign the pattern must have

[82] Nef, *Rise of the British Coal Industry*, VOL. I, p. 85.

been wholly gratifying to Scottish merchants, though perhaps less gratifying to Scottish housewives. From low but erratic points the figure leapt in 1589 to 177 lasts, the equivalent of over two million fish. Thenceforth the trend was decisively upwards to a peak in the 1620's when the annual average of about 570 lasts represented 6 to 7 per cent of all the herring shipped into the Baltic.

Fynes Moryson, a contemporary, ranked cloth with skins as Scotland's chief export to the Baltic.[83] Any attempt at precise quantitative statement is frustrated by the general absence of detailed port records relating to exports, and by the different units employed for customs purposes in Scotland and at the Sound. So though the Scottish customs returns in the Exchequer Rolls give a reasonably adequate summary of total cloth exports, it is not possible to say what proportion of this went through the Sound. We know that Scottish merchants sent coarse wool cloth, notably plaiding; linen; hempen and harden;[84] but, whatever the Sound figures mean in terms of yards, it is probable that Scottish shipments were, in the economist's sense, marginal, and certainly were never more than a small fraction of those from England.[85] The Scottish figures show striking fluctuations over time. Beginning with a steady fall from the 1560's to the early 1600's, they reveal an upward movement after 1616 swelling to a peak in 1643. The early decline may reflect no more than a diversion of cloth to other markets. The revival after 1616 is almost certainly associated with the official stimulus then being given to cloth-making in Scotland, and, less certainly, with the activity of Scottish pedlars. When discussions were afoot for commercial union with England after 1603 the London merchants objected that the Scots competed unfairly because their pedlars "trade after the meaner sort . . . by retayling parcells and remnants of cloth . . . upp and downe the countries, which we cannot doe with the honor of our country."[86]

On the question of the balance of trade between Baltic and North Sea countries, economic historians have engaged in

[83] Hume Brown, *Early Travellers*, pp. 85 ff.

[84] E.g. *Wedderburne Compt Buik*, p. 84; and Aberdeen Customs Book for 1583, MS in Register House, Edinburgh.

[85] Astrid Friis, *Alderman Cockayne's Project and the Cloth Trade*, 1927, p. 104.

[86] *Cal. S.P. Dom., James I, 1603-10*, No. 3.

stimulating controversy.[87] The question, in so far as it is confined to Scottish trade, seems to turn in part on the trading methods employed. It is clear that in the more advanced Baltic ports, notably those where Hanse and Dutch influences prevailed, money was regularly employed and credit mechanisms were being devised. The Scots merchant was in business for profit, yet the indications are that in his foreign dealings he regarded money, ideally, as an intermediate commodity, held temporarily between the sale of one lot of goods and the purchase of another. In other words Scottish traders in the Baltic aimed at a form of "retorno" in which each shipment was turned into money and that money immediately converted back into goods for the return cargo. This system obviously sufficed so long as the value of Scotland's exports to the Baltic could be kept closely in step with her demand for Baltic produce. Exactly how it responded to differential price movements is, in the absence of adequate price data, a matter of guesswork. One can only assume that if Danzig flax were dearer than the Scots expected, they brought back less of it, adjusted their own linen prices, and the next year sent rather more salt or fish than hitherto. The more serious strain on the "retorno" system came from the instability of Scottish demand, stemming, as we have seen, from crop failures in Scotland and the urgent need for Baltic grain to which they gave rise.

The response to urgent food demands was conditioned by the relative rigidity of Scotland's export capacity and by the Baltic's monopoly of certain essential goods. For obvious reasons the output of skins and hides, Scotland's main export to the Baltic, could not be increased in the short run. If crops failed more fish might be caught, but merchants would be under strong legal and moral pressure to feed their own countrymen, and in some famine years herring exports in fact dropped to zero. To compensate for greater corn imports, expenditure on flax, iron, or tar might be reduced, but only at the risk of dislocating industrial life at the very moment when it most needed stimulation. Assuming that our analysis of trading methods is correct, there could be no question of a

---

[87] Christensen, *Dutch Trade to the Baltic*, p. 428; C. Wilson, "Treasure and trade balances," in *Ec. H.R.*, 2nd ser., II (1949), pp. 152-61; E. F. Heckscher, "Multi-lateralism, Baltic trade and Mercantilism," in *Ec. H.R.*, 2nd ser., III (1950), pp. 219-25.

carry-over of credits from previous years. The inference that grain was bought, in part anyhow, for coin carried to the Baltic by skippers and factors, is substantiated by Wedderburne's account of his own trading activities. The years 1595 to 1597 all saw heavy grain shipments. In each of these years Wedderburne either took or sent coin to Danzig, Königsberg and Lübeck,[88] and his instructions to his factors repeatedly refer to the purchase of rye and peas. This pattern is repeated in the early 1620's. In the years 1617 to 1620 Scottish grain shipments from the Baltic were of negligible dimensions. A sharp rise began in 1621, producing a total for 1623 comparable to the peaks of 1587 and 1597. The next year, 1624, the Privy Council reported to the King on the strains imposed by these heavy purchases on the domestic economy of Scotland. "The importatioun," they said, had been "so exceeding grite . . . as the most pairt of the moneyis of this kingdome hes bene bestowit to that use," producing such a scarcity of money that numbers of people of all ranks had been unable to give satisfaction to their creditors.[89] John Acheson had these experiences in mind when writing one of his notes on monetary proposals in 1633. Opposing Briot's plan to lift the face value of certain Scots coins, Acheson argues that this would harass merchants trading with the "eastern countreyis quhairfra in tyme of famene we most buy victuall" because, he said, in such times Scotland had nothing to send except money.[90]

While it is more difficult to generalise with certainty about the balance in years of normal trade, there is reason to think that then also some drain on Scotland's precious metals occurred. It was plainly in the interests of merchants to argue that their trading was, in the mercantilist sense, favourable to their own nation, yet it was merchant representatives who, in 1622, "declairit upoun thair grite aoth that the said trade [i.e. the Eastland trade] cannot be, nor never was, interteynit with the native commodityies of the countrey, bot that of necessitie some moneyis must be exportit to that effect."[91]

The date of this statement is significant, for British trade with the Baltic had very recently experienced a crisis of alarm-

[88] *Wedderburne Compt Buik*, pp. 46, 71, 72.
[89] Melros Papers, quoted in Hume Brown, *Scotland before 1700*, p. 283.
[90] Cochran-Patrick, *Coinage*, VOL. II, pp. 82-3.
[91] *R.P.C.*, VOL. XIII, p. 120.

ing proportions. Though, as we saw in Chapter II, Scotland provides no evidence of any internal economic depression in 1620 comparable to that in England, it is nevertheless plain that her total trade with the Baltic ran at a relatively low level from 1618 to 1621. The number of laden Scottish vessels passing the Sound was lower than it had been since 1592-3 and was not again to fall so low until the outbreak of the Bishops' War in 1639; but the detailed pattern of the trade is anything but simple.[92] Salt and herring exports, for example, were at their worst in 1618 but were fairly good in 1620, and though flax and hemp imports had poor years in 1617 and 1620, iron imports were particularly high in 1619 and 1621 and were well above normal in 1620. "The rising of the moneys"—the coinage debasement—in the east Baltic countries, of which the English traders complained so bitterly,[93] must have posed certain problems also to the Scots, but Scotland was lucky in that these were years when her external grain requirements were low. Furthermore, if our basic supposition be correct, the Scots' willingness to take good West European coin would ensure for them a welcome which did not necessarily await those who merely took merchandise.

The general statements about the balance in the Baltic trade, coupled with what we know of individual transactions, prompts speculation as to how Scotland acquired the coin and the precious metals to supplement her export of goods to the Baltic lands. Where, to cite a specific case, did Wedderburne get the "lx lib worth gold," the dollars, the crown ducats, the "ryellis of xl," the "ryellis of 8," and the chains and rings of gold which he carried with him to Königsberg in 1596 and 1600?[94] The nationality of coins provides no clue, for most of them enjoyed international circulation and might have been away from their country of origin for years. It is tolerably clear that in some branches of her foreign trade Scotland operated on "favourable" terms, thus building up a floating stock of miscellaneous coin and precious metal which went to supplement the export of goods in other branches. A guess— with no statistical basis—would be that in some periods at

[92] *Sound Toll Registers* for years cited.
[93] For the depression in English trade see R. W. K. Hinton, *The Eastland Trade and the Common Weal in the Seventeenth Century*, 1959, pp. 14-20.
[94] *Wedderburne Compt Buik*, pp. 46, 122.

least the profits of trading with the Dutch and the French covered deficits on trade with the Baltic. What alone is certain is that though each branch of trade was superficially bilateral, the whole commercial system of the country rested on elementary multilateral adjustments.

VI

ECONOMIC RELATIONS WITH FRANCE AND SPAIN

THE FRANCO-SCOTTISH ALLIANCE

With the cry "Gardyloo," once a familiar warning as housewives flung their slops into the streets of Edinburgh, there echoed the memory of the most lasting voluntary alliance in Scottish history. This alliance with France can be traced back to the twelfth century when both Scotland and France were threatened by the Angevin monarchy, and, on the diplomatic level at least, the continuing basis of Franco-Scottish friendship was mutual hatred and fear of England. As such the alliance acquired an emotional appeal in Scotland which distinguishes it from the rest of the country's external links. Nothing in the cold forests of the Baltic or in the wet polders of the Netherlands could so move the hearts of Scotsmen as the white irises of France.

When our period opens this alliance with France was still the decisive factor in Scottish diplomacy. In perspective the attempted Anglo-Scottish *rapprochement* by the marriage of James IV and Margaret Tudor—the Thistle and the Rose of the Scottish poet—was a momentary lapse, for the old enemy was to show his true colours again at Solway Moss and Pinkie. In the middle decades of the sixteenth century the cultural and political links with France were remarkably strong and intimate. The symbol—indeed the finest tangible memorial —of the alliance was the South Range at Falkland Palace, built by French craftsmen, or Scots trained in France, mainly between 1537 and 1542. There, twenty years later, the most French of all Scottish monarchs was to spend some of her happiest days in Scotland, revelling with her "Four Maries" in "all the sparkling wit of Ronsard and Châtelard."[1] In politics the

[1] I. Moncreiffe, *The Royal Palace of Falkland*, National Trust for Scotland, n.d., p. 19.

regency of Mary of Lorraine and the marriage of the child Queen to the Dauphin seemed decisive; indeed, as Professor Mackie writes, "between the years 1550 and 1560 Scotland was in some danger of becoming a French province."[2]

But the tide of popular opinion was beginning to turn. Loyal Scots resented over-much French intervention in their country's domestic life; the attitude of the Crown no longer faithfully mirrored the views of the entire nation; in 1559 the Lords of the Congregation, rising against the government of the Queen Regent, sent Maitland of Lethington to seek Elizabeth's aid and, in 1560, welcomed the arrival of an English naval squadron in Leith Roads. This was a crucial moment in both Anglo-Scottish and Franco-Scottish relations. The progress of Protestantism in Scotland, meat to the Scottish Anglophile party, was poison to the official French alliance. Nevertheless the death was lingering. Loyalties sealed over four centuries were not likely to melt overnight; by and large the French kings continued to cultivate the goodwill of Scotsmen and, even after 1603, to discriminate between them and Englishmen.[3] In some areas of Scotland the substantial groups of Roman Catholics who resisted the Reformation looked to their co-religionists in France for succour and deliverance; conversely in those areas of France under Huguenot domination, fellowship in the New Religion gave fresh life to the old friendship, so that, in commercial centres such as Dieppe and La Rochelle, Scots and French could meet without embarassment either to bargain or to pray.

The place of the "auld alliance" in the economic history of Scotland, in so far as it relates to the period covered by this book, can be examined in response to two questions: what material benefits did it bring to Scotland; and, secondly, did Franco-Scottish economic relations reflect the political cooling-off after 1560 and especially during the reign of James VI? In answer to the first question, Dr Grant has written that "in trade, as well as in other ways, Scotland had to pay heavily for her rather one-sided friendship with France."[4] The costs may be briefly expressed. Friendship with France involved English

[2] J. D. Mackie, "Henry VIII and Scotland," in *Transactions of the Royal Historical Society*, XXIX (1947), p. 112.
[3] E.g. in the Bordeaux wine trade. See below, p. 209.
[4] Grant, *Social Development*, p. 338.

hostility. This in turn meant physical damage to ships and buildings and to cattle and crops, diversion of scarce resources to military preparedness, and, in consequence, a general aggravation of the poverty of Scotland. Secondly, it meant that trade with England was imperilled and, at times, reduced to a comparative trickle. Instead, Scotland developed her main trading axes with the lands across the North Sea, so that her trade routes were extended and became vulnerable to the depredations of English and other privateers.

This is, of course, a prejudiced assessment of the net advantage. If Scotland had broken with France before the time of James VI she might well have fallen under the same kind of English overlordship as was suffered by Ireland. Quite apart, however, from guarding Scotland against that dismal fate, the alliance was attended by positive and tangible benefits. From the opening years of the sixteenth century Scotsmen traded in certain major regions of France as members of a favoured nation. They had the privilege—valuable in English eyes at any rate—of direct access to the wine growers of the Bordeaux hinterland and, in Normandy, they enjoyed exemption from most customs duties.[5] With the marriage of Mary and the Dauphin in 1558 the removal of the barrier of nationality between their two peoples meant an enormous immediate widening of the range of privilege: Frenchmen became naturalised Scots and Scots became naturalised French with all the consequent benefits of free movement and social intercourse.[6] All this made towards greater intimacy between two peoples whose economies were largely complementary. We know, for example, that Scots merchants were often sufficiently familiar with the French language to dispense with the services of interpreters in their commercial dealings in France.[7] When John Barton was preying on the English merchantmen out of Calais in the 1540's, one of his crews included twenty Frenchmen from Dieppe "speaking good Scots and disguised even in their garments."[8] The first major literary work by John Napier (a theological treatise) was translated into French and published at La Rochelle in 1602 by George Thomson, a Scotsman

[5] See e.g. *R.P.C.*, VOL. VII, pp. xxxii-xxxiv.
[6] Lesley, *History*, VOL. II, p. 379.
[7] Trocmé and Delafosse, *Le Commerce rochelais*, p. 85.
[8] B. Winchester, *Tudor Family Portrait*, 1955, p. 242.

domiciled there. Edinburgh appears to have maintained a regular corps of factors in Dieppe,[9] where, writes M. Mollat, Scotsmen were so much at home that they "semblent avoir été absorbés par la population indigène."[10]

We shall examine presently the pattern of Franco-Scottish trade which grew up in this favourable environment. Suffice it for our present purpose to say that Scottish imports fell into two fairly well defined groups: raw materials such as salt and dyestuffs, and exotic semi-luxuries such as wine, fruits, and quality textiles. That the latter group contributed to the enrichment of Scottish social life is undeniable. France was the main sixteenth-century avenue through which the new standards of culture and of social behaviour came to Scotland. The impact is visible in a multitude of instances. It was a French scholar, Pierre de Marsilliers, induced by John Erskine of Dun to settle at Montrose, who prepared the raw youth Andrew Melville for entry to St Andrews, equipping him with a grasp of Aristotle's Greek which amazed the logicians in the University who hitherto had not ventured beyond the Latin translations.[11] Especially in the days of Mary of Lorraine and her daughter, the *haut ton* of France set the standards of housekeeping and attire which the top levels in Scottish society sought to emulate with wares imported from France. Thus Eustatius de Coquill, a French merchant, writes to Mary of Lorraine that his servant is en route for Scotland with merchandise of such distinction that none may see it until the Queen Regent has made her own purchases, and that if she or her ladies need tapestries or other fine goods he can supply them.[12] It was from similar sources that the young Queen Mary got her coach, her fans and precious stones, and her little canopy of satin designed to "mak schadow befoir the queen."[13] Where royalty led, the nobility followed: Boissonnade speaks of "la clientèle élégante en Écosse"[14] to which the French sent their fine wares. On their dining-tables, French fruits and

---

[9] *Edinburgh Records*, VOL. V, p. 314; *Convention Records*, VOL. III, p. 103.
[10] Mollat, *Le Commerce maritime normand*, p. 508.
[11] Melville, *Autobiography and Diary*, p. 39.
[12] *Foreign Correspondence with Marie of Lorraine*, ed. M. Wood, Scottish History Society, VOL. I, 1923, Letter CX.
[13] J. Warrack, *Domestic Life in Scotland, 1488-1688*, p. 73-4; *Accounts of Lord High Treasurer*, VOL. XI, p. 499.
[14] P. Boissonnade, "Mouvement commercial", p. 8.

confections gave variety and distinction, while in all substantial households the drinking of rich French wines was "a sign of almost ostentatious civility."[15]

To the purchase of these goods, especially the wine, Scotland diverted more of her resources than either a seventeenth-century moralist or a twentieth-century economic planner would think justified. Though no direct check was imposed on the import of wine, and though, as we saw in Chapter III, the wine duties imposed about 1600 had a strong fiscal motive, official opinion in Scotland was periodically perturbed both by the economic cost and the social consequences of heavy wine-drinking. It was bad enough for the nobility and the gentry to prefer foreign wines when "most helthful drink" might be made from home-grown grain, but the time for action was clearly at hand when the "unsatiable thrist and druckin dispositioun of the husband, specialie of workmen within townes" led to the spending of whole days in taverns, leaving "the wyff and children at home to famishe for hunger."[16] In effect the Council was admitting that by 1600 wine-drinking had become general through most classes of Scottish society. Here, if nowhere else, the masses in the Argyle Gait in Dundee and the Shoe Gait in Perth shared, with the great ones of the land, in the fruits of the alliance with France.

It was wholly beneficial for a country on the periphery of European society to experience a consciousness of intimacy with one of the great nations within that society. The consciousness could be highly personal, as when David Wedderburne, in the middle of a series of entries in his *Compt Buik* about purely family affairs, recorded that "4 May 1610 The Kyng of France wes slayn."[17] Lithgow, who cordially disliked Frenchmen, nevertheless acknowledged the "fond conceites" his countrymen had "of the fantasticke French";[18] and, whether knowingly or not, every Lowland Scot paid lip service to France in his everyday vocabulary. And one wonders what curious distortion of friendship lay behind the Inverness practice of branding the "fluir ye lyis" on the cheeks of female slanderers.[19]

[15] Mathew, *Scotland under Charles I*, p. 109.
[16] *R.P.C.*, VOL. IX, p. 551.   [17] *Wedderburne Compt Buik*, p. 127.
[18] Lithgow, *Totall Discourse*, p. 438.   [19] *Inverness Records*, p. lxviii.

In the diplomatic sphere, as we have seen, the friendship was cooling after the Scottish Reformation; and, as a first economic result, the trading privileges enjoyed by Scotsmen in France became less secure. Their survival, even in attenuated form, can be attributed partly to the momentum of happier days, partly to the influence of the Protestant groups in French political life, and partly—perhaps mainly—to the constant exertions of the Convention of Royal Burghs in sending envoys and representations to the French authorities.[20] Yet in the long run the closer relations with England, above all the Union of the Crowns, meant the erosion of Scotland's peculiar trading rights in France. Furthermore the harmony of Scotland's economic relations with the French was disturbed by the religious and civil wars which divided France herself. A letter from John Mail, written from Dieppe to Alexander Robertson in Aberdeen in 1596, is one piece of evidence of the dislocation of Franco-Scottish trade consequent upon the wars. "As for the market heir," he writes, "ther is na dispeche for na sort of waris and al becaus the cuntray is become peur be raisson of the weris."[21] Yet the ultimate outcome might have been worse. The wars left France virtually split into regions of Catholic and regions of Protestant influence, and it was a matter of good fortune to the Scots that many of their traditional haunts, La Rochelle, Dieppe, and the like, were strongholds of Protestantism.

In short, the influences bearing on Franco-Scottish trade did not suddenly veer into hostility. The continuing strength of pro-French sentiment in Edinburgh so late as 1624 is shown by the decision of the Town Council when, hearing the news of the betrothal of "our dearest and most hopefull Prince" and "the most illustrious and worthie Princes, Marie" (Henrietta Maria), they ordered that every householder should light a bonfire under peril of a £20 fine for non-compliance.[22] The sentiment was kept aglow by the steady consumption of French wine. The Edinburgh Treasurer's Accounts from 1611 to 1625 show that the annual sale of this wine in Edinburgh, over 1100 tuns in 1611-12, fell to little more than 500 in 1617-18, but

[20] *Convention Records*, VOL. I, pp. 140. 182, 211, 270-2 *et al.*
[21] *Aberdeen Council Letters*, VOL. I, pp. 64-5.
[22] *Edinburgh Records*, VOL. VI, p. 259.

rose again briskly to almost 1200 in 1623-4.[23] Over the same period, sales of wine from the only alternative source, Spain, only once exceeded a hundred tuns and showed no significant trend.[24] The following figures, extracted from the Dundee Shipping Lists, point to the same conclusion.

Date	Total vessels arriving at Dundee	From France
1580-1	42	14
1599-9	77	12
1614	48	15
1617	48	12
1620	61	11

In so far as such samples can be taken as representative, it looks as if the volume of Franco-Scottish trade persisted strongly in the first two decades after the Union of the Crowns. The indications are that the real turn came about the time of the death of James VI. By then Scotland was becoming more fully implicated in England's foreign relations, and the Anglo-French War of 1626 marks a clear milestone in Scottish commercial history. The French remained remarkably tolerant. In the summer of 1626 some 120 English and Scots vessels went to Bordeaux in what Sir James Balfour called "the tyme of wintage."[25] All were at first arrested, but, in "respecte of the ancient leauge," the Scots were quickly released. Later that year, however, Charles I wrote to Scotland "inhibitting the importatione of aney wynnes from France,"[26] and in 1627 Buckingham's expedition to La Rochelle included some 3,000 Scots troops under the Earl of Morton.[27] Thus the old economic alliance ended. In the Leith Customs for 1627-8 and in the Dundee Shipping Lists for the years about 1630, references to direct trade with France are few and scattered.

TRADE WITH NORTH-WEST FRANCE

In France, Scotsmen traded in two geographically distinct regions from which they procured two broadly distinct groups of commodities. For simplicity—though at the sacrifice of some geographical precision—we can speak of the one region as Normandy and focus our attention on Scots trade through

---

[23] *Op. cit.*, App. xv.   [24] Ibid.
[25] Balfour, *Annals*, VOL. II, p. 158.
[26] *Op. cit.*, p. 153.   [27] *Op. cit.*, pp. 158-9.

Dieppe and Rouen. The other, to which we turn later, can similarly be labelled the Biscay coastlands, with their leading commercial centres at La Rochelle and Bordeaux. The ports of Normandy could provide Scotsmen with a variety of vegetable products, grown either in the hinterland or in those Mediterranean countries with which the Normans, since the later fifteenth century, had maintained direct contacts.[28] Sometimes, for example, a cargo of grain might be obtainable.[29] Woad, one of the commonest dyestuffs of our period, came mainly from Picardy, but was also grown along the banks of the Somme and was sent from there to Scotland via Dieppe. Through these Norman ports came also a minor tributary of the great river of French wine which flowed steadily to Scotland.[30]

The real interest, however, of the Normandy trade lies in the sophisticated manufactures and the services which it made available to Scotsmen and women. The cargo of the *Grace*, arriving from Dieppe in the spring of 1615, consisted almost wholly of haberdashery and stationery: silk buttons, thread buttons, silk points, passments (lace embellishments especially for livery), men's belts, "bairnis belts," hats, whalebone, paper, pens, inkhorns, sponges, and cards.[31] The cards which occur so often in this traffic present a problem: some think that they were instruments for textile workers,[32] but the "11 gross playing kerts" in the cargo list of the *Andro* in 1616 supports the more light-hearted interpretation.[33] Perhaps both kinds came from France. The textiles which occur even more often were simply examples of the embroidery, lacework, tapestry, and so forth for which the French were already famous. They came to Scotland both in the piece and made up into clothing. "Les bourgeois de villes d'Écosse," wrote Boissonnade, "comme les nobles, se flattent de suivre le goût de nos tailleurs"; and he quotes as an example the "habit de drap noir de Paris" which George Buchanan wore in mourning for Queen Mary.[34] Wedderburne similarly—though for a different reason—

[28] Mollat, *Le Commerce maritime normand*, pp. 238 ff.
[29] E.g. cargo of the *Jonas*, Dundee Shipping Lists, p. 243.
[30] For a selection of these wares see Dundee Shipping Lists, pp. 221, 236.
[31] Dundee Shipping Lists, p. 255.
[32] Mollat, *Le Commerce maritime normand*, p. 159. *Convention Records*, VOL. II, p. 375, supports this interpretation.
[33] Dundee Shipping Lists, p. 266.
[34] Boissonnade, "Mouvement commercial," p. 8.

bought "sa mekle of the Frensche blak claythe as wil be a clok to me."[35]

Alternatively Scotsmen might avail themselves of the skill of the French dyers. Wedderburne in 1604 sent two parcels to Rouen and another to Dieppe or Rouen in 1613.[36] One parcel contained twelve ells of "thicket blew worzet clayth to be littit [dyed] ayther tanny or els rusche broun." The Rouen tawny dye was an old-established favourite in Scotland: Lady Catherine Gordon had had a gown of it a century earlier.[37] The other parcel in 1604 prompts exciting speculations: seven and a half ells to be dyed "fyn scarlit to be my lassis weyle cottis." The scarlet dye, commonly called kermes, was extracted from the bodies of insects and had been used in Mediterranean countries since Roman times. The "lass" for whom the cloth was intended would be Wedderburne's eldest daughter Helen, and a glimpse of her scarlet petticoat must have brightened the winter days in the Mercat Gait of Dundee.

Frivolities like playing cards and scarlet cloth occupied only a small place in the cargoes passing from Dieppe and Rouen to the ports of east Scotland. So long as France and Scotland maintained close diplomatic alliance, the Scots could look to France for arms. Thus in the troubles of 1546-7 a dozen Scottish vessels were freighted at Dieppe with artillery, munitions, and powder for Scotland,[38] and in June 1571 the Bishop of Ross recorded in his diary: "This day Jhone Chesolm departit furth of Diep towart Scotland, with money and munitione."[39] The same kind of industrial skills, directed to civilian ends, enabled the French to sell to the Scots a variety of ironware, notably iron pots and barrel girds, and small manufactured articles. Of the latter precise details are scarce, but the "lytill knok with ane walkner" which was found in the *Neptune* of Dieppe at Burntisland in 1564 must have been among the first alarm-clocks in Scotland.[40] To sum up, therefore, we find a close resemblance between Scotland's imports from north France and those from the Low Countries. Both

[35] *Wedderburne Compt Buik.* p. 147.   [36] *Op. cit.*, pp. 45, 111.
[37] This was a "sea-gown" provided at James IV's command when Lady Catherine sailed from Ayr with her husband, Perkin Warbeck, in 1497. *Accounts of Lord High Treasurer*, VOL. I, pp. 343-4.
[38] F. Michel, *Les Écossais en France, les Français en Écosse*, 1862, VOL. II, p. 511.
[39] Lesley, "Diary," in *Miscellany of the Bannatyne Club*, VOL. III, p. 127.
[40] *R.P.C.*, VOL. I, p. 308.

areas had their own distinctive vegetable products, both had a relatively high level of industrial technique, both served as entrepôts for exotic goods from further afield.

TRADE WITH THE BISCAY PORTS

In bulk these imports from north France were completely overshadowed by the great shipments of salt and wine from the ports of the Bay of Biscay. Notwithstanding the increasing domestic production of salt which we have already considered, Scotland remained a substantial importer and, like almost every other north-west European country, she looked for supplies mainly to the salines along the Biscay coasts. The great centres of production lay on the beaches of sheltered bays and lagoon-like inlets between the mouths of the Loire and the Gironde where, in the summer and early autumn, sunshine and drought were continuous enough to evaporate sea-water trapped in shallow pans, producing the coarse and not over-clean "great" salt.[41] Except when production was upset by war or civil commotion, the price of Biscay salt was highly competitive, even in north European markets. The method of manufacture by solar evaporation involved little cost other than that of peasant labour; because of the location of the pans no handling was involved other than the loading of barrels or sacks aboard ship; because of its coarse grain the salt withstood the rigours of shipment, even over very long distances. In some countries, notably the Netherlands, this great salt was further refined, but generally it was used in the crude state for preserving food, packing fish, preparing leather, and a host of similar purposes.

Partly because the trade was seasonal, partly for mutual protection, the salt ships generally moved into the English Channel and North Sea in convoy, and a typical convoy of the sixteenth century would consist overwhelmingly of Dutchmen and Hansards, many of them bound for the Baltic. Some impression of the scale and regularity of Scottish participation can be derived from the record of arrivals at Dundee from 1580 onwards.[42] In a normal year five or six salt cargoes entered the port; with rare exceptions they came in the second

---

[41] A. R. Bridbury, *England and the Salt Trade*, 1955, pp. 41 ff.
[42] Dundee Shipping Lists, *passim*.

half of the year; and the place of departure was almost always La Rochelle, the commercial capital of the Salines d'Aunis. Almost invariably salt made up the whole cargo and belonged to the owners or the skipper of the ship. The conversion of sixteenth century units of bulk into modern units of weight is fraught with difficulty: all one dare say is that a fair cargo of Biscay salt to Scotland in 1600 was likely to be of the order of 20 or 30 tons.

In the long run, however, the relative importance of Biscay salt in Scottish economic life was tending to decline. Throughout the closing decades of the sixteenth century La Rochelle and its hinterland was the scene of civil and religious war; in some years, such as 1575, salt prices rose very steeply; by about 1600 production in the Salines d'Aunis was beginning to decline.[43] Simultaneously, as we saw in Chapter II, Scotland's own salt production was expanding quickly and the quality was improving. Though the decline of the Franco-Scottish salt trade coincided with the cooling of diplomatic and cultural relations, its causes were basically economic; whatever had happened to their Crown and Church, Scotsmen would have bought less French salt.

Further south along the Biscay coast, in the estuary of the Gironde, Scottish traders bought a commodity for which there was no home-made substitute and for which domestic demand was limited only by the extent of the nation's purchasing power. Wine, the great staple of the Bordeaux-Scotland trade was, as we have seen, not only a symbol of urbanity. To the rank and file of the people of Scotland it was a pleasurable reminder of French friendship; in spite of the counter-attractions of ale and beer, brogat and whisky, it was easily the most popular alcoholic drink; and to procure it Scotsmen were prepared to pay heavily in effort and goods. Scotland has seldom experienced leaner conditions than those of the mid-1590's, when crops failed and, by great maritime endeavour and financial outlay, heavy grain imports were brought from the Eastlands. Yet in 1596, in the midst of the dearth, a fleet of "four score sale . . . being for the most part Scotsmen" proceeded to Bordeaux to load wine.[44]

---

[43] Trocmé and Delafosse, *Le Commerce rochelais*, pp. 114-5.
[44] *R.P.C.*, vol. v, p. 537.

By no means all the wine drunk in Scotland came from Bordeaux. Some, as we shall see later, came from Spain; some came from Normandy, or at least through the Normandy ports; in 1600, as in the time of Andrew Halyburton a century before, there are occasional references to Canary and Rhenish wines.[45] None the less the trading records, confirmed by burghal and private papers, reflect a great preference for the wines shipped from Bordeaux, broadly the Sauterne group of white and the Médoc group of red. These preferences were echoed in the language of Lowland Scotland. That distinctively Scottish vessel, the tappit-hen, most likely got its name from the French claret measure, the taupinette. When the Dundee Gildry generalised about the town's wine measures, they talked about "claret-stouppis."[46] The Scots port and customs officers rarely made fine distinctions, and generally entered the Bordeaux cargoes as either "wyne" or "land wyne." The latter, coming from the Haut Pays and subject to a rather lower rate of duty at Bordeaux,[47] was sufficiently familiar to taverners and drinkers in Scotland to pass under the corrupt name of "hoypyis."[48]

We can get a reasonably close-up picture of the Bordeaux-Scotland wine trade from the activities of two brothers, William and Andrew Kinnereis (the name is variously spelled) in their flyboat, the *Hope for Grace*. William in particular features prominently in Dundee burgh affairs in the early 1600's— burgess in 1602, town councillor in 1615, bailie in 1628 and ultimately provost in the 1640's. Their ship, as we have already seen, was of a type recently introduced and its great storage capacity and its low operating costs fitted it admirably for the conveyance of barreled wine.[49] Between December 1612 and March 1618 the *Hope for Grace*, with either William or Andrew as her master, bore thirteen consecutive cargoes from France to Dundee, four of them of salt, the other nine predominantly of wine.[50] The normal pattern emerges very clearly: salt in August, wine in November or December and again in May or June. Invariably many merchants shared in the cargo—no

---

[45] E.g. *Edinburgh Records*, VOL. I, p. 235.   [46] *Burgh Laws of Dundee*, p. 138.
[47] M. K. James, "Fluctuations in the Anglo-Gascon wine trade," in *Ec. H.R.*, 2nd ser., IV (1951), pp. 170 ff.
[48] E.g. *Edinburgh Records*, VOL. II, p. 185.   [49] See above, p. 132.
[50] Dundee Shipping Lists for relevant years.

less than twenty-eight in that which arrived in May 1617—but unfailingly some part of the cargo belonged to the brothers, besides which they often imported small lots of wine in other people's ships. Though they traded in other commodities and with other regions, so much of their energies was focused on Bordeaux and on wine that they must have been as highly specialised as any Scottish trading family of the period.

Enough is known of them and of similar wine-shippers to create some rough impression of the scale of the wine trade as a whole. The various contemporary measures, the pipe, the hogshead, the pece, and the terce, can in most cases be resolved into the standard wine unit, the tun, which contained 252 old "wine" gallons or 210 modern Imperial gallons. Converted into these recognisable terms, the cargo of a typical Scottish wine ship of the years about 1600 would be of the order of 10,000 gallons, and it seems reasonable to suppose that a minimum of fifty such cargoes reached Scotland annually. According to the Council in 1610, "the most pairt of the wynes broght yeirlie within the kingdome ar ventit within the burgh of Edinburgh and the town of Leyth."[51] No other area possessed the same concentration of purchasing power, nowhere else was public hospitality dispensed on such a scale. From the Edinburgh Treasurer's Accounts of the revenue from the local wine impost between 1610 and 1625 it can be deduced that yearly wine sales there ranged from 175,000 to 250,000 gallons.[52] By contrast Dundee, almost certainly Edinburgh's nearest rival in this trade, imported up to 100,000 gallons in a heavy year like 1616,[53] but oftener a good deal less.

The trade was fraught with danger, risk, and frustration. Alleged leakage from barrels, especially on board ship, was a constant source of dispute and loss: in an action before a Dean of Gild Court the loss from leakage was put as high as $17\frac{1}{2}$ per cent;[54] and under the Book of Rates of 1612 merchants were entitled to a rebate of 10 per cent of the import duty to cover their "lekkage."[55] On sunny afternoons in the English Channel mariners naturally acquired a thirst; when the boat lay be-

[51] *R.P.C.*, VOL. IX, p. 551.   [52] *Edinburgh Records*, VOL. VI, App. xv.
[53] Twelve cargoes of wine arrived at Dundee in 1616, Dundee Shipping Lists, pp. 265-78.
[54] *Burgh Laws of Dundee*, p. 152.
[55] Printed in *Ledger of Andrew Halyburton*, p. 283.

calmed off Spurn Point a barrel of claret would provide a welcome release from boredom; hence the ruling that, "becaus it is notarlie knowen that the merchandis are heavilie hurt . . . in drinking and drawing of thaire wines coming furth of burdeous . . . upon the sea principally,"[56] skippers were henceforth to be personally responsible for loss. And even if the cargo escaped the attentions of the crew it might fall into the hands of pirates to whom wine ships offered the tempting prospect of a cost-free bacchanalia. If he survived all the perils of the open sea the skipper might still have to break the terms of his charter-party in the interests of safety—hence a dispute in 1572 over the *Margaret* which, with 48 tuns of Bordeaux wine for Aberdeen, was diverted into Leith on the orders of the Lord Admiral.[57]

The more strictly commercial risks arose from the combination of an open market in Bordeaux and a relatively controlled market in Scotland. In France, wine prices fluctuated considerably from both month to month and year to year. The technique of conservation was not yet well developed—it has been said that "vin vieux égale bon vin est une formule moderne"[58]—and the immediate sale of the current vintage is directly reflected in the highly seasonal character of the export trade from Bordeaux. The effect on prices of crop variations was distorted and complicated by internal political conditions in the vineyard regions of France, and by the unevenness of total overseas demand. Thus in 1559 a sudden upsurge of demand more than outweighed the effect of a very heavy harvest, and prices rose. In short, while the long-term price trend at the French ports was upwards, there were sharp and unpredictable variations from season to season.[59]

When he got back to Scotland, the wine importer passed from this free economy and became subject to various controls. Under an Act of 1540, the King, the prelates, and the barons enjoyed the right of pre-emption on wines entering the kingdom.[60] As payments would be strictly based on statutory prices, and as this privileged group included some notoriously

---

[56] *Burgh Laws of Dundee*, pp. 16-17.   [57] *R.P.C.*, VOL. II, p. 128.
[58] Trocmé and Delafosse, *Le Commerce rochelais*, p. 176.
[59] For the price of vin blanc d'Aunis see Trocmé and Delafosse, *op. cit.*, pp. 178-80; and for claret prices in England see Beveridge, *Prices and Wages in England*, VOL. I, pp. 114, 148.   [60] *A.P.S.*, VOL. III, p. 373.

slow payers, it is not surprising that the Act met with keen resistance and was applied only with the reinforcement of a series of Privy Council enactments. Administrative action, high-handed even by sixteenth-century standards, was authorised, as when the royal "simleir" (or sampler) was given the power to break open lockfast places and to search ships, using "our soveriegn Lord's keys to that effect."[61]

Under these regulations, one-tenth of the wine imported was liable to pre-emption. The entire import was subject to price control as it passed into consumption, for under the same statute of 1540 the burghal authorities were charged with the duty of fixing retail prices, based, theoretically, at least, on the bulk prices paid in France.[62] As we saw in Chapter III, this form of retail price-fixing persisted into the seventeenth century, but in some periods it was overlaid by a more rigid system of national prices which, covering bulk as well as retail transactions, was based mainly on a statute of 1551 and Privy Council acts of 1552 and 1562.[63] The motives behind this statutory price-fixing varied. We encounter the familiar complaints about the machinations of evil forestallers who deliberately created a "dearth" of wine. In 1562 the story was that wine traders were carrying coin out of the realm to make payments in France, and that a brake could be put on this by controlling the price which they were able to command in Scotland. What the Council said at any one time may well have had real relevance to the immediate circumstances, but basically it was fighting a losing battle against the secular price rise and against the depreciation of the Scottish pound in terms of the French livre.

The statutory price schedules of the 1550's and 1560's throw light on the pattern of the trade. Thus under the Privy Council's schedule of 1562,[64] Bordeaux wine, brought home by the "East Seas," could be sold in bulk at £18 a tun. For Rochelle and other somewhat inferior French wines, the corresponding price was £14. In this, as in all the national wine-price schedules of the period, there was a differential of

---

[61] *R.P.C.*, VOL. I, pp. 128, 299, 426. For the operation of pre-emption in Dundee see Maxwell, *History of Old Dundee*, pp. 193-4.

[62] On the operation of these price-fixing arrangements in Edinburgh see Robertson and Wood, *Castle and Town*, p. 282.

[63] *R.P.C.*, VOL. I, pp. 128, 212.   [64] *R.P.C.*, VOL. I, p. 212.

the order of £2 a tun between the prices of wines brought by the East Seas and the West Seas, the latter being always the lower. In the Notarial Notebook of John Mason[65] (Clerk of the Burgh of Ayr 1582-1612) there are enough agreements between burgess-merchants and skippers to demonstrate a fairly steady direct trade with Bordeaux, and scattered references show that wine was directly imported to Dumfries, Irvine, and the Clyde ports,[66] but it is inconceivable that the volume of trade by the west seas was so great as to produce bulk economies and justify lower prices. Possibly the differential was intended as an encouragement to traders to use the west coast ports: certainly Glasgow in the 1560's and 1570's could do with all the encouragement it could get. It has been suggested that the lower west coast price reflected an attempt to counter the illicit traffic in wine by English pirates by whom it was carried up the Irish Sea and reset to the coast-dwellers of Galloway and Ayrshire.[67] Such commercial immorality existed, but geography may provide a better explanation for once past Ushant the Scottish skipper's journey to the Clyde was two hundred miles shorter than to the Forth or the Tay, and freight charges could be correspondingly lower.

Though the Bordeaux-Scotland trade was dominated by wine, and though wine determined both the timing and the direction of sailings, it rarely completely monopolised the cargo-space of the typical Scots vessel. Vinegar, literally the "bitter wine" made from lees or from inferior wines, was brought regularly in fair quantity. Olive oil, the "oyle doly" or "oly doly" of contemporary Scottish records,[68] rarely came in bulk; but shipments of a dozen barrels of prunes were not exceptional. The Scots word for these—"ploomedamis" or "pruindames"—suggests Damascus plums, and they might well have come overland to Bordeaux from the Mediterranean. They were widely used by Scottish housewives in a variety of recipes, some as unexpected as "a pullet with some prunes in the broth." Judged, however, by value, woad was certainly the second biggest single item in Scotland's purchases at Bordeaux, bearing out Boissonade's claim that "la France

[65] Mason, "Notarial Notebook," pp. 218, 220.
[66] E.g. *R.P.C.*, VOL. I, p. 227.
[67] Introduction to *Accounts of Lord High Treasurer,* VOL. XI, p. lxxiv.
[68] E.g. *Wedderburne Compt Buik*, p. 46.

était le grand centre de production des ingrédients végétaux indispensables à l'art des teinturiers."[69] In Scotland, woad from Bordeaux and Dieppe, and potash from the Baltic, constituted the two principal exotic raw materials of the wool cloth industry.

Scottish Exports to France

The economy of sixteenth-century France must have appeared to outsiders as remarkably balanced and self-contained. It offered the foreigner a narrow range of valuable wares, and the question which had puzzled Omar must have had continuing relevance:

> I often wonder what the vintners buy
> One half so precious as the goods they sell.

Fortunately for the wine-drinking world, even vintners are not exempt from the basic needs for food and raiment. By the standards of the time France had a remarkably heavy population, predominantly Roman Catholic, with its chief concentrations mostly remote from the sea. In consequence it offered a great market for fish, and—to draw again on Boissonnade— "parmi les poissons importés figuraient surtout les saumons qui provenaient des golfes sinueux d'Ecosse . . . ."[70] When John Barton set out from Scotland to Le Havre in 1548 on a piratical expedition and wished to disguise his ship as a typical innocent Scots merchantman, he carried salmon and skins.[71] Scots vessels intercepted by English pirates while en route for Dieppe in 1586 had cargoes of salmon.[72] In the Aberdeen Customs Accounts for 1617 salmon to Dieppe is the most prominent export,[73] and almost every time Wedderburne mentions salmon in his Compt Buik the reference is to transactions with France. Generally the outcome seems to have been satisfactory, though there was a sorry incident of a barrel of "salmon" which "quhen I wenturit thame to the mercat in France they were found grissillies".[74]

In bulk, however, exports of salmon were almost certainly

---

[69] Boissonnade, "Mouvement commercial," p. 2.
[70] *Op. cit.*, p. 200.
[71] Winchester, *Tudor Family Portrait*, p. 240.
[72] *Edinburgh Records*, VOL. IV, p. 466.
[73] *Ledger of Andrew Halyburton*, p. xcvi.
[74] *Wedderburne Compt Buik*, p. 160.

exceeded by those of herring. In earlier chapters we have examined the pattern of the herring fishery and seen that, at times, supplies were artificially diverted into the home market. All contemporary accounts, however, testify to the normally high level of exports, and the value of the herring in Franco-Scottish trade was emphasised by Scotsmen and foreigners alike.[75] Though the data are inadequate for any overall statistical assessment of the scale of exports, it is possible to trace in Wedderburne's *Compt Buik* and in the Notarial Notebook of James Mason the course of individual shipments from the arrangements between merchant and skipper in the Scots port to the sale of the consignment in Rouen, La Rochelle, or Bordeaux.[76] The subsequent inland distribution throughout Poitou of fish landed at La Rochelle[77] was a typical final stage in the long journey which might have started in Loch Broom or off the shores of Lewis.

As we have seen elsewhere, the rural economy of Scotland was based heavily on pastoral farming and hunting, and the products of both were marketable in France. As one would expect, raw wool found its readiest sale in the northern and north-western parts, French Flanders and Normandy. Somewhat before our period Scotland was so promising a source of wool that the great entrepreneur clothier, Guillaume de Varyte, sent his agents to seek supplies;[78] and it is likely that as the English became increasingly reluctant to export wool, Continental buyers turned even more confidently to Scotland. Similarly the skilled clothing and footware trades of north France provided a ready market for the cured skins and hides which the Scots could offer in a great quantity. Further south, in La Rochelle and Bordeaux, where native cloth industries were less prominent, the Scots could sell textiles. In August 1590, for example, Wedderburne sent some 230 ells of linen with Andrew Mortimer, 96 with David Rollock and 250 and a barrel of salmon with James Rankine, to be sold on his behalf and the "fre money" to be used in the purchase of wine and woad.[79] Again in 1598 he sent both linen and white wool cloth

[75] E.g. Craig, *De unione*, p. 454.
[76] E.g. Mason, "Notarial Notebook," pp. 223, 225, 231.
[77] Trocmé and Delafosse, *Le Commerce rochelais*, p. 83.
[78] Mollat, *Le Commerce maritime normand*, p. 85.
[79] *Wedderburne Compt Buik*, pp. 144-5.

with James Neilson, "the fre money to be warit on fyn Bordeaux wynis half clarit half quhyt."[80]

Apart from fish, skins, wool, and cloth, visible exports were slight, though we find occasional references to a cargo of coal,[81] and in 1564-7 horses were being sent to Bordeaux in such numbers that the Privy Council found it desirable to impose a ban.[82] Invisible exports, however, seem to have been of substantial dimensions. A clue to one invisible item is given in correspondence between King James and his Scottish Council in 1619, when a proposal to regulate the freighting of Scottish ships to foreigners was met by the argument that this would ruin Scottish shipowners, "insamickle as the best ships of Scotland are continually employed in the service of Frenchmen . . . whilk is ane chief cause of increase in the number of Scots ships."[83] This was not new. In the last quarter of the sixteenth century, 81 Scottish vessels sailed for the Baltic alone from French ports;[84] in 1590 we have direct evidence of Scotsmen in the French coasting trade;[85] and two years later the Scots clergy tried, without success, to prevent this use of Scottish ships by Catholic charterers.[86]

The inevitable question of how far these exports paid for Scottish imports from France involves an assessment of very conflicting evidence. As will be apparent from the few instances of Wedderburne's trading methods quoted above, a great deal of the Franco-Scottish trade was on a near-barter basis in the sense that a merchant sent a parcel of goods to be sold and the "free" money was immediately employed in the purchase of other goods for the return trip. Contemporary French opinion supports this interpretation. Estienne Perlin, writing in the 1550's, says: "les Ecossais ne payent pas en argent le vin qu'ilz pregnent de ceulx de Bordeaulx, mais leur baillent d'autre merchandise au lieu de ce."[87]

While this may have been generally true, it is abundantly plain that the physical transfer of coin was by no means uncommon, though especially in the early part of our period it

---

[80] *Op. cit.*, pp. 72-3.   [81] Robertson and Wood, *Castle and Town*, p. 279.
[82] *R.P.C.*, VOL. I, pp. 286, 561.
[83] *Op. cit.*, VOL. XI, p. 202; VOL. XII, p. 107.
[84] *Sound Toll Registers* for 1575-1600.   [85] *R.P.C.*, VOL. IV, p. 526.
[86] *Convention Records*, VOL. I, p. 402; W. Chambers, *Edinburgh Merchants*, p. 13.
[87] E. Perlin, *Déscription des Royaulmes d'Angleterre et d'Écosse*. The passage here cited is quoted in Michel, *Les Écossais en France, Les Français en Écosse*, VOL. II, p. 129.

was often the consequence of the current military or diplomatic relationship between the two nations. Thus in 1551 so much money was flowing through the pouches of French troops in Scotland that it became necessary to fix the value of the sou in terms of Scottish currency,[88] and in 1560, while the French garrison was still in Leith, Richard Paine reported to Sir Thomas Gresham that a French vessel had left Flushing for Leith with much money aboard, "all in Frensch." "I wold wel," he added, "our schippes might mete with hym."[89] Additionally, however, there is enough evidence of strictly commercial transference of money to show that Franco-Scottish trade was not always in a state of natural balance. We have already seen that in 1562 the Privy Council acted in the belief that gold and silver were being drained from Scotland to purchase French wines,[90] and, a generation later, Wedderburne sometimes sent coin to Bordeaux for this purpose.[91] But there is at least as much scattered evidence of the movement of cash balances to Scotland. Wedderburne was sometimes in a position to direct that the money realised by the sale of his wares in France should be brought home or left on loan,[92] and we have, in 1583, one clear case of a substantial loan of 4,000 livres to the King of France.[93] It had been negotiated by the Seigneur de Meyneville, and was repayable to the merchants who had advanced it either in Rouen or in Edinburgh. Sir Thomas Craig, writing his *De unione regnorum tractatus* in 1605, had no doubts on this matter. He says that the herring exports to France from the Forth and Clyde pay for foreign articles of consumption and yield "gold and silver, regularly and in great quantity."[94]

Yet whether, in the long run, the trade was in this sense profitable to Scotland, must remain an open question, for neither Scotland nor France possesses the data on which a precise answer can be based. It can, however, be postulated that the trade tended to become more difficult for Scotsmen.

---

[88] Cochran-Patrick, *Coinage*, VOL. I, p. 75.
[89] *Calendar of State Papers, Foreign Series, of the Reign of Elizabeth . . . preserved in H.M. Public Record Office*, VOL. III, ed. J. Stevenson, 1865, p. 157.
[90] See above, p. 180.
[91] *Wedderburne Compt Buik*, pp. 145-6.
[92] *Op. cit.*, e.g. pp. 135, 140.
[93] Michel, *Les Écossais en France, les Français en Écosse*, VOL. II, p. 131.
[94] Craig, *De unione*, p. 454.

N

As we have seen, they relied heavily on fish to cover their purchases of French wine. For various reasons, notably Dutch competition, fish prices were kept relatively low, so that most north European fish producers were finding it desirable to diversify their exports. On the other hand French wines had, in Boissonnade's phrase, "en effet sur les marchés d'Europe une sorte d'empire incontesté,"[95] and as we have seen, wine prices rose briskly. As a hypothesis, therefore, it may be suggested that the terms of trade were tending to move against Scotland in the sense that she would have to send an increasing amount of fish to purchase a constant amount of wine. So while there was no sudden collapse in Franco-Scottish trade in response to the changing political relationship, it may be that the conduct of that trade, even on narrowly economic grounds, was becoming less attractive to Scotsmen.

TRADE WITH SPAIN AND THE MEDITERRANEAN

Until the closing decades of the sixteenth century, Scotland's economic relations with Spain seem to have been virtually restricted to small purchases of a limited range of Spanish products in the markets of the Low Countries. In the generation after 1560 the peoples of the two countries became deeply and bitterly divided on religion, yet it was precisely in this period that economic contacts between them became more extensive and certainly more direct. It is true that, particularly in the later 1580's, there was a significant pro-Spanish element among the Scottish nobility and that, in an attempt to take England in the rear, Philip II courted James VI with the utmost assiduity. James's decision to reject these overtures may have been based primarily on his belief in the value of friendship with England, for despite the predominance of the Protestant parties in Scotland, the popular attitude was by no means clear-cut. To the ardent Protestant, Spain symbolised all that was most abhorrent in religion, and in the Netherlands Scottish troops fought to free the Protestant Dutch from their Spanish overlords. Yet when the survivors of the broken Armada sought refuge in Scottish ports, the sympathy of seafarer for seafarer proved stronger than religious antipathy. At Ayr, for example, the "pure Spainyardis" were shod and

[95] Boissonnade, "Mouvement commercial," p. 221.

fed at the town's expense, and, on the opposite coast, equal
generosity was displayed at Anstruther.[96]

It was a different matter for a Protestant Scot to venture
within the metropolitan jurisdiction of the Spanish Inquisition.
The sad tale of William Lithgow comes first to the mind.[97] A
traveller with 36,000 miles—mainly on foot—to his credit, he
entered Iberia where, at Malaga, he underwent Inquisitorial
tortures so barbarous that on his return to Britain in 1621 he
had to be borne to the presence of the King on a feather bed.
So robust, however, was his constitution, that he shortly revived
to deliver a violent physical assault on the Spanish Ambassador
and to live on to 1660—some say in his native Lanark—with
the undignified nickname of "Lugless Will." Equally famed
in his day, the young David Kinloch, later a royal physician,
is reputed to have escaped *auto-de-fe* by curing the sickness of
the Grand Inquisitor.[98] John Murray and his fellow mariners
in the *Susanna* of Aberdeen had neither the luck of Lithgow nor
the skill of Kinloch. Having sailed under foreign charter from
Middleburg to San Lucar in Spain, John encountered there an
old foe, one "cristeane papa," master of a Breton ship. On the
original accusation of being "theiffis and pirattis," John and his
crew were acquitted by the Spanish authorities, but Christian
then craftily changed his ground and "accusit ye said Johne
and his equippage as protestantis and lutheranis." The outcome is grimly recorded: "sum brunt, sum committit to ye
gallais, sum to slaverie, utheris died in presoun."[99] As the
ministers of the Scottish Church were already objecting to
direct dealings with Spain because of the inherent spiritual
risks, such revelations of the physical risks must have strengthened their voice; but when the issue was forced to a head in
1593 and both the Convention of Royal Burghs and the
Edinburgh Burgh Council agreed to a ban,[100] the merchants
showed great determination to continue the trade. Admittedly
their reason—that they had to go to Spain to collect outstanding debts—seems a trifle thin, but the ministers let them have

---

[96] *Ayr Burgh Accounts*, p. 161; Chambers, *Domestic Annals*, VOL. I, p. 186.
[97] The full account with all the hair-raising details is in his own *Totall Discourse*.
[98] Millar, *Roll of Eminent Burgesses of Dundee*, pp. 92-4.
[99] "Testimonalis grantit be ye Bailies," in *Miscellany of the Third Spalding Club*,
VOL. II, pp. 24-5.
[100] *Convention Records*, VOL. I, p. 402; *Edinburgh Records*, VOL. VI, pp. 95-6.

their way as otherwise "this mater had turnit to a great popular scisme."[101] In fact the Church can scarcely have had the wholehearted backing of the Convention, for not many years later this same body was arranging the appointment of an agent to represent Scottish commercial interests in Lisbon, then within the dominion of the Spanish crown.[102]

The willingness of Scottish merchants and skippers to challenge the rulings of their ministers, to take their ships through notoriously troubled waters, and to expose themselves to the perils of Inquisitorial persecution, all testify to the economic attractiveness of the Spanish trade. The first clue lies in the widening rupture between Spain and England—the phase of semi-official privateering and then, with the preparation of the Armada, open war—during which English vessels could not enter Spanish ports except under disguise. There are indications that during the phase of open war a substantial contraband trade was conducted by Englishmen carrying passports from the King of Scots, and apparently these were available with no great difficulty for, according to the contemporary testimony of Bartholomew Cole, Scottish papers could be "obtained . . . for any bribe."[103] Alternatively the English chartered Scottish ships. Thus when the *New Ship* of St Andrews and a sister ship of Leith were in the Thames taking on cloth and metals for Spain, it was reported that though the packages bore "the leaden seal of Edinburgh" the goods were English, and that the seal was "placed on them to deceive."[104] Fynes Moryson, writing in the late 1590's, summarised the results of Scotland's participation in this trade: it had brought her, he said, wealth and experience.[105]

There seems little doubt that this illicit carrying trade gave natural birth to a substantially increased direct trade between Scotland and Spain. Despite the peril to conscience, Spain had obvious attractions for Scots merchants: the two nations were at peace; Spain was reputedly a high-price market and a rich reservoir of precious metals; it offered much the same

[101] *Historie and Life of King James the Sext, being an Account of the Affairs of Scotland, 1566-1596*, ed. T. Thomson, Bannatyne Club, 1825, pp. 254-5.

[102] *Convention Records*, VOL. II, p. 279.

[103] *Tudor Economic Documents*, VOL. II, pp. 82-3.

[104] *Calendar of Letters and State Papers relating to English Affairs preserved in the archives of Simancas*, VOL. IV, 1587-1603, ed. M. A. S. Hume, 1899, No. 191.

[105] Moryson, *Itinerary*, PT. III, BK. iii, p. 155.

assortment of commodities as south-west France where political conditions were often alarming. Scottish domestic papers show how widely Spanish wines were available in the country. The Thane of Cawdor, on his tour of 1591, drank Spanish wine in Glasgow, Stirling, Linlithgow, and Edinburgh;[106] and the same wine could have been served to him at Balloch, for they kept a stock in the cellars there.[107] He could have bought it in almost any east coast port. At Dundee, for example, the Gildry dealt in 1620 with a dispute about a "leakage" of serious dimensions from butts of Spanish wine lately arrived at the harbour,[108] and an examination of the Edinburgh records of wine sold there between 1610 and 1625 shows that in some years one pint of Spanish was drunk for every ten of French, though generally the ratio was lower.[109] A century earlier these wines might well have come to Scotland via the Spanish Netherlands; that they now came direct from Spain is proved equally by entries in the Dundee Shipping Lists and by the news, reported by the Venetian Ambassador in 1587, of Scots wine ships awaiting clearance at Seville.[110]

In the same way, and for the same reasons, Iberia was an alternative source of salt, woad, and some minor luxury wares. Quantities were never great, but the assortment of luxuries from Spain is another indication of the introduction of variety and colour into the life of upper-class Scotland. The Glenorchy Inventory[111] lists "of silk bedis, ane contiening four curtaines of red Spanische taffite,' and 'ane uther blew silk bed, conteining thrie curtaines of blew Spanisch taffite." In 1599 David Wedderburne instructed James Neilson, then bound for Spain, to "fill my litel barrele with confectionis," and in 1619 he again directed a skipper to bring "murmblade" or "confectionis" for him from Spain.[112] The marmalade of Wedderburne's day was most likely the quince preserve, made mainly in Portugal and highly esteemed in Britain; the confections

[106] "The Thane of Cawdor's western journey," printed in *The Book of the Thanes of Cawdor*, ed. C. Innes, Spalding Club, 1859, pp. 200-8.
[107] Household Book of Breadalbane, printed in *The Black Book of Taymouth*, p. 309.
[109] *Burgh Laws of Dundee*, p. 152.
[109] *Edinburgh Records*, VOL. VI, App. xv.
[110] *Calendar of State Papers relating to English Affairs existing in the Archives of Venice*, VOL. VIII, 1581-91, ed. H. F. Brown, 1894, p. 254.
[111] Quoted in Innes, *Sketches of Early Scotch History*, pp. 509-10.
[112] *Wedderburne Compt Buik*, pp. 114, 182.

were probably caraway seeds dipped several times in sugar solution to form spherical sweets.

Among the miscellaneous Spanish exports to Scotland there are also some which sound a bold masculine note. Thus Wedderburne's instruction to one of his factors that he should "remember to by the gudeman of Ardowny a suird"[113] is a reminder that the classic period of the Toledo blade had opened. Somewhat later Duncan Campbell, writing from Islay to his brother Colin about a stallion for his mares, specifies "Cromerties old Spanis hors, provyding he be of reasonable pryce."[114] The old stallion would be a Spanish jennet, of suitable size to breed with the native strain which, though spirited and hard-working, was comparatively small. In Andrew Halyburton's day Spanish iron had been imported to Scotland via the Spanish Netherlands; by James VI's reign some at least came direct from Spain. Thus in 1587 a merchant of Ayr, "at his last being afield in Spain," disposed of goods for a fellow-townsman and brought in return 83 stones of iron;[115] and at Haddington about the same period "Spanis irn" was being forged in the smithy.[116]

To purchase these goods, Scotsmen sent to Spain a collection of dull but worthy merchandise. The fairly regular parcels of cloth and the periodic shipments of wheat, barley, leather, and wax, reflect the character of Spain's domestic economy in her age of imperial greatness. The neglect of basic industries— especially after the expulsion of the Moors—and the low status of arable farming left Spain dependent on outsiders for her elementary needs, in the satisfaction of which her treasure flowed out over Western Europe. Thus Wedderburne in 1596 sent "auchten scoir fourten elnis lyning" in the *Falcon* to be sold in Spain.[117] He gave his factor two options for the disposal of the proceeds, with the significant proviso that if neither were practicable he was to put the money in his "purs and send it in ryellis of 8." Here, in miniature, is the pattern of Spain's economic relationship with her European trading associates.

---

[113] *Op. cit.*, p. 114.
[114] Quoted in Innes, *Sketches of Early Scotch History*, p. 422.
[115] Mason, "Notarial Notebook," p. 243.
[116] "Haddington Records; Books of the Common Good," in *Transactions of the East Lothian Antiquarian Society*, VII (1958), p. 66.
[117] *Wedderburne Compt Buik*, p. 71.

If Scotland could have participated more extensively, her own trading position—and her domestic coinage—would have been stronger.

For a ship of Protestant Scotland, the voyage to Cadiz was high adventure; east thereof, hazard and apprehension must have increased mile by mile. Algerine, or "Barbary," piracy was in its heyday of sin. Once he had secured the backing of the Turks against Spanish intrusion, and having in consequence exchanged the title of sultan for that of pasha, the local ruler in Algeria, Hayradin, had fortified the port of Algiers and made it the base for the most outrageous piratical campaigning in all history. But the Algerines were open to bargain for captives, provided always that reason was well coated with ransom. References to ransom show that Scottish sailors, serving in foreign ships or under foreign charters, certainly knew the seas east of Gibraltar. Thus in the 1570's the Burgh of Aberdeen made voluntary contributions for the relief of Scottish mariners from Ayr and other places then held captive by the Algerines and Turks.[118] Edinburgh could scarcely be less generous. In 1603 its Town Council voted 100 merks towards the ransom of three Dundonians "laitlie tayne be the Turks gailleyis cumand throws the straitts from Cartagen furth of ane schip of Sanct Mallowas."[119] Similarly in 1613 a further vote of £10 sterling went to help eleven Leith sailors "captives in Turkie and relieved be James Fraser, Scottishman thair"; and again in 1622 one David Peebles, merchant burgess of Edinburgh, was "captive in Turkie."[120]

The ship of St Malo was not the only Frenchman sailing in the Mediterranean with Scots in her crew. John Spens of Leith died on board a Dieppe ship en route from there to Pisa in 1606—or so his wife alleged three years later when she wanted to remarry.[121] When Lithgow was at Naples in 1616 he came upon a fellow-countryman whose experiences almost rivalled his own.[122] This man, George Gibb of Bo'ness, had lost his own ship to "the Turkes," recovered her in Sardinia in a worm-eaten state and sold her in Naples, had been engaged

---

[118] Kennedy, *Annals of Aberdeen*, p. 176.
[119] *Edinburgh Records*, VOL. V, p. 317.
[120] *Op. cit.*, VOL. VI, pp. 135, 233.
[121] *South Leith Records*, p. 6.
[122] Lithgow, *Totall Discourse*, p. 403.

by an Englishman as pilot of his ship, and from the English ship had been removed by the French by whom he was "fast chained to an oare, with shaven head and face." Nor was service—voluntary or compulsory—restricted to French ships, for another of Lithgow's remarkable episodes involves a Flemish vessel en route from Crete to Venice, "the Maister being a Scotchman, John Allen, borne in Glasgow, and dwelt in Middleborough in Zeland."[123] It is equally clear that Gibb was by no means unique in taking a Scottish ship into the Mediterranean, for in the early 1600's when much discussion was afoot about foreign shipping in Scots ports the burghs told the King that many of their vessels were employed by the French "within the bounds of Spain, Italy and Barbary, where lies their trade."[124]

Similarly by the later years of King James's reign Scotland was maintaining tenuous—but none the less direct—contacts with Italy. The presence of Scotsmen in Rome needs no explanation, though they were not all of the old religion; for Robert Meggat, "borne neere to Newbattle," secreted Lithgow when the Inquisition sought him, and Patrick Baxter, a Dundonian, connived in his escape.[125] Direct trade with Italy was at least beginning in 1627 when William Dick of Edinburgh, with typical enterprise, chartered a Yarmouth ship to carry fish, grain, and wax from Leith to Leghorn or Venice.[126] East of Italy the record fails, and one wonders what strange journey had brought to Palestine the Scotswoman who was found there by an English traveller happily dandling her babe on her lap and crooning "Bothwel bank thou blumest fayre."[127]

In truth the evidence about the Mediterranean is sparse and fragmentary. On a map of European trade in the early part of the seventeenth century the imprint of direct Scottish activity would thin rapidly south of Bordeaux, and beyond Cadiz it would melt into a vague haze.

[123] *Op. cit.*, p. 92.
[124] *Convention Records*, VOL. III, pp. 66-7.
[125] Lithgow, *Totall Discourse*, p. 20.
[126] "The Entress of the Ships, Guidis and Geir transportit at the Port of Leith," MS in General Register House.
[127] This story appeared originally in R. Verstegan, *Restitution of Decayed Intelligence in Antiquities*, 1605.

VII

ECONOMIC RELATIONS WITH ENGLAND

THE RAPPROCHEMENT

During the span of years covered by this book affairs in Scotland were determined by three major influences: the Reformation, the re-establishment of effective central government, and the reconciliation with England. At many points the three were interrelated. The hostility of the English, which stretched back to the days of Edward I and Robert Bruce, had been an irritant in Scotland's domestic politics, a steady drain on her material and human resources, and, indirectly, the lasting cement of the Franco-Scottish alliance. Events in the sixteenth century led inevitably towards a re-appraisal of Anglo-Scottish relations. The English, decisively checked in their Continental ambitions, had then turned in part to maritime expansion and in part to exploiting the political and economic potentialities of the British Isles. A settlement of the old feuds with Scotland thus became an essential element in English policy. "Imprimis," wrote Secretary Cecil in 1559, "it is to be noted, that the best worldly felicity that Scotland can have, is either to continue in a perpetual peace with the kingdom of England, or to be made one monarchy with England, as they both make but one island, divided from the rest of the world."[1] The tactics might vary—the gentle approach in the person of Margaret Tudor, the "Rough Wooing" of Henry VIII, the skilled diplomacy of Cecil and Dr Wotton at Edinburgh in 1560—but the underlying purpose of Tudor policy remained constant. Strains and frictions remained to be resolved, blood

---

[1] "A Memorial of certain points meet for restoring the realm of Scotland to the antient weale," printed in Robertson, *The History of Scotland during the reigns of Queen Mary and King James VI*, VOL. II, App. I.

was yet to flow, but in the long perspective it is evident that the
year 1560, which saw the Treaty of Edinburgh and the official
Scottish Reformation, is as clear a milestone in Anglo-Scottish
relations as either 1603 or 1707.

Though the old hostility was basically political, it contained
certain economic elements. Thus in the valuable trade of the
Low Countries the two nations were often open rivals, and in
commerce generally the English maintained that the lower
standard of life of the Scot enabled him to engage in "unfair"
competition.[2] Judged by the available statistical evidence the
extent of personal penetration by Scotsmen into the domestic
life of England seems comparatively slight. The "testimonialis"
granted by the Aberdeen bailies between 1589 and 1603, listing
Aberdonians either as testators or legatees all over Europe from
the Baltic to Italy and Hungary, contain not a single reference
to an Aberdonian either bequeathing or receiving estate while
resident in England.[3] The statistics of aliens dwelling in
London in the early years of Elizabeth's reign point to the same
conclusion, for among some 4,500 persons so returned in 1571
fewer than 40 claimed Scottish nationality.[4] But it was easy—
and convenient—for a Lowlander to explain his speech as
some remote English dialect, and there were certainly more
people of Scots birth in Elizabethan England than these figures
indicate. In the *Complaynt of Scotlande*, written some time about
1550, the ardent nationalist Dame Scotia deplores the current
degree of familiarity, especially along the Borders, and she
says that in the previous fifty years some 3,000 Scots had
migrated to England.[5] Miserable renegades they were in her
eyes, for "nocht ane of them dar grant that thai are Scottis
men," each having sold his birthright for a mess of English
pottage.

The once intimate maritime trading relationships between
the two lands were embittered and frustrated by the piracy
and privateering born of political hostility. The guilt was fairly
divided. "Worshipful Sir," wrote an English agent to his

---

[2] See below, p. 208.
[3] "Testimonalis grantit be ye Bailies," in *Miscellany of the Third Spalding Club*,
VOL. II, *passim*.
[4] *Return of Aliens Dwelling in the City and Suburbs of London*, edd. R. E. G. and
E. F. Kirk, Huguenot Society, 1907-8, VOL. II, pp. ix, 121.
[5] *The Complaynt of Scotlande*, ed. Murray, pp. 103-6.

employer, "it may please you to be advertised that a Scottish ship, which keepeth about Havre, hath taken seven English ships."[6] "On Wednesday," wrote Randolph to Cecil, "I was sent for before the Council [i.e. the Scottish Council], but it was only for a Dundee ship taken by one of the Queens majesty's," and he went on to warn Cecil that he would hear more about it.[7] He was right, and he might have added that there would be many more such complaints from both sides until the crowns were united in 1603.[8] When war threatened, this desultory piracy gave place to wholesale organised seizure. "Quhen," says Lesley, "our Marchantes, quha feirit na Ill" had gone forth on their lawful errands abroad, "the Inglismen lyeing in wayt in sum nuikis and bosumis of the sey" seized twenty-eight of the returning Scottish ships, and when the Scots protested to England all they got was "wrang upon wrang."[9] Little wonder that for long periods no Scot dared venture to English markets or to France via England without a safe conduct from the English Government.[10]

We begin, then, in an atmosphere so charged with mistrust that so late as the 1580's Elizabeth's government could receive and preserve a detailed plan for an "arteficiall fortyficacion," a great earthen rampart across the Border to serve as a new Hadrian's Wall.[11] Behind this plan, as behind the contemporary defence works at Berwick, there lay centuries of diplomatic strain and friction punctuated by periodic bouts of fighting which had produced an artificial estrangement between the English and the Lowland Scots. The question of how far the official reconciliation in the later sixteenth century and the official intimacy after 1603 were reflected in any substantial integration of the social and economic lives of the two nations must occupy a central place in the present study.

The effect of reconciliation was most immediately evident in the solution of one of the most intractable mutual problems,

---

[6] Quoted in Winchester, *Tudor Family Portrait*, p. 241.
[7] *Calendar of the State Papers relating to Scotland and Mary, Queen of Scots, 1547-1603*, edd. J. Bain *et al.*, 1898-1952, VOL. II, p. 31.
[8] E.g. the complaints made by the English in 1596; *op. cit.*, VOL. XII, p. 224.
[9] Lesley, *Historie*, VOL. II, p. 252.
[10] *Calendar of State Papers relating to Scotland*, ed. M. J. Thorpe, 1858, VOL. I, pp. 187-9.
[11] *Calendar of letters and papers relating to the Affairs of the Border of England and Scotland, preserved in H.M. Public Record Office*, ed. J. Bain, 1894-6, VOL. I, pp. 300-2.

the lawlessness of the Borders. This wide frontier zone, a maze of moor and dale, peat bog and woodland, had resisted complete fusion into either kingdom. Within its confines local hereditary or traditional leadership meant more than the remote kingship in London or Edinburgh, and, as family ties often lay athwart the national frontier, border feuds did not of necessity conform to a national pattern. Thus, on the English side, the Barony of Alnwick suffered more by the depredations of the "riders of Tyneside than by the open enemies, the Scots";[12] and, on the Scottish side, Bishop Lesley contrasted the relatively law-abiding men around Berwick with "the rest of the bordirmen . . . quha [who] nathir in peace or weire can be stainchit [restrained] from takeing the pray."[13] Local feuds, both across the Border and parallel to it, were a jagged edge to national hostility. Stable economic development in the whole Border zone was impossible; hence, as Andrew Borde wrote in about 1540, "the people of the borders toward England lyveth in much pouertie and penurye, hauying no howses but such as a man may buylde wythin iii or iiii houres."[14] The Borderer's life was a compound of inherited hatreds and loyalties, of watchfulness and ruthlessness, relieved by an almost primitive belief in the supernatural.

> From Craik-cross to Skelfhill-pen,
> By every rill, in every glen,
> Merry elves their morris pacing
> Emerald rings on brown heath tracing,

and "a stark moss-trooping Scott" would listen awe-struck to the tale of how, for a kiss beneath the Eildon Tree, Thomas the Rhymer was borne off by the Queen of Elfland herself to serve a seven-year term in her fairy kingdom.

Family feuds and local lawlessness were by no means solely responsible for the economic stagnation of the Border region. Periodic armed incursions—southward by the Scots and northward by the English—contributed heavily, and news of them reaching London and Edinburgh, exacerbated the ill feeling of national governments. Periodic truce-days, which often ended in brawls, and the appointment of joint commissions

---

[12] Quoted in A. L. Rowse, *The England of Elizabeth*, 1953, p. 101.

[13] Lesley, *Historie*, VOL. I, p. 10.

[14] *Introduction of Knowledge made by Andrew Borde, of Physyeke Doctor*, Early English Text Society, 1870, p. 136.

to balance claims for stolen property, were feeble palliatives for a condition which called for firm handling from both sides.[15] The Tudors were not likely to tolerate lawlessness even on the periphery of their realm, and, during the reign of Elizabeth, the long term of Lord Hundson (her cousin) as Lord Warden of the Marches was marked by an increasing regard for law and order. The massive defences of Berwick, a triumph of sixteenth-century military engineering, remain to this day a symbol of the firmness of Elizabethan frontier policy. On the Scottish side, where central government was less stable and less efficient, the defence and pacification of the Borders lacked the insistent resolution of the Tudors. None the less periodic attempts were made. The Prior of St Andrews headed an expedition in 1561; Mary went in person to keep company with Bothwell in 1566; during the regencies of Moray and Morton vigorous action was undertaken. Yet so late as 1596, in spite of twenty years of increasing co-operation between the Scottish and English Governments, William Armstrong— "Kinmont Willie" of the ballad—was abducted by the English on a truce-day and, after the failure of appeals for his release, was rescued from Carlisle Castle on a misty morning by two hundred horsemen led by the Scottish Warden, Walter Scott of Buccleuch.[16]

The fact was that the Borders would continue to jeopardise friendship between the two countries and to retard the economic progress of the whole frontier region until the forces converging on them came under unified control. Thus the union of 1603 was decisive. The very week that James set off for London, the Armstrongs moved south along a parallel course, harrying the country down to Penrith and earning a retribution which foreshadowed the shape of things to come to Border malefactors. A joint Anglo-Scottish force under the commander of Berwick invaded Liddesdale,[17] the Armstrong country, performing its task to such effect that men found it safer to disown even the name of Armstrong. This joint action was consolidated in the

[15] The general Border history in the following sentences is drawn from F. H. Groome, *A Short Border History*, 1887; and R. B. Armstrong, *History of Liddesdale, Eskdale, Wauchopedale, and the Debateable Land*, 1883.

[16] The story is told, free from later embellishments, in *Historie and Life of King James the Sext, being an Account of the Affairs of Scotland, 1566 to 1596*, pp. 366-71.

[17] See the various instructions issued to William Bowyer, Captain of Berwick, in *Cal. S.P. Dom., James I, 1603-10*.

establishment of a mixed commission, set up in 1605-6 under
the Earl of Dunbar.[18] In 1606, says Balfour, Dunbar hanged
"above 140 of the niblest and most pouerfull thieves in all the
borders, and quha were most obnoxious to the publicke-peace:
and fully reduced the other inhabitants ther to obedience."[19]
Across to the south-west, among the fells and dales of Cumberland, the Grahams, "the chiefest actors in the spoil and decay
of our country," were equally on the anvil of royal displeasure.
Three boat-loads of them were shipped from Workington in
1606 and 1607 to settle in Ulster, and others were forced to take
service in the armies in the Low Countries.[20]

During the two decades of James's rule from London, this
vigorous policy went on unabated. "Broken men," the outlaws
of the Scottish Middle March, were rounded up for compulsory
service in armies on the Continent; peel towers, the symbols of
local suspicion and wariness, were demolished; and as the
respectable gentry of Cumberland denounced the Grahams, so
Scott of Harden banded himself with Scott of Tushielaw and
Gladstone of Cocklaw to uphold the King's writ among their
kinsmen and retainers.[21] The report conveyed to James in
1609 that the "Middle Shires" of his combined kingdom were
as peaceable as any part of Christendom[22] was perhaps opti-
mistically premature, but "Jethart Justice" in its various forms
did its work quickly and did it well. Old habits die hard, and
it is scarcely surprising that the courts in the Border shires
continued to hear innumerable charges of sheep-stealing and
the like,[23] but as a political matter the old Border problem no
longer existed by about 1620.

Building works, so often a mirror to their age, symbolise the
change. The Elizabethans left their imprint on Berwick in
defensive walls and fortifications; James was responsible for the
fifteen-arch bridge over the Tweed, at once a physical link and
an emblem of union between his two realms. Begun in 1611, it
took thirteen years to complete at a cost—according to Brereton

[18] *R.P.C.*, VOL. VII, pp. 486, 504-6, 543, 728-9.
[19] Balfour, *Annals*, VOL. II, pp. 16-17.
[20] J. Nicolson and R. Burn, *The History and Antiquities of Westmorland and Cumberland*, 1777, VOL. I, pp. cvi cxxix.
[21] Groome, *A Short Border History*, p. 120.
[22] Hume Brown, *History of Scotland*, VOL. II, p. 207.
[23] R. Grierson, "Nithsdale at the Union of the Crowns," in *S.H.R.*, XIII (1916),
pp. 245-65.

—of £17,000.[24] The road was being cleared for the Scots courtiers and craftsmen drawn by duty or prospects to the court of James VI and I. Equally significant are the regulations promulgated from 1603 onwards about postal services between Edinburgh and London.[25] But how much trade crossed the Border nobody can say. There were accusations and counter-accusations of goods being smuggled along "fels and other by-passages," and the English said that lambs and young sheep, bearing a "kind of Hairy and very coarse wooll" were driven in considerable flocks to markets on their side.[26] Similarly the linens which the weavers of Paisley and other towns made for English housewives may very well have been sent along the land routes,[27] but the truth—sad to an historian—is that the data are too elusive to justify any firm conclusions about the volume or the composition of overland trade as a whole. What is clear is that the pacification of the Borders prepared the way for economic advance on the estates of the Border families and on the fringing areas hitherto exposed to their depredations. On the south side better estate management, applied in an atmo-sphere of unprecedented security, produced so sharp a rise in rentals that—to give one example—the northern lands of the Percys were yielding twice as much revenue in 1617 as they had done ten years before.[28] On the Scottish side Sir William Seyton could speak in 1623 of the spectacular increase in wool production in the southern shires generally, attributable he said, to the "solid government" which had prevailed "since his sacred majesties happie arryvall to the commandement of both kingdomes."[29]

ECONOMIC ASPECTS OF THE UNION OF THE CROWNS

The notion of union was by no means novel. John Elder, a native of Caithness, had addressed a firm proposal to Henry VIII in 1543,[30] and four years later James Harryson, "Scottishe-

---

[24] Brereton, *Travels*, p. 94.
[25] *R.P.C.*, VOL. VI, pp. 567-71.
[26] *Convention Records*, VOL. I, p. 455; "On the Union of the Crowns," British Museum, Harleian MS 1314, henceforth cited as Harl. 1314.
[27] Thomson, *The Weaver's Craft*, p. 81.
[28] G. R. Batho, "The finances of an Elizabethan nobleman: Henry Percy, ninth Earl of Northumberland (1564-1632)," in *Ec. H.R.*, 2nd ser., IX (1957), p. 442.
[29] *R.P.C.*, VOL. XIII, p. 774.
[30] Printed in *Collectanea de Rebus Albanicis*, pp. 23 ff.

man," wrote his *Exhortaton to the Scottes to conforme themselves to the godly union.*[31] As Elizabeth aged and remained unwed the prospects improved, with James as the future occupant of the common throne. The growing attempts to harmonise Anglo-Scottish relations in the last two decades of the sixteenth century reflect James's determination to consolidate his prospects; and it was, in part at least, because of these more cordial relations that his succession in 1603 was smoothly effected and generally accepted by both nations.[32]

Nevertheless, as so often happens in human affairs, the event preceded a full examination of its implications. There was nothing exceptional in a monarchy common to two distinct nations—it prevailed for example in contemporary Iberia—but the King himself regarded his journey to London as the prelude to union rather than as its consummation. "He hasteneth," wrote Bacon after his first interview with James, "to a mixture of both kingdoms and nations, faster perhaps than policy will conveniently bear."[33] Bacon's response, a tract drawing suggestive parallels between natural and political processes, launched the King onto a sea of prurient metaphors: "I am the husband, and the whole isle is my lawful wife"; the aim of policy should be to bring the two nations "at the first to shake Hands, and, as it were, Kiss other, and lie under One Roof, or rather in One Bed, together";[34] or, to change the location but retain the spirit, "England and Scotland should join and coalesce . . . as two twins bred in a single belly."[35] Small wonder that his English subjects should, in reaction, coin the phrase "platonical communion."[36]

What could be done towards economic unification without parliamentary approval, James did at once. By proclamation of 8 April 1603—only fifteen days after Robert Carey's breathless arrival at Holyrood—he made the £6 Scots gold piece legal tender in England at 10s. sterling, thus confirming the existing ratio between the two currencies.[37] The following year Napier

[31] Printed with *The Complaynt of Scotlande,* ed. Murray.
[32] D. Nobbs, *England and Scotland, 1560-1707,* 1952, p. vii.
[33] Letter to the Earl of Northumberland, quoted in J. Spedding, *The Life and Times of Francis Bacon,* henceforth cited as *Bacon,* 1878, pp. 413-4.
[34] *Journal of the House of Commons, 1547-1628,* henceforth cited as *Commons Journal,* 1803, p. 359.   [35] *Op. cit.,* p. 230.   [36] Harl. 1314.
[37] R. Ruding, *Annals of the Coinage of Britain and its Dependencies,* 1840, VOL. I, p. 360.

of Merchiston, General of the Mint in Scotland, went to London where "the witt and knowledge of the general wes wonderit at be the Englischmen."[38] Negotiations ensued on a project to reduce the monies of the two countries to "a conformity and equall goodnesse," which, said the proclamation of November 1604, was not only "a necessar preparation for the union of the saids Kingdomes, bot ane essentiall pairt of the samen."[39] The immediate practical outcome was the issue of sets of gold and silver coins, headed symbolically by the Unit, by which it was hoped to "unite the gold coinages of England and Scotland as James had united the Crowns."[40] Apart from the mint marks and "ane littill thrissell" on the horses' trappings on the Scottish silver crowns and half-crowns, the English and Scottish issues of the new coins between 1605 and 1609 were of identical design and enjoyed equal freedom of circulation throughout the two kingdoms. The close relationship maintained between the two coinages after 1604 must, indeed, stand high among the tangible economic results of the Union of the Crowns. In 1611, for example, it was found that the Unit was worth one-tenth more abroad than in Britain, and "all utheris his maiesties coynes rateable." To redress the balance and restrain the "insatiable desyre of lucre and gayne" which induced men to export coin, the face value of the new gold coins in England was raised by one-tenth.[41] Two days later the same action was taken in Scotland, so that henceforth the Unit was current at £13. 4s. Scots and 22s. sterling.[42]

The accomplishment of the King's desire for complete commercial integration hinged on the conclusion of a treaty of union, which, as events were to show, was more than his English Parliament would swallow. But shortly after his accession he was able, by the employment of his prerogative powers and by the temporary compliance of his subjects, to secure a considerable easing of the conditions on which Scotsmen traded in England and Englishmen in Scotland. One result of this can be readily illustrated by an examination of

---

[38] "The Diary of Robert Birrel," in *Fragments of Scottish History*, ed. Dalyell, p. 62.
[39] Gordonston Papers, printed in full in Cochran-Patrick, *Coinage*, VOL. I, pp. 210-5.
[40] A. E. Feaveryear, *The Pound Sterling*, 1931, p. 81.
[41] *Cal. S.P., Dom., James I, 1611-18*, p. 92.
[42] Cochran-Patrick, *Coinage*, VOL. I, pp. clxvi, 220-1.

the collection of import duties at English ports in the early 1600's.[43] The "subsidy," calculated at a shilling in the pound on the official value of the goods concerned, was levied on all imports from abroad, irrespective of the nationality of the importer. Above this the "custom," 25 per cent of the subsidy, was levied on merchandise brought in by aliens. Thus on 17 December 1604 the *Gift of God* arrived at Boston (Lincs.) from Scotland with a cargo of salt, on which the Scottish owner paid 16s. subsidy and 4s. custom. If the vessel had been held up for nine days the owner of the salt would have saved 4s., for from Christmas 1604 the custom was no longer levied on Scottish-owned goods. The change is symbolised in the terminology of the English Port Books. Henceforth the Scottish merchant, hitherto designated "Al" (alien), becomes "Scot" or "Brit."[44]

In Scotland the remission of duties meant virtual free trade, at any rate for native commodities, so that the mercantilist trend which we detected in Scottish commercial policy in the 1590's received a partial reverse. As early as June 1603, the Scottish Council held that "Adrian More, Inglishman . . . now being our Souerane Lordis subject, sould be frie of all outward custome";[45] and an action in 1605 against certain Scots for exporting wares to England contrary to an Act of 1593 failed on the ground that the commerce of both nations was now freed.[46] The scale of these remissions of Scottish customs is indicated by the plea addressed to the Council by the farmers of the customs. For the year November 1605 to November 1606 they reckoned that their takings would be down by £13,000, though, with somewhat suspicious readiness, they settled for a reduction of £10,000 in their annual obligation to the Crown.[47]

Once, however, it became apparent that the negotiations for a permanent commercial treaty between the two nations were likely to prove abortive, this spirit of liberal goodwill evaporated. There is an ominous warning in 1607 when the Scottish Council ruled that while no duties should be levied, merchants should be required to find caution for payment in

[43] *Boston Port Books,* p. xxiv, and entries for 1604.   [44] *Op. cit.,* p. xxii.
[45] *R.P.C.,* VOL. VI, p. 577.
[46] *Op. cit.,* VOL. VII, pp. 80, 117.   [47] *Op. cit.,* VOL. VII, p. 392.

case of sudden resumption.[48] By 1611 all pretence was dropped: in Scotland the pre-1603 duties on both imports and exports were revived and the Privy Council seized the opportunity to undertake a general tightening-up of the customs organisation.[49] Each nation accused the other of abusing its privileges by surreptitiously re-exporting custom-free goods to foreign markets; Scotland especially missed the revenue collected before 1603 on English goods entering the country. But behind these minor arguments lay the breakdown in the formal parliamentary negotiations for more perfect union to which the remission of customs had been a gesture of royal encouragement.

With this breakdown the prospect of perfect commercial integration was ruled out, and free trade, in the sense in which a skipper might freely carry native wares from Hull into Newcastle, did not apply in Anglo-Scottish relations until the 1650's.[50] Furthermore, despite the professed willingness of both nations after 1603 to repeal "hostile laws," the movement of particular commodities, notably wool, was still from time to time prohibited.[51] Even the relief of Scotsmen from trading discrimination as aliens survived only in the face of English sniping. Thus in 1612 the Convention of Royal Burghs heard with concern that customs officials in London, Hull, Lynn, and elsewhere were trying to reimpose the old alien dues on Scottish traders.[52] To provide some protection the Convention revived a proposal, originally made by James in 1599,[53] for the appointment of a Scottish commercial agent in London. In the event the choice of occupants of the new office proved unhappy. The first agent, Robert Mure, apparently regarded the office as a sinecure;[54] the second, John Brown, was active but collected more than his authorised fees and, having failed to appear before the Convention in 1617, was summarily dismissed.[55] In the same period a special mission, led by Andrew Forret, protested successfully in London against the imposition of dis-

[48] *Op. cit.*, VOL. VII, p. 347.   [49] *Op. cit.*, VOL. IX, pp. lxvi, 262 ff.
[50] T. Keith, "The economic condition of Scotland under the Commonwealth," in *S.H.R.*, V (1908), p. 275.
[51] E.g. *A.P.S.*, VOL. IV, p. 369.
[52] *Convention Records*, VOL. II, p. 462.
[53] Pagan, *The Convention of the Royal Burghs*, p. 190. Aberdeen had vigorously opposed this proposal; *Aberdeen Council Register*, VOL. II, pp. 189-92.
[54] *Convention Records*, VOL. II, p. 379.   [55] *Op. cit.*, VOL. III, pp. 25, 31.

criminating dues on Scottish shipping using English harbours.[56] Meanwhile, in 1615, an English royal proclamation re-asserted the ruling that the goods and ships of Scotsmen should be subject to no dues in English ports other than those payable, in like circumstances, by Englishmen, and that reciprocal treatment should be accorded to Englishmen in Scottish ports.[57] In short, Scottish wares were still regarded as foreign wares, but Scottish traders were not foreign traders—a compromise which fell far short of full commercial union.

The reasons for the failure to achieve complete and permanent commercial fusion must be sought in the oral and literary debates over the draft Treaty of Union. Prodded into action by the King, the English Parliament took up the "matter of the union" in the early summer of 1604.[58] A joint Anglo-Scottish conference was convened—a shining example, according to Bacon, of "a grave and orderly assembly"[59]—which quickly produced an instrument for submission to the Parliaments of the two nations.[60] Various hindrances, notably the plague and the Gunpowder Plot, delayed formal parliamentary consideration until 1606-7. Then, in its "Act anent the Unioun",[61] the Scottish Parliament accepted the recommendations of the Joint Conference, subject to the vital proviso that nothing take effect until the English passed a similar statute. That this was improbable was immediately apparent from the violence of the criticism, which fell especially on the articles regarding nationality and commercial integration.

To resolve the tricky problem of common nationality, the Conference of 1604 recommended a dual solution whereby the *antenati* (i.e. those born before 1603) would have a restricted, and the *postnati* a full common citizenship. A torrent of legal and economic argument, heavily embellished with polemical abuse, was thereupon released. So far back as 1593 the Jesuit Robert Parsons, writing his tract on the succession to the English throne,[62] had maintained that Scotland could "bring

---

[56] *Op. cit.*, VOL. III, p. 10; *R.P.C.*, VOL. IX, pp. 263-7.
[57] *Cal. S.P., Dom., James I, 1611-18*, p. 282.
[58] The preliminaries are described in *R.P.C.*, VOL. VII, pp. xxix ff.; and in *Commons Journal*, p. 318.   [59] Bacon, *Works*, VOL. VI, p. 426.
[60] The Instrument is printed in *R.P.C.*, VOL. VII, pp. xxxii-xxxiv, and in *Edinburgh Records*, VOL. VI, App. III.   [61] *A.P.S.*, VOL. IV, pp. 366-71.
[62] Published under the pseudonym "R. Doleman," *A Conference about the Next Succession to the Crown of England*, Amsterdam 1593.

no other commodity to England than increase of subjects";
and after 1604 no zoological metaphor went unused to illustrate
how, given the chance, the hordes of Scotland would swarm
into England. In the Commons debate in February 1606, "Sir
Christopher Piggot, Knight . . . arose . . . and entered into by-
matter of Invective against the Scotts . . . using many words of
scandal and obloquy."[63] In a relatively mild passage he
described Scotland as "the barrenest land in existence" from
which—to summarise his point in the words of another English
contemporary—"Pharaos Lean Kyne will feed upon our full
pastures." A fellow member, Nicholas Fuller, in a speech
lasting all day, maintained that England was already overfull,
her merchants were hard pressed to make ends meet, her
universities were producing more graduates than could find
employment, and much more in the same strain.

There was no shortage of answers, founded in economics, in
equity, and in law. In his tract of 1605, Sir Thomas Craig (a
Scottish representative at the 1604 Conference) argued loyally
that poverty had its own virtues and that, under perfect union,
English skill and money would flow to Scotland to blend with
the abundant labour already there.[64] Furthermore, he said, if
Scotsmen were to give up their special privileges in France, they
should in all equity be allowed chances of employment and
office in England. In the House of Commons Bacon ridiculed
the fearful prospect of an England overcrowded with Scotsmen:
there was plenty of scope for labour on the land and on the sea,
fen and waste awaited the hand of the cultivator, Ireland and
Virginia could take many thousands of colonists, men were
the sinews of military power, Scotsmen were too sensible to
move south unless they had prospect of employment in some
such capacity. I do not speak, he said, with courtier-like
flattery of the King's views, but "out of the foundation of my
heart."[65] None the less the King very soon afterwards appointed
him to the office of Solicitor General at £1,000 a year.

It was well-timed advancement, for the last word in this
matter of common nationality was to lie with the English courts.
During the parliamentary debates the English judges held, in

[63] The debate is recorded in *Commons Journal*, pp. 333 ff.
[64] *De unione*, pp. 277, 329, 333, 431 ff.
[65] *Commons Journal*; E. A. Abbott, *Francis Bacon*, 1885, pp. 114-5.

an opinion tendered to the Lords, that the *postnati* were automatically naturalised; but neither the Commons nor the joint Lords-Commons Committee in 1606-7 were prepared to accept this view so long as the two nations retained their distinct legal systems.[66] A collusive suit was accordingly brought in 1608 before the English judges, to whom Bacon delivered one of his greatest forensic speeches.[67] By an overwhelming majority—thirteen concurring against two dissenting —the judges in the Exchequer Chambers held that the *postnati* were automatically naturalised.[68] Like the masons on the new bridge at Berwick, they applied the spirit of union which the King himself embodied.

But the spirit was very far from all-pervading. The broader project of commercial fusion, even with the important exceptions accepted by the 1604 Conference, was more than the English Parliament would swallow, and without parliamentary approval perfect integration could never be realised. Action under the prerogative, wrote an English commentator, was but a girdle to clasp the outer trappings of union; the blood of union, he said, "cannot run into the Veynes of the Commonwealth without an Act of Parliament."[69] In a draft preamble to the Conference's report (in the event another preamble was used) Bacon argued that "for so much as the principal degree to union is communion and participation of mutual commodities . . . it appeareth to us . . . that the commerce between both nations be set open and free . . . for the better sustentation and comfort of all parts."[70] "Comfort of all parts" was a tall order, but the concept appealed to James. "Whereas," he wrote, "some may thinke this Union will bring preuidice to some Townes and Corporations within England; it may bee a Merchant or two . . . may have an hundred pounds lesse in his packe; But if an Empire gaine and become the greater, it is no matter."[71]

These spacious views were hardly likely to commend themselves either to the average English merchant or to the burgess

[66] Spedding, *Bacon*, VOL. I, pp. 497-501; S. R. Gardiner, *History of England*, *1603-42*, 1883-4, VOL. I, pp. 325 ff.

[67] Bacon, *Works*, VOL. VII, pp. 641-79.

[68] Spedding, *Bacon*, VOL. I, pp. 524-5.

[69] Save where otherwise indicated the quotations and opinions in the following paragraphs are taken from Harl. 1314.

[70] Spedding, *Bacon*, VOL. I, p. 496.   [71] *Commons Journal*, p. 361.

members of the House of Commons, and it is not surprising that when the articles of commerce in the proposed treaty came before the English Parliamentary Committee in December 1606, its Reporter found "nothing to report but confusion and disorder." The merchants' parliamentary mouthpieces, though "roundly shaken up by the Lord Chancellor" in committee and harangued by the King in a speech which occupies six pages in the *Commons Journal*,[72] clung tenaciously to their objections.[73]

The objections were founded on two broad propositions. Firstly, and chiefly, it was argued that the proposal to admit the Scots to English trade on terms of complete equality would damage the financial resources, the commerce, and the security of the realm of England. Even exemption from the "aleyn or petit Custome"—the extra 25 per cent levied on aliens— would mean loss of revenue to the King. To allow the Scots to convey goods duty free between English and Scottish ports was simply an invitation to fraud, for the London officials had no effective means of preventing re-export to foreign lands from some remote Scottish port. Furthermore it was held that, given equality of opportunity, the Scots would undercut the English in both carrying and selling. Whereas the English ships, massive in build and heavily armed, had relatively little storage space and required big crews, the Scots ships were built "wholly for stowage and nothing for Warr." Whereas the English seamen demanded assured wages and a lordly diet of beef, pork, beer, and the like, the Scots, "even to the least boy on the ship," found for themselves, carried their victuals from home, baked their "oaten cake made of bean flour," and fried their salt fish on the ship's fire, and were allowed to eke out their meagre pay by private trading. A further alleged national characteristic, the impetuousity of the Scots, might apparently be a defect or a virtue according to the circumstances. "The Scotch, being hasty and giddy headed, impatient of delays," were, according to the English objectors, thereby unfitted for responsible office; but when the Scottish skipper's impatience of delay led him to put to sea in a favourable wind while his

---

[72] Spedding, *Bacon*, VOL. I, pp. 494-5; *Commons Journal*, pp. 332-3, 357-63.
[73] Harl. 1314; and Objections of the London Merchants, Answers by Salisbury and the Scottish Merchants, in *Cal. S.P., Dom. James I, 1603-10*, pp. 336-7.

English rivals were still feasting ashore off a Michaelmas goose, it constituted a kind of opportunism which threatened civilised maritime behaviour.

The same characteristics, so the argument proceeded, made for unfair commercial competition. The English, with their faith in regulated trade and organised companies, regarded the small-scale private enterprise of the Scots with a mixture of derision and fear. The entire crew of the Scots ship, they said, down to the "meanest ship's boy" (who must have been flattered if he heard of these remarks in high places), carried cloth or other wares to sell on their own account. The Scots merchants—in the Commons Fuller bluntly called them "pedlars" —traded in small lots with negligible overhead costs, little risk, and quick returns. In short, the English argued, if these people have open access to the goods and ports of England, they will undercut both our mariners and our merchants, "and so our great ships, being the gard of the land, would decay."

A second set of English arguments against complete trading equality was based on the contention that the Scots enjoyed superior trading privileges in France. These privileges, the English reasoned, were based historically on the old Franco-Scottish alliance against England. The Union of the Crowns had removed the basis of the alliance, and consequently the continuance of special privileges in France was no longer justifiable. By arguments not overloaded with economic logic, the English held that so long as the privileges persisted, the Scots could not fairly be allowed to compete directly with Englishmen, especially in Franco-English trade. The Conference of 1604, after diligent enquiry, had found that at Bordeaux, when all was "reckoned and well weighed on either side," there was little to choose between the terms on which the two nations traded. In Normandy, in spite of the English treaty of 1572[74] with Charles IX, it seemed to the Conference that the balance of advantage lay with the Scots. Recent events there were certainly not reassuring to the English, for in 1598, in the belief that imported English cloth was harming the Norman industry, a ban had been imposed on all English cloth stretched by tentering, and a whole batch had been

---

[74] B. Reynolds, "Elizabethan traders in Normandy," in *Journal of Modern History*, IX (1937), pp. 289-90.

confiscated at Rouen, and the condition of Anglo-Norman trade remained highly precarious until the removal of the ban in 1606.[75] Faced with this fluid situation, the Conference of 1604 obviously showed discretion in recommending that "ffower meete persons" be sent to investigate on the spot.

In general the Scots accepted this summary of the relative privileges in France. Any surviving advantages they enjoyed in Normandy were, so they said, offset by those extended to the English in other trading localities, while the greater distance between Scottish ports and Bordeaux put their wine traders at a positive disadvantage there in competing with Englishmen. The English, on the other hand, were far from accepting the Conference's findings,[76] especially in the matter of relative privileges at Bordeaux. No Englishman, they alleged, might buy wine save through a "broaker" appointed by the French, though the Scots could deal direct with the vintners; the English were barred from direct access to the "high country," though the Scots could buy their wine anywhere; the English were forced to unship their wares onto the "open key" where damage "by wett" often occurred, whilst the Scots could sell direct from the holds and decks of their ships. Furthermore they argued that the greater distance between Scotland and Biscay was no real handicap to those Scots masters who engaged for part of the year in the English carrying trade, and who passed to Bordeaux at the appropriate season from their last English port of call.

Though the debate engendered a great deal of hot blood, it was in a sense academic because neither nation seriously desired close economic integration. The arguments employed were often specious, reflecting more truly the depth of national antipathy than the economic realities of the time. Thus the Scottish merchants had little difficulty in countering the charges laid against them, and their reply had the backing of Salisbury who, if he did not accept the idea of closer union with any enthusiasm, had at least too balanced an outlook to be swayed by propaganda.[77] But apart from the King and Bacon, it would be hard to name any person of influence in London

---

[75] E. Moir, "Benedict Webb, Clothier," in *Ec. H.R.*, 2nd ser., x (1957), pp. 256 ff.

[76] Again I summarise the arguments in Harl. 1314.

[77] *Cal. S.P. Dom., James I, 1603-10*, pp. 336-7.

whose attitude was positively favourable. The English Parliament, its worst suspicions confirmed by James's favouritism towards Scotsmen at his Court, was increasingly unamenable to royal pressure, and the establishment of common nationality in defiance of English parliamentary opinion clearly damned any prospect of a change of heart. In the eyes of English mercantile spokesmen the proposed arrangements were one-sided: "It will be a want of policy and discretion in the English, and a kind of fraud and deceiving in the Scottish, to robb Peter to cloath Paul withall"; "Change is commonly said to be no Robbery, but such a change as yield not *Quid pro Quo* is not much less than Robbery"—so the Englishmen of Bacon's day used Baconian language to contravert his arguments.[78]

The changing tone of official pronouncements in Scotland reveals a suspicious willingness to withdraw from the negotiations. In 1604 the Scottish Parliament was "Ravished in admiration with ane so fortunate beginning" and looked forward to "the fruition of sik ane effectuall union,"[79] but by the spring of 1607 the Scottish Council was enquiring whether, in view of the violence of English parliamentary criticism, the whole matter should not be shelved.[80] Sir Thomas Craig and Lord President Fyvie[81] (later Earl of Dunfermline) emerge as leading Scottish protagonists—the former's *De unione tractatus* was the outstanding Scottish literary contribution to the cause—but their views were not representative of the Scottish nation as a whole. Indeed James in 1607 admitted to the English Parliament that the Scots "did never crave this Union of me . . . norever once did any of that Nation presse me forward."[82] Economic union, as the experience of the ages has shown, is a sensitive plant, and neither the soil nor the climate was kindly enough in 1603. There is, indeed, wisdom in Hume Brown's belief that had the treaty been forced through then it might have exacerbated the "mutual repugnance" of the Scots and the English and so delayed the parliamentary Union of 1707.[83]

What then were the material results of the Union of the Crowns? The principal, though in many respects the least

[78] Harl. 1314.   [79] *A.P.S.*, VOL. IV, p. 263.
[80] *R.P.C.*, VOL. VII, p. 512; Calderwood, *History of the Kirk of Scotland*, VOL. VI, p. 633.   [81] *R.P.C.*, VOL. VII, p. 23.
[82] James VI, *Political*, p. 301; see also C. S. Terry, in his Introduction to Craig, *De unione*, p. vi.   [83] Hume Brown, *History of Scotland*, VOL. I, p. 194.

ponderable results, emerged from Scotland's changing political condition, in which the Union was the outstanding landmark. In a sense the Union was the fulfilment of the Tudor ambition to stabilise the political link between England and Scotland and so to remove those sources of friction which had frustrated and distorted their relationships through the preceding centuries. Similarly, within Scotland, the Union marked a crucial point in the establishment of more effective central executive government; for though the authority of the Crown was certainly increasing in the 1590's, it was only after 1603 that James could rule from a position of strength and security. The immediate tangible result, the pacification of the Borders, represented a substantial addition to the economic potential of both Scotland and the northern counties of England. More generally the new political stability created an environment which enabled Scotland to participate—admittedly as a poor late-comer—in the economic advance and expansion which more favoured lands had been experiencing since the middle decades of the sixteenth century. In short, as we have seen in earlier chapters, the political changes of which the Union was both the symbol and the climax, altered the whole outlook for the Scottish economy in the first forty years of the seventeenth century.

But while, in this sense, political association with England was materially beneficial to Scotland, its cost was far from negligible. The removal of the King to London meant that Scotland became inevitably embroiled in English foreign policy. The direct financial burden thus imposed on Scotland was considerable:[84] over a million pounds Scots in 1621 to subsidise the Elector Palatine, and £400,000 in 1625 for war against—of all people—the French. Furthermore the active participation of Scottish troops against the French[85] was the last straw on the back of the Old Alliance. As we saw in Chapter VI, Franco-Scottish trade continued strongly through the chilling days of Reformation and Anglo-Scottish diplomatic *rapprochement*. After 1603 its survival was at best problematic: after 1625 its collapse was inevitable.

The question of how far the political association with

---

[84] T. Keith, *Commercial Relations of England and Scotland, 1603-1707*, 1910, p. 33; Hume Brown, *History of Scotland*, VOL. II, pp. 224-5.
[85] Balfour, *Annals*, VOL. II, p. 158.

England led to closer social and economic integration can be
illustrated, if not precisely answered, by reference to two
specific themes, migration and trade. It must have seemed by
about 1610 that the ending of personal discrimination against
the Scots as aliens in England had cleared the way for southward migration. There were certainly powerful attractions.
The occupation of the throne by a Scottish-born and Scots-
speaking king aroused in the minds of Scottish gentlemen the
vision of lucrative office at Court: already in 1603 James
replaced Raleigh as Captain of the Guard by Sir Thomas
Erskine; Lord Kinloss became Master of the Rolls; Sir George
Hume Master of the Wardrobe; fellow-Scots filled the posts of
Gentlemen of the Bedchamber and Masters of the Harriers.[86]
Their migration, Sir Thomas Craig complained, transferred to
London a great volume of Scottish purchasing power which
would otherwise have stimulated trade and manufactures in
Scotland.[87] Englishmen, and their ladies, voiced other complaints, protesting against the King's prodigality towards his
compatriots and deploring the change in fashions at Court as
compared with the old Queen's time. There was ostentation
galore—too much of it by some accounts—but the tone fell:
"We were all lousy," wrote Lady Anne Clifford, "by sitting in
the chamber of Sir Thomas Erskine."[88]

The progress of Scotsmen at Court, coupled with the known
extravagance of Queen Anne and the mythical wealth of native
Londoners, was a powerful magnet to an assortment of fortune-
hunters and practitioners of many skills. David Ramsay went
to London to continue his duties as watchmaker and horologer
to the King, and, according to another credulous fellow, to
seek with hazel rods for treasure buried under the floor of
Westminster Abbey.[89] George Heriot, jeweller to the Queen,
grew from strength to strength. Already a rich man by
Scottish standards, he crowned his fortune in London, married
into the nobility, and left enough in 1623 to endow handsomely
"ane hospitall for orphanes" in his native Edinburgh.[90] For,

---

[86] Gardiner, *History of England*, VOL. I, pp. 94-6. For James's defence of these
appointments see James I, *Political Works*, ed. McIlwain, pp. 294-5.
[87] *De unione*, p. 448.
[88] *The Diary of Lady Anne Clifford*, ed. V. Sackville-West, 1923, p. 4.
[89] *William Lilly's History of his Life and Times from 1602 to 1681*, 1826 edn., p. 46.
[90] J. and J. Johnstone, *Historical and Descriptive Account of Heriot's Hospital, with
a Memoir of the Founder*, 1827.

one hopes, loftier motives, Thomas Young joined them in about 1612. A son of a Perthshire manse and the possessor of an inferior M.A. ("minus potentes") of St Andrews, he became a London curate, coached a boy called John Milton, and eventually became Master of Jesus College at Cambridge and a leading light of English puritanism.[91]

Once it was apparent that the southward migration was not limited to men of substance or skill, even James was prepared to apply a brake. "Hark ye, Richard," says Sir Walter Scott's Nigel, "in this paper the Lords of the Council set forth that, 'in consideration of the resort of idle persons of low condition from his Majesty's Kingdom of Scotland to his English Court, dishonouring the royal presence with their poor and beggarly persons' . . . these are to prohibit the skippers of vessels . . . from bringing such miserable creatures."[92] "I marle," replied Richie, "the skipper took us on board." "Then you need not marvel," went on Lord Nigel, "for here is a clause which says that such idle suitors are to be transported back to Scotland . . . and punished for their audacity with stripes, stocking or incarceration." Cynics said that the King's real purpose was disclosed in a specific ban on Scotsmen who sought to approach the Court under the pretext of collecting old debts, which, not surprisingly, was "of all kinds of importuning, most unpleasing to his Majesty."[93] There were, however, more dignified motives behind the anti-migration edicts. The King was genuinely anxious to deprive the English of the satisfaction of ridiculing the nation of which he was the head. The participation of an active coloniser, Sir William Alexander, in the publication of the edict of 1619[94] suggests that James accepted the theory that foot-loose Scots would be better employed in Ireland or in Nova Scotia than in begging their way to London. It is equally clear that restrictive action was associated with outbursts of anti-Scottish feeling in London. Thus the Scottish Council's Act of 1612,[95] with its unchivalrous reference to Elizabeth Maxwell whose presence in London would "produce mater of scandaill," reveals a sensitiveness to London opinion. The Scot in London in 1612 moved in the shadow of the

---

[91] D. Laing, *Biographical Notices of Thomas Young*, 1870.
[92] Sir Walter Scott, *The Fortunes of Nigel*, 1842 edn., p. 25; *R.P.C.*, VOL. IX, p. 377.
[93] *R.P.C.*, VOL. XII, pp. 274-5.   [94] Ibid.   [95] *Op. cit.*, VOL. IX, p. 327.

gibbet on which, much to the delight of the mob, swung the corpse of Lord Sanquhar, hanged for the murder of a fencing-master.[96]

For though outspoken comment might be dangerous—John Marston and his fellow playwrights were lucky not to lose their ears for slighting remarks in *Eastward Hoe*—there was plenty of criticism, especially in London, as each fresh Scot arrived to help his countrymen "gnaw old England's bones." Yet taking England as a whole, the southward flow of Scotsmen does not seem to have been numerically formidable; certainly there is nothing comparable to the movement in the eighteenth century. After 1603 the trilled R was heard in the buzz of conversation about the Court, and the Scot in London infuriated his audience by his claims to personal acquaintanceship with "Jamie" or Anne. Once outside the Court and its periphery we drop far down the social scale, to the pedlars and the "highlandmen" on the roads, before we encounter any considerable number of Scottish migrants. Naturally they were likeliest on the main routes between Scotland and London, where their readiness to lead the horses and their ability to touch the heart-strings drew money from wealthier compatriots. James Nesbit encountered them when, in 1613, he carried to London a wedding gift from the town of Edinburgh to its godchild, the Princess Elizabeth. For assistance in finding the way from Stilton to Huntingdon he paid 2s. 6d. to the guide—"being a fine boy, a Scottis boy"; at Royston he gave 1s. to "ane puir Scottiswoman"; in London another 13s.—all duly entered on his expense account—was disbursed among "sindrie necessitous Scottis pepile."[97]

But in the solid core of English economic life, the realm of the trader and the farmer, the Scottish migrant made little apparent impact. Some ghostly figures cross the pages of English colonial history in 1625 when John Wedderburne was authorised to administer the estates of certain Scots lately deceased in "the Indies,"[98] but it is not until the 1630's that we have clear proof of a Scot—John Burnett of Aberdeen—engaging in the Plantation trade alongside the English.[99] The

[96] *Op. cit.*, VOL. IX, p. xxviii.   [97] *Edinburgh Records*, VOL. VI, App. XX.
[98] *Calendar of State Papers, Colonial Series, East Indies, 1625-29*, ed. W. N. Sainsbury, 1884, p. 10.
[99] *Calendar of State Papers, Colonial Series*, VOL. VI, 1574-1660, ed. W. N. Sainsbury, 1860, p. 277.

merchants of the English chartered companies need not have feared that hordes of frugal opportunist Scots would immediately overrun their preserves. Looking at migration as a whole, down at least to the eve of the Civil War, we find little to modify the conclusion of a now classic Scottish historian that "even the pungent satirist cannot run up a very formidable score against the hungry invaders."[100]

In one of his passages on the economic effects of the Union of Scotland, Sir Thomas Craig considered possible reorientations of Scottish overseas trade. Why, he asked, should Scottish traders hazard their lives in distant waters "if with less trouble and expense they can dispose of their goods at their own door?"[101] We have seen that after 1603, and especially down to 1611, extra-parliamentary action in England seemed to offer encouragement to the expansion of Anglo-Scottish trade. How far traders responded to this encouragement in particular and to the changing national relationship in general can be best judged in the context of a complete assessment of Anglo-Scottish trade over the seventy-five years with which we are concerned.

THE CHARACTER AND COURSE OF ANGLO-SCOTTISH TRADE

The essential basis of Scottish trade with most foreign countries can be explained in terms of different natural endowment. Trade with England admits of no such simple explanation. There was not, for example, enough difference between the soil and climate of the two countries to promote a regular interchange of specialised agricultural products. Furthermore, because of the nature of Anglo-Scottish political relations, trade between them since the fourteenth century had been disjointed and chancy. Through the centuries the life of the Anglo-Scottish trader had been hazardous when goods, ships, and men's lives were small counters in the game of North Sea diplomacy. And yet, as Dr Grant points out,[102] whenever a truce prevailed, as after the Rough Wooing in the later 1540's, economic contacts were eagerly renewed. The strong urge to

---

[100] J. H. Burton, *The History of Scotland*, 1873, VOL. v, p. 398.
[101] *De unione*, p. 273.
[102] Grant, *Social Development*, p. 336. This contention is borne out by the spate of applications for safe-conducts; *Calendar of State Papers relating to Scotland, 1547-1603*, VOL. I, e.g. pp. 187-9.

trade which over-rode political antipathy was based in part on geographical proximity: the short and relatively safe voyage between port and port and the consequent reduction of both physical and commercial risks. But this alone would have provided a frail basis for trade had not the domestic economies of the two countries advanced at different rates and with different forms of specialisation. In most branches of industrial production the English had clearly attained a higher level of technical skill, but there were a few manufactures in which the Scots—by specialisation and low costs—could effectively compete, especially in eastern England. In a broad sense the difference in the stage of economic growth reached in the two countries is reflected in the exchange of English manufactures for those raw or near-raw materials which could be sent to London and other English coastal towns more expeditiously and probably more cheaply than from the remoter parts of England itself.

Neither the volume nor the composition of this trade can be described with complete precision until all the English Port Books have been examined and their contents analysed, an immense task which is only now beginning.[103] What follows here is based primarily on the use of sample books for the principal English ports involved in the Scottish trade; and though the conclusions reached are necessarily tentative and guarded, it becomes clear that the level of Anglo-Scottish trade was appreciably higher than has often been supposed, particularly for the years before 1603.

Fynes Moryson, writing in 1598, required only four operative words to sum up Scotland's exports to England: "Linnen cloathes, yarne and salt."[104] Twelve years earlier the townsmen of Boston in Lincolnshire had furnished a rather longer list. In the past, they said, their chief traffic had been with the Hansards and the Merchants of the Staple; "but now the trade remaining is with the Scottes, for salt principally and secondlie for fish, herynge, course dyaper, lynnen cloth, course tapistry."[105] The Boston men, though they were grinding an axe against a proposed salt monopoly, were probably justified in

---

[103] As has been done for Boston by Dr Hinton in *Boston Port Books*. There are, of course, limitations to the value of the Port Books for this purpose.

[104] Moryson, *Itinerary*, PT. III, BK. iii, p. 155.

[105] *Tudor Economic Documents*, VOL. II, p. 258.

their use of the words "salt principally" for the period in which they wrote and for the region with which they were familiar. Eastern England south of Flamborough Head, which relied almost wholly on seaborne supplies of salt to satisfy the needs of its fishing ports and its relatively populous agricultural hinterland, constituted a market into which the Scots entered as vigorous and successful competitors. Of eleven cargoes from Scotland to Hull in 1581-2,[106] seven were mainly of salt; the three cargoes to Ipswich in 1589-90[107] similarly were mainly of salt; in the early 1600's virtually every ship from Scotland to King's Lynn and Boston carried salt;[108] London in 1599-1600 received 504 weys (a wey being 40 bushels), in 1620-21 1,336 weys, and in 1625-6 575 weys.[109] With relatively few exceptions the salt was carried in Scottish vessels and was owned either by a Scottish merchant or by the master of the vessel. To the smaller English ports, especially those on the silt-ridden rivers of the Wash, typical cargoes were of the order of 16 to 18 weys; to London some were much greater, as in 1599-1600 when the *Fortune* of Kirkcaldy and the *Margaret* of Leith each carried over seventy weys.[110] As we shall see presently, it was almost normal for a salt ship to London to carry small parcels of textiles or other packaged goods.

The assertion of Lynn and Boston in the 1580's that Scottish salt sold at "half the somme" demanded by the English salt monopolists,[111] while no doubt a piece of propagandist exaggeration, indicates a high opinion of the competitive ability of the Scots; and though there were some local withdrawals, it seems that Scottish salt retained a strong position in eastern England until at least the middle decades of the seventeenth century. But further north, in Northumberland, Durham, and the North Riding, the Scottish salt exporter encountered sharply rising competition from local makers,[112] especially around Shields, where methods of production were substantially the same as those of the Forth and Fife. It is, therefore, even stronger testimony to the competitive ability of the Scots salt

---

[106] Port Books, E/190/312/6.   [107] Port Books, E/190/593/23.
[108] Port Books, E/190/433/12.
[109] Port Books, E/190/11/2, E/190/24/4, E/190/31/5.
[110] Port Books, E/190/11/2.
[111] *Tudor Economic Documents*, VOL. II, pp. 259-60.
[112] Hughes, *Studies in Administration and Finance*, p. 48.

P

exporters that so late as 1610-11 they could still penetrate the enemy territory to the extent of four cargoes to Whitby (one of them in the *Durtie Megge* of Burntisland) and one to Scarborough.[113]

But away from the ports the typical Elizabethan Englishman, if he thought of Scottish produce at all, would think of fish. Fish from Scotland, or at least fish with a name suggestive of Scotland, was kept in every well-stocked English larder. Thus in the surviving housekeeping books, from that of the Northumberlands in the very early 1500's[114] to that of Lady Penelope Spencer in 1622-7,[115] "haberdine fish" or "haberdine warps" (a couple of fish) appears with unfailing regularity as the verbal equivalent of barrelled cod.[116] Throughout our period all the three main classes of Scottish fish, cod, herring and salmon, together with occasional barrels of fish oil, were being sent south, though their relative contribution to the overall value of Scotland's exports to England almost certainly declined. In the middle decades of the sixteenth century whole shiploads of fish were fairly common: thus in 1572 John Moncur was in serious trouble at home for slipping out of the Tay with a cargo of white fish for England without either paying custom or showing a cocquet;[117] and ten years later the East Fife ports, Crail, Anstruther, and Dysart, were sending shiploads to Hull and Newcastle.[118] In the early 1600's what must have been full cargoes—77 lasts of herring in the *Hope* of Kirkcaldy and 37 lasts in the *Elizabeth* of Leith—arrived from time to time in London;[119] but generally shipments of fish to England appear after about 1600 as smallish consignments accompanying a bulk cargo of salt or coal. It would not, in fact, be a matter for surprise if Scottish fish exports to England underwent an absolute decline, for the English were vigorously expanding their own fisheries, while the remarkable increase in Scottish fish

[113] Port Books, E/190/486/10, E/190/213/5.
[114] *The Regulations and Establishments of the Household of Henry Algernon Percy, the Fifth Earl of Northumberland, Begun Anno Domini MDXII,* 1770, especially pp. 136, 427.
[115] J. N. Simpkinson, *The Washingtons,* 1860, App. III, p. xxix.
[116] The etymology here implied conflicts with that now commonly advanced in dictionaries, but Englishmen had bought cod from Aberdeen for centuries, and they often spelled the name of the town as "Haberdyne" or "Haburdyn".
[117] *R.P.C.,* VOL. II, p. 141.
[118] Port Books, E/190/312/6, E/190/185/6.
[119] Port Books, E/190/24/3.

exports to the Baltic could hardly have been possible without some diversion from other markets.

It is significant that neither of the contemporary lists of Scottish exports to England quoted at the beginning of this section included coal. But as we saw in Chapter II, by the last two decades of the sixteenth century Scottish coal-mining was entering a phase of vigorous growth, and the Scottish "great" coal—"charbon d'écosse"—was rapidly acquiring a high reputation, especially in London where its comparative cleanliness appealed to the fastidious wives of prosperous burgesses. The same qualities commended it to industrial users; indeed in the early 1600's it was commonly regarded in London as the only coal suitable for glass-making.[120] In a typical year in the later part of the reign of King James, the smaller English ports might each receive two or three cargoes of ten or twenty chaldrons (a chaldron was something like two tons); but it seems certain that London was the outstanding single market. In the London Port Books for 1620-21[121] it is possible to identify twenty-five separate cargoes of Scottish coal ranging from the 77 tons in the *Barbara* down to the 24 in the *Jacob*. All told in that year London imported 1,334 tons from Scotland, and though there were surrounding years when the total fell to as little as 500 or 600 tons, there were others, such as 1615,[122] when it rose to over 3,000.

The more strictly rural products sent to England fell into two groups: grain and skins. The grain trade presents constantly changing patterns, partly because the balance into or out of Scotland depended upon her own harvest conditions, and partly because some part of the grain appearing among Scottish exports originated in the eastern Baltic and was in fact a re-export. As we have seen, each of the three closing decades of the sixteenth century had its spell of deficient harvests and Scotland rarely had any genuine surplus of grain. Throughout 1602 and 1603 the movement of grain in Anglo-Scottish trade was towards Scotland.[123] In those years all but one of the twenty-four ships freighted out of Boston for Scotland carried either beans, peas, barley, or malt, though especially in 1602

[120] Nef, *The Rise of the British Coal Industry*, VOL. II, pp. 118-20.
[121] Port Books, E/190/24/4.
[122] Port Books, E/190/18/6.
[123] E.g. *Boston Port Books*, pp. 18-19.

the individual quantities were often small. Thenceforth in the early 1600's grain shipments to Scotland seem rarer, while in some years substantial quantities went from Scotland to England. Several cargoes of grain from Scotland arrived at Scarborough in 1610-11 and at Lynn and Yarmouth in 1611-12, and in 1614-15 two of rye arrived at Boston.[124] Over substantially the same period the run of better harvests in Scotland enabled her to aid King James in easing that chronic headache of all Tudor and Stuart governments, the feeding of London. Shipments from Scotland to London fluctuated with a general upward trend, reaching in 1625-6 a total of nearly 7,000 quarters, mainly of wheat.[125]

Though the great outlets for Scottish skins and hides were in Continental markets, a substantial demand existed in England especially for what the London customs clerks recorded as "goat-in-hair" and "kid-in-hair." In peak years such as 1621-2 up to 8,000 goat and 16,500 kid-skins were sent to London.[126] The rest went in very small lots; a few thousand raw cow hides, 170 stag hides in 1625-6, a few dozen ownce furs (wild cat?), and, in 1599-1600, 200 "red" skins. In some years, indeed, these minor groups of skins and hides were equalled in value by the traffic in feathers, which rarely, in the early 1600's, fell below a ton a year and in 1629-30 reached eight tons to London alone.[127]

Anglo-Scottish trade in raw wool demands separate consideration, not so much because of its intrinsic value in either direction as for the highly controversial atmosphere in which it was conducted. The English suspected, perhaps with justification, that Scotland was a back door through which precious English wool was surreptitiously carried to her cloth-making competitors on the Continent. "Much wool," Sir George Coppin told the English Privy Council in 1613, "is carried to Scotland and from thence to Camphire in the Lowe Countries, where there is a staple of wool."[128] This was precisely the kind of leakage the English merchants had forecast in their objections to the commercial clauses in the proposed Treaty of Union;

---

[124] Port Books, E/190/312/8, E/190/433/12, E/190/482/2.
[125] Port Books, E/190/31/5.   [126] Port Books, E/190/24/4.
[127] Port Books, E/190/34/2.
[128] Sir Julius Caesar's Notes on Privy Council Meetings, quoted in Friis, *Alderman Cockayne's Project*, p. 459.

and when the English, a few years later, reissued their periodic ban on wool exports, it is significant that they specifically included Scotland among the prohibited areas. On the Scottish side, as we saw in Chapter III, the export of wool was often subject to restriction; but peace and security, especially after 1603, promoted sheep-farming in the upland regions of the south. Indeed by about 1620 it could be confidently stated— admittedly by a representative of the landed interests—that the store of wool was "sua increased" that a surplus existed beyond all reasonable domestic requirements, and in recent years export had been resumed under licence.[129]

The English cloth-makers, still licking their wounds after the débacle of Cockayne's Patent and the slump of 1620, launched at this point an obvious attempt to secure a monopoly of Scottish wool exports. In response to this the King, in 1622, called on the Scottish Council to send representatives to London to consider "how the woll of this kingdom [Scotland] not draped and wrought at home mycht be sent to England . . . and that no exportatioun of woll frome this kingdome sal be els."[130] Considerable deliberation followed both in London and in Scotland, where the gentry and barons of the sheep-rearing shires debated the proposals with representatives of the burghs. The outcome in Scotland was almost unanimous hostility. Recent export under licence, according to the manufacturers from the burghs, had already induced a sharp rise in price, threatening unemployment to the artisan weavers, especially in the north.[131] The sheep-rearers saw straight through the English plan. If the English got their monopoly, they said, their buyers would "contemne and scorne to give pryces for our wool,"[132] our merchants and shippers would refuse to handle it at the prices offered, it would remain unsold in the farmers' storehouses, and the gentry and barons would lose their rents. Furthermore, all groups argued, if the Scots were denied the right to carry their wool to Continental markets, their purchases of iron, hemp, and the like would either be restricted or would involve the export of coin or other scarce commodities. One group of gentry, those of East Lothian,

[129] The spokesman was Sir William Seyton. *R.P.C.*, VOL. XIII, p. 774.
[130] *Op. cit.*, p. 70.
[131] *Op. cit.*, p. 218; *Convention Records*, VOL. III, p. 160.
[132] *R.P.C.*, VOL. XIII, p. 775.

suggested a compromise whereby the sale of the annual clip would be unrestricted until Michaelmas and confined to England from Michaelmas to Christmas, but the general opinion, with which the King finally agreed, was that the prime consideration should be the needs of the Scottish cloth industry itself.[133]

The debate ended on a note of anti-climax. In June 1623 the Council's representatives returned from London with the news that after several meetings with "the commissionaris on the Inglish syde" it had been agreed that the whole matter was not of sufficient importance to warrant any action.[134]

In view of the technical superiority of England in most branches of textile production, it is at first surprising to find "Linnen cloathes" and "yarne" at the head of Fynes Moryson's brief list of the goods imported from Scotland. We saw, however, in Chapter II that Scotland possessed certain relative advantages in the production of the linen fabrics and yarn, and of the wool knitted goods which formed the third main group in Scotland's textile exports to England. On such goods of relatively high intrinsic value, the additional cost of sea transport was insignificant, especially as the almost invariable practice was to send textiles in smallish lots along with bulk cargoes of coal or salt.

For the early part of our period the data are too scarce for any deduction of trends, but for the later part it looks as if yarn—variously called "linen yarn" or "Scotch yarn"—was of increasing importance, with London as the main single market. In the 1620's annual shipments to London of the order of 30,000 or 40,000 lb. were common,[135] and once, in 1620-21, the shipment was almost 73,000 lb. Linen cloth appears periodically in Scottish shipments to most English ports and regularly in those to London, and the 18,000 ells entered, without distinction of variety, in the London Port Books of 1599-1600 gives a fair impression of the overall scale of the trade at the turn of the century.[136] Ticking, the close-woven material used for mattresses and pillow-cases, features prominently whenever varieties are distinguished, and there

---

[133] Hence the decision to set up the Standing Committee on Manufactures. See above, p. 95 and *R.P.C.*, VOL. XIII, pp. 235, 773.

[134] *Op. cit.*, p. 233.   [135] Port Books, E/190/24/4, E/190/31/5, E/190/34/2.

[136] Port Books, E/190/11/3.

was obviously a widespread English demand for the coarser harden and packing canvas made either of flax or hemp.

The quantity and range of knitted stockings sent from Scotland to London, especially in the early 1600's, provides a footnote to the history of Jacobean English dress. Worsted stockings, according to the London customs clerks,[137] might be either "mens" or "womens"; the heavier "wadmoll" stockings would commend themselves to seamen; the short worsted and short wool stockings which were separately listed were presumably for children. At Leith, where many of the stockings were knitted, the customs officers, perhaps less dress-conscious, lumped the lot together as boot hose.[138]

A narrow range of other made-up textile products, generally in small parcels, appears fairly regularly: 180 "wadmoll mittens"; 21 "coverlets for bed at 8s. each"; cushions, sometimes 40 or 50 dozen a year; three or four dozen carpets. Apart from "coarse drinking glasses," manufactured goods other than these textiles rarely appear among Scotland's minor exports to England, and the catalogue is completed by a string of items many of which were clearly re-exports: tar, whale oil, deals, pipe-staves, "1400 lb. psyllium in the oil," resin, and the cargo of wine which reached Scarborough in 1582, in "Le Mychael de Wemes ab Dunde."[139]

The assumption that, in return, England should have provided Scotland with the products of her more advanced industries is, on the whole, increasingly justified as our period progresses; though even after 1600 Anglo-Scottish trade was never a simple exchange of English manufactures for Scottish raw materials and linens. In the early decades at least, coal and lead were shipped to Scotland from Newcastle;[140] in 1588 the *Eagle* carried wool and "barkit [tanned] skinnis" from London to Dundee;[141] smallish lots of skins were often brought from Boston in the early 1600's, perhaps for reshipment to the Baltic;[142] in 1613 the *Gift of God* sailed for Scotland from "ye Iyle of Wicht" with what the Scots clerk recorded as "frensche salt" but what, by its place of shipment, was more likely

---

[137] Port Books, E/190/31/5.
[138] "The Entress of the Ships, Guidis and Geir transportit at the Port of Leith, 1627-8," General Register House.
[139] Port Books, E/190/308/1.   [140] Port Books, E/190/185/6.
[141] Dundee Shipping Lists, p. 217.   [142] *Boston Port Books, passim.*

Lymington salt;[143] and in the early seventeenth century parts of south-west Scotland certainly imported English salt. The expansion of the Scottish leather-tanning industry is reflected in the imports of English oak bark, whole cargoes of it from Lynn and Newcastle;[144] in spite of English protests, small consignments of wool made their way to Scotland; and, as we have seen, there were periods in which Scotland looked to the English farmer for supplies of grain.

But taking one year with another, Scotsmen encouraged English arable farming mainly by their evident liking for English beer. The background is familiar to students of sixteenth-century England: how the brewing of beer, as distinct from ale, had developed with astonishing rapidity until, by the 1580's, London alone was producing annually something like 650,000 barrels of 36 gallons each.[145] By this time English beer was already coming to Scotland in fair quantity—it formed the bulk of the exports to Scotland from Ipswich in 1589-90[146]— and after 1600 it often constituted the entire cargo of Scotland-bound ships;[147] but in spite of this scale of shipment Scottish demand was not thoroughly sated. Whereas, said the Privy Council, the proclaimed price, allowing reasonable profit margins to all concerned, "was xviii d the pynt . . . it is of treuth that the said Englishe beir is commonlie sauld in all pairtis of the countrey for xxxii d the pynt and above."[148] Nor was the liking confined to beer. "Send," noted David Wedderburne in 1596, "with Thomas Cokburn 3 lib stirling . . . to be warit [spent] on Inglis cider."[149]

We have already seen that by the 1590's Scotland was seeking both to reduce the inflow of English cloth and to stimulate her own textile industries. English textiles continued to arrive in Scotland, but their composition—small parcels of specialised and often fairly costly goods—suggests that they were complementary to Scottish textile production rather than competitive. In the cargo lists of Scottish vessels leaving London for Scotland

[143] Dundee Shipping Lists, p. 237.
[144] E.g. Port Books, E/190/185/4, E/190/433/12; Dundee Shipping Lists, p. 239.
[145] J. U. Nef, "Industrial growth in France and England, 1540-1640," in *Journal of Political Economy*, XLIV (1936), pp. 647-8.
[146] Port Books, E/190/593/22.
[147] E.g. Dundee Shipping Lists, p. 240, which records the arrival of two such cargoes on one day.
[148] *R.P.C.*, VOL. IX, p. 508.   [149] *Wedderburne Compt Buik*, p. 71.

in the fiscal year 1611-12[150] it is possible to identify over eighty separate consignments of cloth of at least twenty-five different kinds. With fabrics with such familiar names as fustian, bayes, and cotton (not, it should be added, the pure cotton of today), the list ranges from "Holland cloth" to "Spanish satin, English making," and from "perpetuances" (a strong wool fabric) to "tamett" (a thin wool fabric). But apart from one of 1,362 goads (a goad was 1½ yards), the normal consignment of cotton cloth was never above a few hundred goads; any individual parcel of fustians of over twenty pieces was exceptional, and, among the less familiar fabrics, parcels as small as two or three pieces or of ten or twenty yards were common.

Along with hats—"lined in the head with taffeta," "plain for men," "plain for children," or merely "unfaced"—the made-up textile goods constituted a fair assortment of haberdashery. Typical items were "thrid snagg" (fringe); "falling bands for women" (collars?); hatbands, both plain and, in the *Jennet* of Kirkcaldy in 1619,[151] embroidered in gold and silver; worsted stockings, worsted garters, silk garters, "crewell" (embroidered) garters, and "gartering for children"; thread and thread buttons; gloves in variety, some fringed with silk; embroidered velvet muffs; but the total quantity shipped in any one year would not have strained the capacity of a single stock-room in modern Princes Street. Indeed Wedderburne's English trans-actions bear out the impression that haberdashery was often imported from England in response to the particular require-ments of private individuals. "Andrew Mores, maryner," he wrote, "hes promisit me a pair of sad gray wolfin shankis [stockings] worth vi lib at his returning fra London this present voage"; "Johne Barry agreit that . . . at his first hamecuming from Ingland he suld gif me a hatt and a string of crep worth 12 s sterling"; while he authorised Peter Man, if he was in England, to spend certain money on "lynt hattis with veluit about the browis and 2 stikis [pieces] fusteonis of trym cullouris."[152]

It seems clear also that as time passed and Anglo-Scottish contacts became more intimate some of the Scottish demand for miscellaneous manufactured goods, which hitherto had been

[150] Port Books, E/190/16/2.   [151] Port Books, E/190/22/9.
[152] *Wedderburne Compt Buik*, pp. 135, 140, 162.

focused on north France and the Low Countries, was transferred to England and especially to London. On board the typical Scots vessel leaving London for Leith in the generation after 1603 there would be, in addition to the kind of textile wares just described, an even more varied assortment of what the Scottish customs clerks entered in "drywair geir." In the *Gift of God* in 1619 there were two gross of bowstrings, a mixed lot of harness and bits, three pairs of tailor's shears, two gross of tobacco pipes, four hour glasses, four small lanterns, 4,000 iron tacks, 2,000 nails, ten dozen hinges, a dozen padlocks, a few horn cups, some jugs and drinking-glasses, and ten "small beard brushes." From other cargo lists of the same period the catalogue can be extended to include a dozen small Bibles, two virginals, horn books, tobacco pipe cases, spectacles and spectacle cases (but not in the same ship), English knives, foreign sword blades and handles (but again in different ships), and enough pins to set a Scottish economist thinking about the problems of division of labour.[153] The list could be prolonged, but the only hardware items which, individually, occupied any considerable ship space were barrel hoops— roughly 30,000 of them were sent from London in 1611-12— and wrought pewter which was being shipped in lots of up to half a ton a time.[154]

While it is true that the pattern of Anglo-Scottish trade underwent no immediate dramatic upheaval after 1603,[155] it is apparent that changes in its composition were afoot and fresh influences can be detected. The ending of the old hostility created an environment more favourable to continuous trading; the changing character of her domestic economy enabled Scotland to compete effectively in supplying the English with a narrow range of raw or near-raw goods and with coarse textile products; and, thirdly, the increasing hindrances encountered by Scottish traders in some of their traditional French markets prompted them to transfer more of their energies to England. The behaviour of Scottish trade at individual English ports is perplexing enough, and anything like an overall determination of changes in value or volume is all but

---

[153] Port Books, E/190/22/9. Sample cargo lists are printed in Friis, *Alderman Cockayne's Project*, pp. 452-3.
[154] Port Books, E/190/16/2, E/190/22/9.
[155] Keith, *Commercial Relations of England and Scotland, 1603-1707*, p. 32.

impossible. At Boston, for example, in some years in the 1580's more than twenty ships arrived with cargoes from Scotland,[156] from 1602 to 1618 the normal figure was between ten and sixteen, but after 1627, when the Boston Port Books resume after a nine-year gap, anything more than a single ship a year was exceptional.[157] Similarly at Hull and Lynn the number of arrivals in a typical year around 1600 was appreciably lower than it had been twenty years earlier, though individual ships may have been of greater capacity.[158] The hypothesis can be advanced that at ports where the foundation of the trade was Scottish fish or salt, there was a likelihood of stagnation or even decline as English domestic production rose or as Scotsmen found it more profitable to sell elsewhere; but where, above all at London, these old staples of Scottish trade were increasingly overshadowed by linen yarn, cloth, and coal, the value and probably the volume of Scottish trade reflected the rising tempo of Scottish economic activity in the later years of James VI. Considered therefore in narrow commercial terms, the Union of the Crowns seems important only in so far as it marked a stage in the ending of the old hostility and in the clearing of the field for the fuller development of Scottish economic potentiality.

The strong association between this English trade and the extractive and manufacturing industries of east-central Scotland is closely reflected in the geographical distribution of the Scottish ports mainly involved. In the surviving English customs accounts for the first two decades of our period the shipping from Scotland is nearly all "of" or "from" Kirkcaldy, Dysart, Crail, Bo'ness, or some other of the neighbouring East Fife-Forth ports, with occasional entries of or from Dundee or Leith.[159] In the trade with English eastern provincial ports the pattern underwent no substantial change. In times of southward grain shipment, as in 1612, an occasional vessel was freighted out of Aberdeen or Montrose,[160] but the regular traffic in coal, salt, and flax products was regularly— and naturally—handled by merchants and skippers of the producing areas, especially by those of Kirkcaldy whose vessels

---

[156] Port Books, E/190/390/15.   [157] *Boston Port Books, passim.*
[158] Cf. Port Books, E/190/308/1, E/190/312/6.
[159] E.g. Customs Accounts 101/9 (Lynn) and 13/15 (Boston), MS in Public Record Office.
[160] E.g. arrivals at Yarmouth, Port Books E/190/484/2.

in some years virtually monopolised Scottish trade with the ports around the Wash.[161] The same place-names appear regularly at London, though there the dominance of the smaller Scottish ports was challenged by Leith, whence, by the end of our period, roughly three departures out of every eight were for London.[162]

By contrast, the evidence of Anglo-Scottish trade along the west coasts is mainly of occasional shipments. It is plain from the history of her medieval commerce that Bristol, the trading metropolis of south-western England, had no tradition of direct dealings with Scotsmen.[163] Welshmen and Irishmen were more accessible, and no doubt more amenable, as suppliers of the animal products and the fish which might have been obtained from Scotland: it is significant that in the early 1600's, when the normal trade between Bristol and Scotland never required more than an occasional ship each year, arrivals from Ireland were sometimes as high as eighty or ninety.[164] The same pattern of small-scale irregular trade is suggested by scattered references to Scottish ships at Dartmouth, Plymouth, and elsewhere in south-west England and Wales; and it was only in the 1620's that the occasional Glasgow ship began to appear in the Thames.[165]

It looks as if Bristol's complaint in 1619 about the extent to which her trade had fallen into the hands of Dutch and Scottish shipping is probably more indicative of the mental depression through which her burgesses were passing than of the true extent of Scottish competition.[166] Nevertheless the Bristol complaint involved arguments which had become widely accepted in England. In our examination of the commercial negotiations after 1603 we found that Englishmen believed that any concessions to the Scots would strengthen their already formidable capacity to compete in the carrying trades between England and foreign countries. The existing participation,

---

[161] *Boston Port Books, passim*; Port Books, E/190/425/5.

[162] "The Entress of the Ships, Guidis and Geir transportit at the Port of Leith, 1627-8," General Register House; Port Books E/190/16/2.

[163] E. M. Carus-Wilson, *The Overseas Trade of Bristol in the late Middle Ages*, Bristol Record Society, VOL. VII, 1937.

[164] Port Books, E/1134/7, E/190/1134/11; P. McGrath, *Merchants and Merchandise in Seventeenth-Century Bristol*, Bristol Record Society, VOL. XIX, 1955, pp. 279-80.

[165] Port Books, E/190/31/5.

[166] G. D. Ramsay, *English Overseas Trade*, 1957, p. 137.

they said, was the thin end of a dangerous wedge. The data available from the English Port Books examined in the preparation of this chapter enable us to estimate approximately how deeply the wedge had in fact been driven during the decades around the time of the Union negotiations.

If, as the English maintained, the Scots could offer low freight rates, then presumably their competition would be most effective in the handling of cargoes of low intrinsic value: coal, timber, and similar bulky goods. In typical years in the closing decades of the sixteenth century thirty or more Scots vessels loaded coal at Newcastle, some invariably bound for the Continent, a few proceeding coast-wise to other English ports.[167] In exceptional instances Scotsmen rather than Scots vessels participated in the timber trade. In 1604 the *Swan* of Bergen, her skipper Thomas Thompson of Kirkcaldy, arrived at Boston with a cargo of Norwegian deals belonging to Archibald Webster of Dysart.[168] But normally at Boston—which seems in this respect to have been reasonably typical of English provincial ports—Scots skippers carried timber in Scots ships, either on their own behalf or on behalf of local English merchants. Thus the *Mary Katherine* of Kirkcaldy arrived from Marienburg with deals belonging to her master, Walter Williamson, while another Scottish master in the *James* of St Andrews brought a cargo of timber from Norway for Isabel Foxley, a member of a well-established Boston merchant family.[169]

Scottish intervention, however, cut across the entire range of English trade with the Continent. In 1611-12 a dozen Scots vessels entered Yarmouth from France, Norway, and the Low Countries, their cargoes made up of salt, wine, timber, cloth, spices, and dried fruit, and in the same fiscal year three left Yarmouth with fish and cloth for La Rochelle and the Mediterranean.[170] About the same period George Balcanquell with the *Bruce* of Kirkcaldy was a regular trader at Boston.[171] In 1610 he left in April and September with cargoes of cloth, returning in July from the Baltic with rye, flax, and iron, and in November from France with vinegar and prunes. The

[167] E.g. Port Books, E/190/185/6, E/190/308/1.
[168] *Boston Port Books*, pp. xxii, 32.   [169] *Op. cit.*, p. xliv.
[170] Port Books, E/190/484/2.   [171] *Boston Port Books*, pp. xlv, 42-3.

year following he left Boston again in April for Elbing with cloth and skins belonging to Matthew Foxley, returning at the end of July with rye, flax, pitch, and glass for the same merchant. On occasions political relationships made it expedient for the English to employ Scottish shipping. In our study of trade with Spain we saw how, in the troubled days of the Spanish Armada, Scotsmen were used to penetrate the Spanish embargo on English imports. Similarly the greater affability of the French towards the Scots provides an obvious explanation of the English willingness to employ them in Anglo-French trade. In 1611-12, for example, Scottish vessels brought two cargoes of Bordeaux wine to Yarmouth,[172] two to Lynn,[173] and one to Boston, and it is significant that even after the outbreak of Anglo-French hostilities in the mid-1620's an occasional Scottish ship still carried French goods to London.[174]

Measured against the great bulk of shipping passing between England and the Continent, the extent of this Scottish participation was small, and there is no indication that it increased materially after 1603. None the less in the context of the Scottish economy the earnings of even a handful of ships could constitute an important item of income. The composition of this income can be deduced from the trading activities of John Black in the *Temperance* of Anstruther, who spent much of 1602 and 1603 in running between Boston and Bordeaux and who, in February 1603, shipped 200 quarters of malt and beans on his own behalf from Boston to Leith.[175] The implication is that his earnings were thus sent to Scotland in kind, and if we make the reasonable assumption that a dozen or twenty ships and crews were regularly employed in this way, their total earnings must have added substantially to the credit side of Scotland's trading account. But any participation of outsiders in their carrying trade was an affront to those English mercantilists who—like the Eastland merchants in 1622—were opposed to "shipping any commodities in strangers' bottoms, either into this kingdom, or out of the same."[176] There is some evidence of heavily-conditioned concessions to Scottish

[172] Port Books, E/190/484/2.   [173] Port Books, E/190/433/12.
[174] Port Books, E/190/34/2.
[175] *Boston Port Books*, p. 18.
[176] Printed in Hinton, *The Eastland Trade and the Common Weal in the Seventeenth Century*, p. 175.

carriers in the 1620's,[177] but on the whole it was no consolation to the shipowner of Hull or Bristol to be told that his competitor shared allegiance to a common monarchy, for the accomplishment of union was too recent and the tradition of hostility too strong for either English or Scots to recognise the existence of mutual economic interests.

"That which," said James VI in a wave of optimism, "hath been sought so much, and so long, and so often, by Blood, and by Fire, and by the Sword, now is brought and wrought by the Hand of God, and to be embraced and received with an Hallalujah."[178] The Conference of 1604 was wiser: full reciprocity between the nations, it believed, might have to be delayed "untill tyme and conversation have increased and accomplished an Union . . . in the hartes of all the people."[179] A century later a Scot could write of "this loose and irregular tye of the Union of the Crowns, a state wherein we are not considered as Subjects nor allies, nor Friends nor Enemies, but all of them, only when, where, how and how long our Task Master please."[180] This was a hard judgment, passed in a moment of deep bitterness for Scotsmen, but, shorn of its polemical overtone, it summarises their attitude to the working of the compromise of 1603.

[177] Friis, *Alderman Cockayne's Project and the Cloth Trade*, p. 190.
[178] *Commons Journal*, p. 315.
[179] *Edinburgh Records*, VOL. VI, App. III.
[180] "Proposals and Reasons for constituting a Council of Trade, 1701," British Museum, MS 1029 a.6 (i).

VIII

TRADE WITH THE LOW COUNTRIES

In each period of history some region has seemed to epitomise the highest qualities in economic skill and enterprise, so constituting a hub around which the commercial history of the period can be written. For the sixteenth and early seventeenth centuries the Low Countries clearly occupy this nodal position. If we consider the great branches of commerce—the Baltic grain trade, the English cloth trade, the Biscay salt trade—the technical and financial expertise of the Low Countries is the factor common to all. The dominance is all the more remarkable when we recall the grim and bloody process by which the Dutch tore themselves free from the Spanish Empire, taking with them into their independent United Provinces the torch of economic leadership which hitherto had burned in Antwerp. Here, in the new state of Holland, lay one of the great control panels of the European economy: a complex of unique contacts, unique financial mechanisms, and technical skill—in some industries at least—unsurpassed in the world.

Close contacts between Scotland and Flanders go back to the earliest days of Scottish town life, when Flemings seem to have served as a catalyst in the process whereby the burghs acquired self-conscious independence. In the Low Countries, Scotsmen were generally well received, for the willingness to be everything to all men was one of the qualities on which both Flemings and Dutchmen built their commercial success. It is true that the Scots possessed but limited purchasing power and offered a limited range of national products; yet among those products were skins, wool, fish, salt, and coal, commodities which could always be handled with profit because they were necessities for which the demand was relatively rigid. The rivalry among the towns of the Low Countries for the privilege of handling the Scottish staple trades indicates the value they set upon this narrow range of goods, and the sixteenth-century Dutch coastal silhouettes of the Forth now preserved in the Maritime Museum at Amsterdam reveal their makers' interest in the main outlet of Scottish exports. Trade with the Low Countries was highly attractive to Scotsmen: a skipper returning to his native Fife could scarcely fail to impress as he described "a general Sea-land: the great Bog of Europe," and recounted—with advantages—how he had bargained with the Dutch on the quay at Middleburg or how he had argued theology in the Conciergery House at Veere. To go to the Low Countries was to go to the emporium of Western Europe: the best products of skill and ingenuity and of art were all there. Furthermore the Dutch could make payment in a currency which kept its value and which was acceptable everywhere.

This mutually advantageous intercourse was neither established nor sustained without serious hindrances, springing in part from the political vicissitudes of the Low Countries themselves. In about 1545, says Lesley, "the king of Ingland throuch fraude, requeist and rewarde, put sik a mynd and intent in thame of fflandiris, that thay ouirthrew . . . xvi scotis shipis," and, "fra this furth at ane tyme we had with Inglis and flandiris baith at anes weiris."[1] In this phase of alliance between the English and Charles V, the overlord of the Low Countries, Scotsmen were engaged in seemingly continuous privateering activities against both Dutch and Flemings, for the "Remonstrance made to the Count of Arran [Regent of Scotland] of the extortions, captures . . . effected on the subjects of His Majesty by the Scots"[2] details fifteen assaults in 1545-6 at points from Norway right down to Biscay. The ending of this hostility, which so seriously imperilled the whole future of Scottish overseas trade, was the subject of rejoicing in both territories in 1550. After a visit to London the Scots envoys, Lord Erskine and Henry Sinclair, sailed to Flanders, "the bande of peace with thame tha mak to the Joy of baith the natiounis";[3] and the first Scots merchant crew to arrive thereafter at Veere, "Jan Fodregem, skipper of Dundee, and

---

[1] Lesley, *Historie*, VOL. II, p. 287.
[2] *Bronnen Tot de Geschiedenis van den Handel met Engeland, Schotland en Ierland,* henceforth cited as *Handel met Engeland,* ed. H. J. Smit, The Hague 1928, VOL. I, No. 788.
[3] Lesley, *Historie*, VOL. II, p. 332.

Q

his companions,"[4] were feted by the townsmen as the harbingers of better times.

The rejoicing was premature, for during the following generation Scottish trade with the Low Countries was liable to dislocation by the internal strife there, especially in the period when the Dutch aspirations to freedom burst into open conflict with their Habsburg overlords. The proceedings of the Convention of Royal Burghs, especially in the mid 1570's, repeatedly reflect "the troubilism estait in Flanderis."[5] The Scottish trading base had "bene removit to syndrie places . . . throwe the occasion of the civill tumultis, quhair wyth the maist pairte off Flanderis hes bene . . . occupiet to the hurt of mony"; so much so in fact that in 1574 the Convention contemplated the complete removal of its commercial representative from the Low Countries to Calais until the fighting was over.[6]

The fixed base, and the organisation that went with it, distinguishes this branch of Scottish trade from all others; for in spite of the existence of colonies of Scotsmen and the concentration of Scots trade in towns such as Danzig and Bordeaux, there was nothing in the world quite comparable to the Scottish Staple in the Netherlands. As three classic studies of the Staple exist,[7] a lengthy survey of its constitution and functions would be redundant, though the brevity of treatment here must not be taken as any measure of the importance of the Staple in Scottish relations with the Low Countries. The attempt to channel Scottish trade through a single town in the Low Countries and the appointment of a Conservator—or agent—to serve there, long precede the beginning of our period, though in the early days the arrangements were generally less formal and certainly less stable than they became after the 1570's. Thus in the early fifteenth century Bruges was the recognised focal point for Scottish trade, but by the end of that century Bruges was in decline, and Andrew Haly-

---

[4] *Handel met Engeland*, VOL. I, No. 856.
[5] *Convention Records*, VOL. I, pp. 21, 38-9: Pagan, *The Convention of the Royal Burghs*, pp. 161 ff.
[6] *Convention Records*, VOL. I, p. 26.
[7] James Yair, *Account of the Scotch Trade in the Netherlands*; Davidson and Gray, *The Scottish Staple at Veere*; M. P. Rooseboom, *The Scottish Staple in the Netherlands*, The Hague 1910. The following three paragraphs are based almost wholly on these books.

burton, the Conservator from 1492 to 1503, seems to have operated mainly in Middleburg. At all events Middleburg, Antwerp, and Campvere (Veere to contemporaries) were competing in the early 1500's with gifts and promises for the possession of the Scottish Staple. After a period of shifts, it was fixed in 1541 at Veere where, apart from the breaks in the 1570's, it remained for two and a half centuries.

The Scottish Staple bore only a superficial resemblance to the English one. While there was always some royal interference, the management of the Scottish Staple was in general the responsibility of the Convention of Royal Burghs. Its local chief officer, the Conservator, administered its affairs in the Low Countries and acted there as both consul and commercial agent, and, in the Conciergery House at Veere, he maintained a hostel and social centre for visiting and resident Scots. His concern was with both commerce and conduct. Thus, under a royal decree of 1532, no ship was to break bulk in Flanders until the merchants had "consulted with the Conservator how the market is." He was, under the instruction of the Convention in 1575, to "suffer no manner of persons to haunt nor to use the trade of merchandise . . . but such as are free merchants known to him, of fame and honesty, and bringing with them the testimonial of their freedom." He was to uphold the fair name of his countrymen and to keep the peace among them; so, for example, "giff they call any ane uther ane knaif or lowne . . . or else gif ane uther ane cuf on the halfit [side of the head], they sall pay ane pund Fleymes."[8]

The central function of the Staple—the canalising of Scotland's "staple" exports—fulfilled two purposes. As we saw in Chapter III, customs duties in Scotland were, until 1597, confined to these staple exports, and the canalisation obviously simplified collection. Secondly, the existence of the Staple meant that in this important branch of foreign trade supervision could be exercised at both ends, and consequently the monopoly of the free burgesses of the Royal Burghs could be the more easily upheld. Though this canalisation was never complete, the Staple none the less represented a considerable limitation on the freedom of trade even of a burgess with the

[8] *Convention Records*, VOL. I, pp. 40, 51-2, 59, 62; Yair, *Account of the Scotch Trade in the Netherlands*, p. 145.

certificate of Edinburgh or Dundee in his satchel. On the other hand it conferred substantial benefits. Unlike the English Merchant Adventurer, the Scottish trader in the Low Countries was never subject to a "stint" or any similar limit to the volume of his trade. He approached Veere in complete confidence, knowing that under agreements with the local rulers there his vessel would be piloted and docked, and his cargo unloaded and warehoused at fixed charges. The Conservator and the local factors would advise on the marketing of his goods, his own chaplain would minister to his spiritual needs, and, in the Conciergery House, he could drink his fill of duty-free wine and beer. Smallegange, describing Veere in the early seventeenth century, believed that the benefits of the Staple were shared between the Scots and the townsmen. "The Scottish nation," he wrote, "increased daily, and selling their goods to the best advantage, they grow richer and more flourishing. Campvere, on the other hand, loses nothing by the bargain."[9] By 1609, when Grimeston published his translation of a recent French work on the Low Countries, it had become a "good sea towne, one of the four of the Island of Walcheren," famous to contemporaries for its support of the reformed religion and for the exploits of its "brave captaines" against the "mightie Spanish fleete."[10]

In the broad context of European affairs, the Staple at Veere symbolised the strength of the mutual interests of Scotland and the Netherlands. As time passed the bonds increased, so that, by the late 1500's, they were just as evident in ecclesiastical relations as in the military support given by the Scots Brigade to the struggle for Dutch independence.[11] But behind all these developments lay the basic cause, the complementary nature of the economies of the two countries. The pattern of trade, which persisted virtually unchanged from the Middle Ages, was determined by Scotland's capacity to supply primary goods and her anxiety to obtain the manufactures and the exotic wares which the Low Countries could either produce or obtain.

When Guicciardini wrote his account of the economic life of

[9] Quoted in Yair, op. cit., p. 216.
[10] E. Grimstone, The Low Country Commonwealth, 1609, p. 165.
[11] Papers Illustrating the History of the Scots Brigade in the Netherlands, 1572-1679, VOL. I, 1899.

Antwerp (*c.* 1560), the focus of Scottish commercial activity in the Low Countries was already passing to Veere, but none the less his short paragraph on trade with Scotland immediately illustrates this basic pattern. "From Scotland," he says, "we are provided with a great number of sheep- and rabbitskins as well as other kinds of fine pelts, and above all of the most beautiful martens. We also import a goodly number of hides, some wool and cloth, but the latter is badly made; beautiful large pearls, though neither so clear and white nor of such price and worth as those of the Orient. We send hardly anything important there, as much because the Scots are poor as because they satisfy their requirements in France and England; however we send them various spices, sugars and madder, silken cloths, all sorts of camlet [a type of cloth], serge made in various ways, linen-cloth and mercery."[12]

Guicciardini's tone is clearly disparaging; he saw Scotland as a very minor participant in the activities of what was then the trading metropolis of the western world. In the Scottish perspective the trade with the Low Countries acquired a vastly different scale. When Fynes Moryson described Scots trade in 1598 he listed "Camphire in Zetland" as the first of the four places with which the Scots had their "cheefe trafficke."[13] Thither, he said, "they carry salt, the skinnes of weathers, otters, badgers and martens." The priority he gave to salt is a reminder that, as the reign of James VI went on, the composition of Scotland's exports to the Low Countries was widened by the products of the Scottish extractive industries. Thus while the toll tables, agreed between the Scots and the town authorities at Veere in 1578 and 1613, provided for Scottish exports of cloth, wool, fish and oil, beef and grain, as well as the usual assortment of skins, the Conservator's return of the duties he collected in 1626 makes it clear that by then coal was prominent among Dutch purchases from Scotland.[14]

It appears, therefore, that the primary products formed the permanent mainstay of Scottish exports to the Low Countries, and in the later decades of our period these fell into three well-

---

[12] *Tudor Economic Documents*, VOL. III, p. 168.
[13] Moryson, *Itinerary*, PT. III, BK. iii, p. 155.
[14] Rooseboom, *The Scottish Staple in the Netherlands*, Nos. 84, 112, 119.

defined groups: products of animals, notably skins, hides and wool; products of the sea and the rivers, notably herring and salmon; products of the earth, notably coal. Of semi-manufactured goods salt occurs increasingly, and metals, especially lead, occasionally. Among manufactured goods, cloth, yarn, and hose are the only significant items. Here, as in other branches of Scottish commerce, individual mixed cargoes often reflected the composition of the trade as a whole. Thus in 1551 a Scots skipper, John Forthringham, arrived in Flanders with 8,950 sheepskins, 1,800 footfells, 1,000 lambskins, 63 dakers of hides (a daker was 10 units), 16 dakers of hart hides, 325 ells of "northlands" cloth, 25 ells of kersey, 15½ barrels of salmon, and 2 barrels of flesh.[15] For a second example we move on nine years to the reports made by Richard Paine to Sir Thomas Gresham on the arrival of Scots ships at Middleburg. "There be 2 schyppys," he writes, "come from Harburdyn Laden with salt, samon, skynnis, hydes and some clothis, kerseys owt of Skotland,"[16] and later in the same year he reports a Dutch "fisherboat" with five lasts of Scottish salmon, hides, fells, and "churchlead" from "Brownt Island."[17]

The prominence of these exports of primary goods directly reflects the strength of Scotland's domestic economy. On the other hand it is at first sight surprising that the Scots could sell textiles in what must have been a highly competitive market served by all Europe's leading manufacturers. Though the customs officers were lamentably sparing in detail, it can be deduced that the Scottish textile exports consisted mainly of plaiding and other wool cloth; linen, hodden and harden; linen and wool yarn; and woollen hose. In the making of plain cloth the low standard of living and the low raw material costs of the Scottish domestic or gild producers would balance, perhaps even outweigh, the greater technical efficiency and superior organisation of the more advanced cloth-making countries. Similarly it was low-cost production which enabled woollen stockings, notably those which the customs officers called "wollen hois maid in Leith Wynd,"[18] to be shipped in

[15] *Handel met Engeland*, VOL. I, No. 877.
[16] *Calendar of State Papers, Foreign Series, of the Reign of Elizabeth*, VOL. III, p. 123.
[17] *Op. cit.*, p. 157.
[18] This expression is used in the Customs Books and in The Book of Rates of 1612.

prodigious quantities to Dutch and Flemish markets in the early 1600's.

In studying the evolution of the Scottish economy, however, interest should be focused less on these routine exports, and more on two items which were gaining in relative importance. We have seen elsewhere how, by the closing decades of the sixteenth century, coal was acquiring a new significance in the Scottish economy. The political influence of the mine-owners enabled them to overcome the official objections to exports;[19] the English policy of imposing duties on exported coal tended to divert foreign customers to Scotland;[20] the coastal location of the Fife and Forth fields was particularly fortunate for shipment across the North Sea.

The employment of stone from Longannet Quarry in Fife for building work in Amsterdam[21] provides another clue to the increasing sale of coal to Dutchmen; for coal, equally scarce in Holland, could equally well be taken aboard as ballast, and it is likely that Scots mine-owners thus secured very favourable freights in outgoing Dutch ships. Furthermore their production costs in Scotland were relatively low, so that, as Professor Nef says, "in parts of Holland, Flanders, and Northern France, Scotch coal could apparently undersell Belgian, and, after the high export tax was imposed in 1599, English coal."[22] It is not surprising, then, to find that in a single year in the mid-1620's, fifty cargoes of Scottish coal were entered at Veere alone;[23] and there is no reason to suppose that these represented more than a part of the total sales to the Dutch. But the real significance of these sales lies not so much in mere quantity as in the manner in which the trade was conducted, and in particular in the willingness of the Dutch to send vessels to buy coal at Scots ports on a cash and carry basis. In the years about 1620, for example, there were loud complaints that while coal was virtually unobtainable not only in Angus and Kincardineshire but even in the Forth valley, scores of Dutch ships were queueing in the Forth waiting their turn to load.[24] The ex-

---

[19] See above, pp. 49, 85.
[20] Nef, *Rise of the British Coal Industry*, VOL. II, p. 223.
[21] R. Noad, "The influence of the Low Countries on the architecture of Scotland," in *Quarterly of the Incorporation of Architects in Scotland*, No. 28 (1928), p. 101.
[22] Nef, *Rise of the British Coal Industry*, VOL. I, p. 114.
[23] Rooseboom, *Scottish Staple in the Netherlands*, No. 119.
[24] *R.P.C.*, VOL. XII, pp. 605 and 645.

planation is simple. The Dutchmen were prepared to pay cash, good stable riksdollars, currency which was acceptable as widely as the markets they themselves served. The coal might go anywhere from Iberia to the east Baltic. Thus in the 1580's Pieter Cornelisz, a skipper of the great Delft firm of van Adrichem, was taking Scottish coal to Portugal,[25] and in some years in the early 1600's a big part of the total coal imports into the Baltic went from Scotland in Dutch ships.[26] It is little wonder that Dysart was popularly called "Little Holland."[27]

In this fashion coal contributed directly to the strength of Scotland's exports and her ability to earn foreign currency. The indirect contribution, in the making of salt for export, was scarcely less important. There were periods when salt exports were officially banned or restricted, but normally the structure of the industry resulted in a more or less rigid division of the product between the home and overseas markets. The proprietors habitually amassed their share of the salt in warehouses —locally "garnels"—where it awaited shipment either south to England or east to the Continent.[28] Any North Sea salt producer inevitably attracted the Dutch, for apart from the enormous demand created by their own fisheries, their grip on Baltic grain exports (and hence the dominance of Amsterdam in the European grain market) depended in large measure on their capacity to carry salt to Danzig and Königsberg. Not surprisingly, therefore, as their main supply from the Biscay coastlands became less dependable and more expensive, they sought alternatives elsewhere, and by the mid-1630's Brereton could write of the Scottish pans between Musselburgh and Stirling that "the greatest part of the salt here made is transported to Holland."[29]

The credit side of Scotland's trading balance with the Low Countries was completed by some imponderable, though certainly small items of income. From 1572 onwards Scottish mercenaries were earning their pay as members of the Scots Brigade in Holland.[30] Two benefactions to Stirling, one from

---

[25] Christensen, *Dutch Trade to the Baltic about 1600*, p. 248.
[26] See above, p. 160.
[27] A. S. Cunningham, *Mining in the Kingdom of Fife*, 1913, p. 38.
[28] The classic account of the structure of the industry is in T. Tucker, "Report."
[29] Brereton, *Travels*, VOL. I, p. 112.
[30] Details of pay and allowances can be found in *Papers Illustrating the History of the Scots Brigade in the Netherlands, 1572-1679*, VOL. I, *passim*.

the Colonel of the Brigade, William Edmond, the other from "Charles Scherar, induellar at Dort,"[31] illustrate the patriotic generosity of expatriates; and it seems reasonable to suppose that such remittances from Scots abroad would exceed the surplus earnings of the few Dutch and Flemish craftsmen working in Scotland. On the other hand the earnings of Scottish ships working under charter for Dutchmen or carrying grain from the Baltic to Holland would almost certainly be outweighed by payments to Dutchmen for similar services to Scotland. In 1561 the Lord High Treasurer authorised the settlement of an account from two Dutchmen for the conveyance of the Queen's horses, mules, servants, and equipment from France to Scotland,[32] and Dutch vessels periodically carried normal commercial cargoes at the expense of Scotsmen.[33] The Notarial Archives at Amsterdam and elsewhere contain a good many instances of the hiring of Dutch vessels by Scotsmen such as Robert Monteith, merchant of Edinburgh, who in 1609 paid 2,900 guilders as the charter price of a ship to carry timber to the Thames.[34] Furthermore Scotsmen periodically incurred charges for technical services in the Low Countries. When the "brazen cok" on the steeple of St Nicholas at Aberdeen became shabby, he was sent to Flanders to be "mendit and owergilt."[35] In 1591, when David Wedderburne's sand glass was broken (no doubt his eighteen-month-old daughter Helen had knocked it over), he sent it with John Ogilvy to Flanders to have a new glass installed.[36] When James Bell went from Glasgow to Holland in 1622, his various commissions included the adjustment of three pairs of scales.[37] At a guess we might assume that the balance on invisible items was against Scotland.

Craftsmanship is the common characteristic of the first group of Scottish imports from the Low Countries. "Soli Deo Gloria: Ian Burgerhuys me Fecit, 1610"; "In the year of grace, 1594, Marcus Knox, a merchant in Glasgow, zealous for the interest

---

[31] Morris, *The Stirling Merchant Gild*, p. 236.
[32] *Accounts of Lord High Treasurer*, VOL. XI, p. 436.
[33] E.g. Dundee Shipping Lists, p. 301.
[34] Gemeente-Archief, Amsterdam, Nos. 114, 115. I am indebted to Mr G. J. Eltringham of the University of Nottingham for supplying me with a note of this entry.
[35] *Aberdeen Council Register*, VOL. II, p. 284.
[36] *Wedderburne Compt Buik*, p. 166.   [37] Bell Notebook.

of the reformed religion, caused me to be fabricated in Holland";
thus church bells, small and great, recite the story of their
birth.[38] The Burgerhuys at Middleburg almost certainly
provided more bells to Scotland than any other contemporary
founders; at least seven were supplied by the first Jan Burgerhuy
(*d.* 1617), and four years after his death the Edinburgh Gildry
paid £1,443. 15*s*. 0*d*. Scots for "thrie bellis that came from
Middleburgh," two of them for the "greit kirk stepill" and the
third for the "Netherbow stepill."[39] Smaller items of Dutch or
Flemish make were entered, no doubt with pride, in the
inventories of private citizens. The Parson of Stobo had "1
dosane of fyne grete cuschingis of Flanderis werk";[40] Colin
Campbell of Glenorchy had "of Holland scheittes ii pair, quhair
of i pair schewit with holie work";[41] and David Wedderburne
in 1598 devoted two pages to a catalogue of "Flanderis waring"
which included silks and velvets, hats, plates, pestles and
mortars, waterpots, and candlesticks.[42] Stowed in one corner
of a "Hollander" ship discharging in the Forth in 1619 were
"little drums for bairns, xii pieces."[43] James Bell's purchases
in Holland in 1621-2 read like the stock-sheet of a Highland
shopkeeper: pins, scissors, sad irons, frying pans, kirk stools,
hammers, textile equipment, candles, ribbon, fringes, and a
whole assortment of dried fruit and spices.[44]

"Groceries," in fact, would be the most apt heading for the
second group of imports from this source. Because of their
dominance over the finance and transport of the European
grain trade, the Low Countries could sometimes help Scotland
a little when her own crops failed; but the regular purchases
were more in the nature of supplements to the staple foods. In
part they were the products of the horticulture in which the
Low Countries were already skilled; in part the exotic, sometimes tropical, products which passed more and more through
the hands of Dutch merchant houses. So the *Fleece*, putting to

[38] R. W. M. Clouston, "The Church bells of Renfrew and Dunbartonshire,"
in *P.S.A.S.*, LXXXII (1947-8), and "The Church and other bells of Stirlingshire," in
P.S.A.S., LXXXIV (1949-50); A. Montgomerie, "The bells of Haddington," in
Transactions of the East Lothian Antiquarian Society, VII (1958).
[39] *Edinburgh Records*, VOL. VI, App. XXX.
[40] Quoted in Warrack, *Domestic Life in Scotland*, p. 53.
[41] Quoted in Innes, *Sketches of Early Scotch History*, p. 510.
[42] *Wedderburne Compt Buik*, pp. 120-21.
[43] *Ledger of Andrew Halyburton*, p. xcviii.
[44] Bell Notebook.

sea from Veere for Scotland in the early part of 1558, had on board wine, figs, raisins, onions, saffron, pears, and soap.[45] Wedderburne bought sugar, "confettis," "sucher candee," onions, and apples; Bell bought raisins, figs, walnuts, barley sugar, and tobacco. In this catalogue of groceries, onions, soap, and apples were, from the point of view of the national economy, the items of greatest value. Whole cargoes of onions arrived at Scottish ports from the Low Countries,[46] to appear, in due course, on the tables of lairds and burgesses in dishes like "smothered rabbit" in which the usual numerical ratio between onions and rabbits was of the order of eighteen to one. Apples were already held in high esteem in Flanders, otherwise the painter Memling would scarcely have made his angels offer them to the infant Christ; and, like onions, they were imported to Scotland in relatively large quantities in an attempt to infuse variety and piquancy into an otherwise stodgy diet.[47]

Finally the Low Countries furnished some part of Scotland's needs in such industrial raw materials as hemp and dyestuffs, especially madder. The quantities, compared with those from other sources, were seldom great; indeed the mere fact that these materials feature at all in this trade demonstrates still further the remarkable entrepôt function of the Dutch and Flemish ports. Quite evidently in the mind of the Scotsmen of our period the Low Countries were the emporium of the western world. Some things might be cheaper elsewhere, but nowhere was the same range available.

To enter so attractive a market, Scots merchants and skippers from the Clyde and south-west ports were prepared to make a long voyage through English-dominated waters. From "Jeens Willz" of Glasgow, who was at Middleburg in 1552,[48] to James Bell who sailed from Dumbarton to Holland in 1621, their activities can be traced in Dutch and Scottish port records. But they were never numerous, for most of the trade with the Low Countries was handled by the ports of the east coast. Their hinterlands embraced much of the potential Scottish market, and the direct North Sea crossing was less exposed to

[45] *Handel met Engeland*, VOL. I, No. 942.
[46] E.g. Dundee Shipping Lists, pp. 199, 238.
[47] E.g. Dundee Shipping Lists, pp. 228, 251, 280.
[48] *Handel met Engeland*, VOL. I, No. 877.

the hazards of storm and piracy than the much longer route from Glasgow or Ayr via the Irish Sea and the English Channel. In the more northerly of these ports, such as Inverness, where normal exports consisted simply of skins and fish, overseas trade was nearly synonymous with Holland trade. By drawing on Dutch records it has been possible to form a rough estimate of how the bulk of the trade was distributed over the major ports from Aberdeen southwards. Thus for the eleven years 1561-71 ships en route for Veere, Middleburg, and Flushing, and paying "ankerage-geld" to the officials of the Province of Zeeland, gave their ports of departure thus:[49]

Leith	225	Kirkcaldy	13
Dundee	79	Montrose	13
Aberdeen	45	Kinghorn	6
St Andrews	16	Others	20

In this context "others" comprises mainly the smaller ports of East Fife and the Forth, with an occasional entry from the west. Though it has been suggested that the exposure of Edinburgh and Leith to assault from the south led to some diversion of their commerce to ports north of the Forth, it is abundantly clear from these figures that they retained a very powerful grip over Scotland's traditional trade with the Low Countries. The reasons are simple. Edinburgh, for which Leith was the outport, offered by far the greatest concentrated market in Scotland for sophisticated and exotic goods. As a point of export, Leith enjoyed the advantage of drawing not only on its natural hinterland in the Forth basin but also on south-east Scotland generally, which had no alternative major outlet. Furthermore the concentration of shipping and of mercantile experience in Leith attracted the attentions of merchants further north who sent their goods coastwise to Leith for reshipment thence to Holland or elsewhere.

If we move on to the mid 1620's, and draw on the return of duties collected by the Scottish Conservator at Veere,[50] the totals of arrivals from Scottish ports over a period of fifteen months appear thus:

[49] Derived from the Returns of Ferdinando Molchman, Water-bailiff at Arnemuiden, printed in *Handel met Engeland*, VOL. I, Nos. 1005, 1023, 1042, 1115, 1133, 1152, 1169, 1183, 1190.
[50] Printed in Rooseboom, *Scottish Staple in the Netherlands*, No. 119.

Dysart	22
Kirkcaldy	14
Leith	13
Dundee	5
Aberdeen	2
Others	6

The new prominence of the Fife ports reflects the rapid expansion of the coal and salt industries in their immediate vicinity, and the amazing extent to which small ports were able to own and man the vessels which carried their local products. If we abstract these bulk cargoes of coal and salt and concentrate on the shipment of what the customs officers called "staple wares," Leith would still hold its place at the head of the list.

To the wider question of the share of the Low Countries in Scotland's total overseas trade, the answer must be even less statistically precise. Contemporary opinion—typified for instance by Fynes Moryson—ranked it very high. If we compare the arrivals in Holland from Leith in the 1560's with the total movement of shipping at that port for the same period,[51] it looks as if the fraction was of the order of one-half, and this impression is almost exactly confirmed by the Leith Customs for the later 1620's.[52] Similarly in the departures recorded in the Aberdeen Customs for some years in the 1580's—admittedly a small sample—the Low Countries are at least as prominent as any other destination.[53] On the other hand an exact count of arrivals at Dundee, as recorded in the Shipping Lists from the 1580's onwards, indicates that not more than one in nine or ten was from any port in the Low Countries. In any event the number, or even the aggregate tonnage, of vessels following the different trade routes would be an imperfect guide to the real significance of the trade between Scotland and the Low Countries because, apart from coal and salt, the goods entering that trade were of relatively high value as compared, for example, with the Norwegian trade. Furthermore the sale of coal and salt to the Dutch represented a firm cornerstone in the structure of Scotland's external economic relationships; for

[51] Robertson and Wood, *Castle and Town*, p. 279.
[52] "The Entress of Ships, Guidis and Geir transportit at the Port of Leith," General Register House.
[53] Aberdeen Customs Books, MS in General Register House, Edinburgh.

by this sale the Scots earned foreign currency which could be employed in other branches of their overseas trade where the natural balance was less favourable to them. The value to Scotland of her European contacts is not to be measured in narrowly economic terms. As the old alliance with France faded from the light of reality into the mists of sentimental memory, so the continuance of the link with the Netherlands became the more vital for Scotland's participation in the cultural and intellectual advance of Europe generally. Thus though Geneva might be the fount of Calvinism, the stream which flowed in Holland was more readily accessible to Scottish theologians. Similarly when George Jameson, a promising young Aberdeen painter, sought advanced instruction in portraiture, he went to Antwerp to become the pupil of Rubens and to study alongside Van Dyck.[54] Resting, as we have seen, on mutually beneficial relationships, these contacts could scarcely fail to vitalise and enrich the life of early seventeenth-century Scotland, for it was in the Low Countries of the time that Scotsmen encountered all that was most progressive in Continental thought, art, and technique.[55]

[54] J. Bulloch, *George Jamesone, The Scottish Vandyck*, 1885, pp. 47-50.
[55] On the impact of the Low Countries on Scottish architecture see Noad, "The influence of the Low Countries on the architecture of Scotland," *passim*.

IX

CONCLUSION

"Wherefore my most esteemed Princess, I shall put an end to this little tract about Scotland, which I have delineated as accurately as I could; and no one ought to be offended if I have said that money is scarce in this kingdom, nor indeed need any one be scandalised thereat, as it behoves an historian to follow truth, and not to lie in anything, but to describe things as they are, without change or alteration." The "Princess" was Marguerite, Duchesse de Berri and sister of Henri II of France; the author was a French ecclesiastic, Estienne Perlin; the "little tract" was published in Paris in 1558. Perlin's object was to advertise the mutual benefits of the Franco-Scottish alliance, and his claim to objectivity rests on his readiness to produce a merit as a counterweight for every defect he found in the Scots. Their land, though admittedly poor in gold and silver, was plentiful in provisions; their men were not well armed, but were bold and gallant; wine was very dear, but the people drank much ale and milk; their bishoprics were small, but very loyal to France; there were savages in the country, but their number was being daily reduced.

Any observer, however sympathetic, could not with honesty disguise the fact that the Scotland of the 1550's was, in Continental eyes, poor, remote, and socially immature. The search for explanations might take us back to the collapse of the "Golden Age" of the Alexanders: to that wild night in 1288 when Alexander III, journeying to Kinghorn to join his young bride, fell from his horse and died, leaving Scotland with no royal heir except the Maid of Norway, herself to die in Orkney four years later. For the next two centuries the central themes of Scottish history are the external battle for national independence, and the internal battle for national solidarity. The crossed swords on the map, from Bannockburn down to

Neville's Cross, symbolise the broad character of relationships with England; in Scottish domestic annals the recurrent figure is the ambitious and over-mighty subject. Respites were rare and generally short-lived. They come mainly in the fifteenth century when there were a few moments of calm optimism, as when Bishop Kennedy steered the nation through the minority of James III, and when, as that century merged with its successor, relations of the Scottish and English monarchies moved onto a plane of personal cordiality.

In his *King James IV of Scotland* Mr Mackie speaks of the middle months of 1513 as "that last summer of a too brief golden age." Whatever or whoever was ultimately responsible for the foreign policy of James IV and the catastrophe of Flodden, the cost lay squarely and heavily on Scotland for the ensuing fifty years. It reopened the old wound of Anglo-Scottish hostility, and this in turn sapped the vitality and resources of the Scottish Crown and aggravated disloyalties and dissensions among the Scottish people. Powerful regional allegiancies, born of the geographical configuration of the land, made centralisation hard enough even when the centre was strong; friction with England, and the untimely death of kings, combined to keep the centre weak.

The outcome, so far as it is reflected in social and economic conditions, forms the backcloth to some of the chapters in this book. The unstable mixture of reaction and anarchy, characteristic of the later Middle Ages, was prolonged in Scotland into the period when, in more politically disciplined countries, economic life was so expanding that the phrase "Industrial Revolution" is a by no means inappropriate description. In such essential characteristics as the vigorous survival of the quasi-independent chiefs and barons, primitive methods of tenure and tillage, subsistence farming, and small towns obsessed by pride and privilege, the Scotland of Queen Mary was a backward province on the periphery of the West European economic system.

Our main conclusion, therefore, is that in the period covered by this book Scotland began a slow and hesitant but none the less significant emergence from this retarded and often disorderly condition. We have emphasised the particular importance of the years about 1560 when Scotland officially broke with the Old Religion and, having reached a fork in foreign policy, chose the road that ultimately led to London. As the reign of King James VI went on, the withdrawal of the old threat of English hostility provided the basic requirement for economic and social improvement in Scotland. In part the impact was direct, notably in the stabilisation of the Borders, but the major contribution of the Anglo-Scottish *rapprochement* was the opportunity it provided for the King to assert the authority of the Crown among the Scottish people. His personal inclinations urged him to seize the chance, and the theory of Divine Right, the very intellectual weapon for his purpose, lay ready at hand. In his exposition of Divine Right, both in *The Trew Law of Free Monarchies* (1598) and in the *Basilikon Doron* (1599), he created, with powerful Biblical support, a concept of kingship wholly at variance with Scottish historical experience:

> God gives not Kings the stile of Gods in vaine,
> For on his throne his Scepter doe they swey,

hence, to the English Parliament in 1609 "if you will consider the attributes to God, you shall see how they agree in the person of a King."

James Welwood, writing his *Memoirs* at the end of the seventeenth century, acutely observed that James VI had pitched the prestige of kingship on so high a plane because "he had been kept short of it in his Native Country." Certainly the contributions to *The Muses Welcome to the High and Mightie Prince James . . . at his Happie Returne to his Old and Native Kingdome of Scotland* (in 1617) are couched in terms of politic adulation, but with due allowance for that they reflect a sharp contrast to the evidence of the low esteem in which kingship had been held in sixteenth-century Scotland. A true poet, William Drummond of Hawthornden, eulogised James as

> Eye of oure western world, Mars-daunting king,
> With whose renown the earth's seven climates ring.

When James arrived at Linlithgow he was confronted with a plaster lion from whose bowels the local schoolmaster, James Wiseman, hailed him:

> Thrice royal sir, here do I you beseech,
> Who art a lion, to hear a lion's speech.

Throughout the burghs of Scotland heraldic devices were refurbished, buildings and pavements restored, and Town Clerks strained their ingenuity and their Latin grammar in the drafting of appropriate scrolls of welcome to the returned monarch.

Seventeen years earlier Henri, Duc de Rohan had said, with reference to James, that "God is wont to bring forth great men to a country when he wishes to change a kingdom from one hand to another." No modern biographer with any claim to objectivity would attribute to James the quality of greatness, and not even his most ardent apologist could call him either "Mars-daunting" or leonine. All the same, the gaucherie and conceit which disfigure his record as James I of England must not obscure the magnitude of his contribution to the material wellbeing of Scotland. By a combination of good luck and personal prudence his reign was prolonged from his mother's abdication in 1567 to his own death—from natural causes—in 1625. By a combination of guile and insight, a fluent tongue and pen, a capacity to justify mundane acts by fine moral theory, and, in his own phrase, a knowledge of the stomach of the Scots, he achieved by Scottish standards a remarkable measure of political success. In establishing a healthy respect for royal authority, James did for Scotland what Henry VII and Henry VIII had done for England, in spite of the formidable fusion of geography and tradition which made his task more difficult and the outcome less decisive. In consequence, especially after 1603, the two basic conditions of economic progress, external security and internal political stability, existed in Scotland to an extent unknown for a century.

The rate of progress was determined by a complex of forces. The King's own policy, developing along mercantilist lines, encountered stiff resistance from a variety of vested interests in Scotland and had at times to be tempered in response to English demands and ambitions. In some important fields, notably the provision of an adequate and stable currency, his Scottish servants never wholly overcame the difficulties. Apart altogether from matters of state policy, Scotland's natural poverty and national conservatism were drags on progress. In the conditions of the time, economic—especially industrial—expansion involved individual initiative, a diversion of capital and labour from traditional employments, a breach with the accepted pattern of labour relationships, greater willingness to accept risks, and, quite often, the discovery of new sources of materials or new markets. In the cloth industries of Flanders and of East Anglia and in the iron industry of the Weald these requirements were already fulfilled; in Scotland nothing comparable could be envisaged, let alone accomplished, until the closing years of the sixteenth century.

An industrially backward country is not, however, necessarily at a disadvantage in international trade. The essentially rural character of Scotland enabled her to supply in considerable quantity such commodities as skins, hides, and fish which contributed heavily and steadily to the creation of her overseas purchasing power. The production of coal, almost certainly the most spectacular Scottish industrial development in our period, was facilitated by the coastal location of the seams both in the east and in the west, by the active participation of local landed proprietors, and by the demand for coal in some of Scotland's traditional Continental markets. Salt-making, intimately associated with the local coal-mining, advanced in response to domestic and foreign demands which could no longer be satisfied so smoothly or so cheaply from the French salines. Scottish linen cloth and yarn and wool hose were fully competitive in the north-west European markets for manufactured goods, a reflection of the fairly high degree of specialisation and the low labour costs which attended their production.

Thus, in spite of stubborn rigidities, the internal economy of Scotland was by no means inflexible. Nevertheless, in contrast to her greater neighbours—Holland, England, France, and Portugal—her overseas trade continued along furrows cut centuries earlier. The broadest and deepest of these furrows emanated from Leith, Kirkcaldy, Dundee, Aberdeen, and the now minor harbours of the Forth and south-east Fife. Landward of these lay a second line of royal burghs, Stirling, Dunfermline, Cupar, and Perth, less conspicuous in direct foreign trade but focal points in both manufacturing and commerce. By the test of her contribution to the Scottish burghs' taxation—the only test we can usefully apply—Glasgow rose from eleventh place in 1535 to fifth place in 1591; yet in 1591 her contribution was still less than one-eighth of that of

Edinburgh, a third of that of Dundee, and only slightly greater than that of St Andrews. Her increasing trade with the Western Isles, with the Plantations in Ulster, and southward through the Irish Sea, might have emboldened a major prophet in the 1620's to foretell the Clyde's future dominance of the Scottish economy, but for ordinary observers the commercial leadership of east Scotland must have seemed firmly established in the trade of the North Sea, the Baltic, and the Bay of Biscay.

Yet both in her external relationships and in her internal condition, the Scotland of 1625 was appreciably removed from that of 1550. The old and valued trade with France was grinding, if not to a halt, at least to a snail's pace, but business with Holland and the Baltic lands was booming. Relations with England had, as events were to prove, a deceptive veneer of stability. Internal peace and the increasing practice of feuing were providing conditions in which domestic food production attained a magnitude and a certainty not known for generations. In the extractive and in some of the secondary industries, in the planting of Ulster and in the attempted colonisation of Nova Scotia, Scotsmen were—on a scale appropriate to their limited capital resources—revealing something of the same spirit of enterprise as had characterised Englishmen of a generation earlier.

Whatever significance we attach to these developments as signs of hope and promise, their outcome fell far short of anything which could fairly be called revolutionary. For the most part their direct impact was limited to particular groups and particular areas; for the overwhelming mass of the people economic life continued to run upon traditional lines. But whether the Scotsman of 1625 tended cattle in a Highland sheiling, fished off Lewis, wove cloth in Fife, or tilled the soil of Strathmore, his material rewards were normally more assured than those of his grandfather, and if he lived anywhere between Berwick and Galloway they were certainly richer than those of his father. In nearly every material respect, life was now more secure; the fear of death by starvation or by violence had receded; local baronial despotism, if not strangled, was at least constricted by the cords of royal authority.

But the life of a society is not accurately reflected in the record of its material achievements alone. In some important respects Scottish society had deteriorated in the seventy-five years of our study. The flames which consumed the mortal remains of Patrick Hamilton outside the gateway of St Salvator's College in 1528 were rekindled again and again as, in Pitcairn's phrase, the "frightful inquisition" of the witch-hunters strove to cleanse Scotland of the Devil's agents. After three hundred years the words "convict and brynt" still chill the spine of the reader, and Lithgow's wit falls flat on modern ears:

> But now belyke the Colles, this happy yeare,
> By burning witches, are growne wondrous deare.

Similarly the discipline of Church and state had united to suppress the time-honoured public holidays and the lusty merrymaking associated with them, either because they savoured too much of Rome or because they provided an excuse for hooliganism. "It is statute and ordanit," runs an Act of 1555, "that in all tymes cumming na maner of persoun be chosin Robert Hude nor Lytile Johne, Abbot of unressoune, Quenis of May, nor otherwyse." So a dull pall of respectability began to settle until by 1630 the burgh of Aberdeen—the "blyth and blissful burgh" of Dunbar's time—could resolve that "the commoun pypar be discharged of all going throu the toun at nicht or in the morning in time comeing with his pypes, as being ane uncivill forme to be usit within sic a famous burgh."

We have said that the economic progress of Scotland in the later years of James VI was founded upon greater physical security. Security did not, however, mean serenity, any more than prosperity meant unanimity, indeed sixty years later Thomas Morer was to say that the Lowlanders were the most factious people in Scotland because they were the richest. Every aspect of national life was characterised by uneasy compromise. The Union of the Crowns, far from establishing a fixed pattern of relationships with England, had linked the heads but not the bodies. The forced reintroduction of unwelcome religious practices under the Five Articles of Perth of 1621 confirmed the belief that the material benefits of effective royal government were of little worth if that same royal dominance was also to penetrate the affairs of the spirit and the conscience. Similarly, on the lower plane of economic affairs, the gilds and burghs were becoming uneasily aware of the novel concepts and the revolutionary forms of organisation which were elbowing their way into the traditionally privileged territories.

Under James VI Scotland took a decisive step on the road from one way of life towards another. By 1625 the country as a whole had certainly reaped material benefits. Equally certainly the step had not brought repose to the hearts and minds of Scotsmen. Henryson's fable of the two mice, with which this book opened, can also supply the last words:

> What vailis then thy feast and royaltie,
> With dreidful heart and tribulation?

BIBLIOGRAPHY AND LIST OF ABBREVIATIONS

This list includes all important works cited. Full details
are given in the notes of certain other works not included
in this list. Works cited by a short title are here listed
under that title. Where there is no author or presump-
tive author the work is listed under its title. Except
where otherwise indicated the works are published in
the British Isles.

Aberdeen Customs. King's College Library, Aberdeen, MS M. 70.

— MSS in General Register House, Edinburgh.

Aberdeen Council Letters, ed. L. B. Taylor. 1942.

Aberdeen Council Register = *Extracts from the Council Register of Aberdeen*, ed.
J. Stuart. Spalding Club. VOLS. I and II, 1844-8.

Accounts of Lord High Treasurer = *Compota Thesauriorum regum Scotorum,
Accounts of the Lord High Treasurer of Scotland*, ed. J. Balfour Paul, VOLS.
IX-XII. 1911-16.

"Accounts of Money Disbursed by the Lord Treasurer on the Silver Mines
at Hilderstone, 1608-13." MS in General Register House, Edinburgh.

"Accounts of the Burgh of Aberdeen, 1596-7," in *Miscellany of the Spalding
Club*, VOL. V. 1852.

ALEXANDER, SIR W. *An Encouragement to Colonies.* 1624.

Analecta Scotica, ed. J. Maidment. 2 vols. 1832.

ANDREWS, C. M. *The Colonial Period in American History.* VOL. I. Yale 1934.

Annals of Banff, ed. W. Cramond. New Spalding Club. 1891-3.

A.P.S. = *Acts of the Parliament of Scotland.* VOLS. III-IV, ed. T. Thomson.
1814-16.

ARMSTRONG, R. B. *History of Liddesdale, Eskdale, Ewesdale, Wauchopedale, and
the Debateable Land.* 1883.

ATKINSON, S. *Gold Mynes in Scotland* = *The Discoverie and Historie of the Gold
Mynes in Scotland.* 1619. Bannatyne Club, 1825.

Ayr Burgh Accounts, 1534-1624, ed. G. S. Pryde. Scottish History Society,
3rd ser., VOL. XXVIII. 1937.

BACON, F. *The Works of Francis Bacon*, edd. J. Spedding, R. L. Ellis, and D. D. Heath. 7 vols. 1857.

BAIN, E. *Merchant and Craft Guilds*. 1887.

BALFOUR, SIR J. *Annals = Annales of Scotland*, in *Historical Works*, ed. J. Haig, VOL. IV. 1825.

BARBÉ, L. A. *Sidelights on the History, Industries, and Social Life of Scotland*. 1919.

The Baxter Books of St Andrews, ed. J. H. Macadam. 1903.

Bell notebook = "James Bell's Notebook." Glasgow University Library, MS BE7—f.14.

BEVERIDGE, W. *Prices and Wages in England*. 1939.

BIRREL, R. "The Diarey of Robert Birrel, Burges of Edinburgh," in J. G. Dalyell, *Fragments of Scottish History*. 1798.

The Black Book of Taymouth, ed. C. Innes. Bannatyne Club. 1855.

BOECE, H. *The History and Chronicles of Scotland, written in Latin by Hector Boece and translated by J. Bellenden*. 2 vols. 1821.

BOISSONADE, H. "Mouvement commercial" = "Le Mouvement commercial entre la France et les Iles Britanniques au XVIe siècle," in *Revue historique*, CXXXIV-CXXXV (1920).

The Book of Dunvegan, ed. R. C. MacLeod. 2 vols. Third Spalding Club. 1937.

The Book of the Thanes of Cawdor, ed. C. Innes. Spalding Club. 1859.

Boston Port Books = The Port Books of Boston, 1601-40, ed. R. W. K. Hinton. Lincoln Record Society. 1956.

BRERETON, SIR W. *Travels = Travels in Holland, the United Provinces, England, Scotland and Ireland, 1634-5*, ed. E. Hawkins. Chetham Society. 1844.

BROWN, P. HUME. *Early Travellers = Early Travellers in Scotland*. 1891.

— *History of Scotland*. 3 vols. 1911.

— *Scotland before 1700 = Scotland before 1700 from Contemporary Records*. 1893.

— *Scotland in the Time of Queen Mary*. 1904.

Burgh Laws of Dundee = Burgh Laws of Dundee with the History, Statutes, and Proceedings of the Guild of Merchants and Fraternities of Craftsmen, ed. A. J. Warden. 1872.

BURTON, J. H. *The History of Scotland*. VOLS. IV and V. 1873.

CALDERWOOD, D. *The History of the Kirk of Scotland*, ed. T. Thomson. 8 vols. Wodrow Society. 1843.

Calendar of Letters, Despatches, and State Papers relating to the Negotiations between England and Spain. VOL. I, ed. G. A. Bergenroth. 1862.

Calendar of Letters and Papers relating to the Affairs of the Border of England and Scotland, preserved in H.M. Public Record office, ed. J. Bain. 2 vols. 1894-6.

Calendar of State Papers, Foreign Series, of the Reign of Elizabeth. VOL. III, 1560-1, ed. J. Stevenson. 1865.

Calendar of State Papers relating to Scotland preserved in H.M. Public Record Office, ed. M. J. Thorpe. 2 vols. 1858.

Calendar of the State Papers relating to Scotland and Mary, Queen of Scots, edd. J. Bain *et al.* 12 vols. 1898-1952.

Cal. S.P. Dom. = *Calendar of State Papers, Domestic Series, of the Reign of James I.* VOLS. I-III, 1603-10, 1611-18, 1619-23, ed. M. A. E. Green. 1857-8. And *Calendar of Letters and State Papers, Domestic Series, of the Reign of Charles I.* VOL. V, 1631-3, ed. J. Bruce. 1862.

Cambridge Economic History of Europe. VOL. II, edd. M. Postan and E. E. Rich. 1941.

CHAMBERS, R. *Ancient Domestic Architecture of Edinburgh.* 1859.

— *Domestic Annals* = *Domestic Annals of Scotland from the Reformation to the Revolution.* 2 vols. 1858.

— *Edinburgh Merchants* = *Edinburgh Merchants and Merchandise.* 1859.

CHRISTENSEN, A. E. *Dutch Trade to the Baltic about 1600.* The Hague 1941.

"The Chronicle of Fortingall," in *The Black Book of Taymouth*, q.v.

City of Edinburgh Old Accounts. VOL. I, *Bailies' Accounts, 1544-56*; VOL. II, *Dean of Guild's Accounts, 1552-67*, ed. R. Adam. 1899.

CLARK, A. *History of the Shipmaster Society of Aberdeen.* 1911.

CLOW, A. and N. L. *The Chemical Revolution.* 1952.

COCHRAN-PATRICK, R. W. *Coinage* = *Records of the Coinage of Scotland.* 2 vols. 1876.

— *Mining in Scotland* = *Early Records relating to Mining in Scotland.* 1878.

Collectanea de Rebus Albanicis. Iona Club. 1847.

Commons Journal = *Journal of the House of Commons, 1547-1628.* 1803.

The Complaynt of Scotlande, ed. J. A. H. Murray. Early English Text Society. 1872.

Convention Records = *Records of the Convention of the Royal Burghs of Scotland.* VOLS. I-III, ed. J. D. Marwick. 1870-78.

CRAIG, SIR THOMAS. *De unione* = *De unione regnorum Britanniae tractatus*, trans. C. S. Terry. Scottish History Society, VOL. LX. 1909.

CUNNINGHAM, A. S. *Mining in the Kingdom of Fife.* 1913.

CUNNINGHAM, W. *The Growth of English Industry and Commerce.* VOL. II, 1919.

DAVIDSON, J. and GRAY, A. *The Scottish Staple at Veere.* 1909.

DOLEMAN, R. (PARSONS, R.) *A Conference about the Next Succession to the Crown of England.* Amsterdam. 1593.

DONALD, M. B. *Elizabethan Copper.* 1955.

DRUMMOND, J. and ANDERSON, J. *Ancient Scottish Weapons.* 1881.

Dundee Shipping Lists = "Ane Buik contenand the Intress of Schippis . . . at ye port of Dundie, 1580-1618," in *Wedderburne Compt Buik*, q.v. After 1618 MS in Dundee City Archives.

Ec. H.R. = *Economic History Review.*

Edinburgh Records = *Extracts from the Records of the Burgh of Edinburgh.* VOLS. III-IV, ed. J. D. Marwick, 1875-82: VOL. V, edd. M. Wood and R. K. Hannay, 1927; VOL. VI, ed. M. Wood, 1936.

ELDER, J. R. *The Royal Fishery Companies.* 1912.

"The Entress of Ships, Guidis, and Geir transportit at the port of Leith, 1627-28." MS in General Register House, Edinburgh.

Exchequer Rolls = *Rotuli Scaccarium regum Scotorum, The Exchequer Rolls of Scotland.* VOLS. XIII-XXIII, edd. G. Burnet, A. J. C. Mackay, and G. P. McNeill. 1891-1908.

Extracts from the Records of the Burgh of Lanark, 1150-1722, ed. R. Renwick. Scottish Burgh Records Society. 1873.

FINLAY, I. *Scottish Gold and Silver Work.* 1956.

FISCHER, T. A. *The Scots in East and West Prussia.* 1903.

— *The Scots in Germany.* 1902.

— *The Scots in Sweden.* 1907.

FLEETWOOD, W. *Chronicum preciosum, or an Account of English Money.* 1707.

FLEMING, J. A. *Scottish and Jacobite Glass.* 1938.

Foreign Correspondence with Marie of Lorraine, ed. M. Wood. 2 vols. Scottish History Society, 3rd ser., VOLS. IV, VII. 1923-5.

FRIIS, A. *Alderman Cockayne's Project and the Cloth Trade.* 1927.

GADE, J. A. *The Hanseatic Control of Norwegian Commerce.* Leiden 1951.

GARDINER, S. R. *History of England, 1603-42.* VOL. I. 1883.

Glasgow Records = Extracts from the Records of the Burgh of Glasgow. VOL. I, 1583-1642, ed. J. D. Marwick. Scottish Burgh Records Society. 1876.

GORDON, R. *Encouragement for such as shall have intention to bee under-takers in the New Plantation of Cape Briton, now New Galloway.* 1625.

GRANT, I. F. *Social Development = Social and Economic Development of Scotland before 1603.* 1930.

GRANT, J. *History of the Burgh and Parish Schools of Scotland.* 1876.

GRIERSON, R. "Nithsdale at the Union of the Crowns," in *S.H.R.,* XIII (1916).

GROOME, F. H. *A Short Border History.* 1887.

"Haddington Books of the Common Good," in *Transactions of the East Lothian Antiquarian Society,* VII (1958).

Handel met Engeland = Bronnen Tot de Geschiedenis van den Handel met Engeland, Schotland en Ierland, ed. H. Smit. 2 vols. The Hague 1928.

HANNAY, R. K. "On the Church lands at the Reformation," in *S.H.R.,* XVI (1919).

Harl. 1314 = "On the Union of the Crowns." British Museum, Harleian MS 1314.

HAY, G. *History of Arbroath.* 1876.

HECKSHER, E. F. *An Economic History of Sweden.* Harvard 1954.

— "Mercantilism," in *Ec. H.R.,* VII (1936).

— "Multilateralism, Baltic trade, and Mercantilism," in *Ec. H. R.,* III (1950).

— *Sveriges ekonomiska historia fran Gustav Vasa.* 2 vols. Stockholm 1935-6.

HENDERSON, G. M. *Scottish Reckonings of Time, Money, Weights, and Measures.* Historical Association of Scotland. 1926.

HINTON, R. W. K. *The Eastland Trade and the Common Weal in the Seventeenth Century.* 1959.

HISTORICAL MANUSCRIPTS COMMISSION *Third Report.* 1872.

— *Ninth Report.* See also *Mar and Kellie Papers.*

Historie and Life of King James the Sext, being an Account of the Affairs of Scotland, 1566 to 1596, ed. T. Thomson. Bannatyne Club. 1825.

HOLMYARD, E. J. *Alchemy.* 1957.

"Household Book of Breadalbane," in *The Black Book of Taymouth,* q.v.

HUGHES, E. *Studies in Administration and Finance, 1558-1825.* 1934.

HULME, E. W. "English glass-making in the sixteenth and seventeenth centuries," in *The Antiquary,* xxx (1894), xxxi (1895).

INNES, C. *Sketches of Early Scotch History.* 1861.

INSH, G. P. *Scottish Colonial Schemes, 1620-1686.* 1922.

Inverness Records = Records of Inverness: Burgh Court Books 1556-1586. New Spalding Club. 1911.

JAMES VI AND I, KING. *The Basilikon Doron of King James VI,* ed. J. Craigie. Scottish Text Society, 3rd ser., VOL. XVIII. 1944.

— *The Political Works of James I,* ed. C. H. McIlwain. Harvard 1918.

KEITH, T. *Commercial Relations of England and Scotland, 1603-1707.* 1910.

KENNEDY, W. *Annals of Aberdeen.* 1818.

KERMACK, W. R. *The Scottish Highlands.* 1957.

KEYMOR, J. "Policies of State" = "Policies of State Practised in various Kingdoms for the encrease of Trade." Edinburgh University Library, Laing MSS, Div. II, No. 52.

Kirkcaldy Records = Kirkcaldy Burgh Records, ed. L. Macbean. 1908.

KNOX, JOHN. *History of the Reformation in Scotland,* ed. W. C. Dickinson. 2 vols. 1949.

— *The Works of John Knox,* ed. D. Laing. VOLS. I-II. Wodrow Society. 1846.

Ledger of Andrew Halyburton, Conservator of the Privileges of the Scotch Nation in the Netherlands, 1497-1503, ed. C. Innes. 1867.

LESLEY, J. "Diary of John Lesley," in *Miscellany of the Bannatyne Club,* VOL. III, q.v.

— *Historie = The Historie of Scotland, wrytten first in Latin by . . . Jhone Leslie, and translated into Scottish by Father James Dalrymple . . . 1596,* ed. E. G. Cody. 2 vols. Scottish Text Society. 1888.

Letters and Documents relating to the City of Glasgow, ed. J. D. Marwick. 1894.

LINDESAY OF PITSCOTTIE, R. *The History and Chronicles of Scotland*, ed. A. J. G. Mackay. 3 vols. Scottish Text Society, VOLS. XLII, XLIII, LX. 1899-1911.

LINDSAY, SIR D. *The Works of Sir David Lindsay of the Mount*, ed. D. Hamer. 2 vols. Scottish Text Society, 3rd ser., VOLS. I-II. 1931.

LITHGOW, W. *Totall Discourse* = *The Totall Discourse of the Rare Adventures and Painefull Peregrinations of long nineteene yeares travayles*. 1632.

LYTHE, S. G. E. *Life and Labour in Dundee from the Reformation to the Civil War*. Abertay Historical Society. 1958.

— "Scottish trade with the Baltic, 1550-1650," in *Dundee Economic Essays*, ed. J. K. Eastham. 1952.

MACADAM, W. I. "Notes on the ancient iron industry of Scotland," in *P.S.A.S.*, IX (1887).

MACEWEN, A. R. *A History of the Church in Scotland*. 2 vols. 1913.

MACGEORGE, A. *Old Glasgow*. 1888.

MACKENZIE, W. C. *History of the Outer Hebrides*. 1922.

— *The Book of the Lews*. 1919.

MACKENZIE, W. M. *The Scottish Burghs*. 1949.

MACKIE, J. D. *The University of Glasgow*. 1954.

McURE, J. *View of the City of Glasgow, its Origin, Rise, and Progress*. 1830.

MAJOR, J. *History of Greater Britain*, trans. A. Constable. Scottish History Society, VOL. X. 1892.

Mar and Kellie Papers = Historical Manuscripts Commission, *Report on the Manuscripts of the Earl of Mar and Kellie, preserved in Alloa House*. 1904.

MARSHALL, T. H. *History of Perth*. 1849.

MARWICK, J. D. *Edinburgh Gilds and Crafts*. 1909.

MASON, JOHN. "Notarial Notebook" = "The Notarial Notebook of John Mason, Clerk to the Burgh of Ayr, 1582-1612," in *Archaeological and Historical Collections relating to Ayrshire and Galloway*. VOL. VI. 1889.

MASON, JOHN. *Brieffe Discourse of the New-found-land*. 1620.

MATHEW, D. *Scotland under Charles I*. 1955.

MATHIESON, W. L. *Politics and Religion, A Study in Scottish History, 1550-1695.* 1902.

MAXWELL, A. *The History of Old Dundee, narrated out of the Council Register.* 1884.

MAXWELL, C. *Irish History from Contemporary Sources, 1509-1610.* 1923.

MELVILLE, J. *Autobiography and Diary of Mr James Melville,* ed. R. Pitcairn. Wodrow Society. 1842.

MICHEL, F. *Les Écossais en France, les Français en Écosse.* 2 vols. 1862.

MILLAR, A. H. *Roll of Eminent Burgesses of Dundee.* 1887.

MILNE, J. *Aberdeen: Topographical, Antiquarian, and Historical Papers.* 1911.

Miscellany of the Bannatyne Club, VOL. III. 1855.

MITCHELL, A. *List of Travels and Tours in Scotland, 1296-1900.* 1902.

MOIR, D. G. "The roads of Scotland," in *Scottish Geographical Magazine,* LXXIII (1957).

MOLLAT, M. *Le Commerce maritime normand à la fin du moyen âge.* Paris 1952.

MONRO, D. "Description of the Western Isles of Scotland, called Hybrides," in Brown, *Scotland before 1700,* q.v.

MONTGOMERIE, A. "King James VI's tocher gude," in *S.H.R.,* XXXVII (1958).

MORRIS, D. B. *The Stirling Merchant Gild and the Life of John Cowane.* 1919.

MORYSON, F. *Itinerary = An Itinerary Written by Fynes Moryson, Gent, . . . containing his ten yeares travell through . . . Germany . . . England, Scotland, and Ireland.* 1617.

MOYSIE, D. *Memoirs of the Affairs of Scotland, 1577-1603,* ed. J. Dennistoun. Bannatyne Club. 1830.

MURRAY, D. "Scottish local records," in *S.H.R.,* XXIV (1927).

The Muses Welcome to the High and Mightie Prince James . . . at his Happie Returne to his Old and Native Kingdome of Scotland. 1618.

NAPIER, M. *Memoirs of John Napier of Merchiston.* 1834.

NEF, J. U. "The genesis of industrialism and modern science," in *Essays in Honor of Conyers Read,* ed. N. Downs. 1953.

— "Industrial growth in France and England 1540-1640," in *Journal of Political Economy,* XLIV (1936).

NEF, J. U. *The Rise of the British Coal Industry.* 2 vols. 1932.

New Statistical Account of Scotland. VOL. X. 1845.

NICHOLLS, G. *A History of the Scotch Poor Law.* 1856.

NOAD, R. "The influence of the Low Countries on the architecture of Scotland," in *Quarterly of the Incorporation of the Architects in Scotland,* No. 28 (1928).

NOBBS, D. *England and Scotland, 1560-1707.* 1952.

Nova Scotia Charters = Royal Letters, Charters, and Tracts relating to the Colonization of New Scotland and the Institution of the Order of Knights Baronets of Nova Scotia, 1621-1638, ed. D. Laing. Bannatyne Club. 1867.

O'BRIEN, G. *The Economic History of Ireland in the Seventeenth Century.* 1919.

PAGAN, T. *The Convention of the Royal Burghs of Scotland.* 1926.

Papers Illustrating the History of the Scots Brigade in the Netherlands, 1572-1772, ed. J. Ferguson. 3 vols. Scottish History Society, VOLS. XXXII, XXXV, XXXVIII. 1899-1901.

Papers relating to the Scots in Poland, ed. A. F. Steuart. Scottish History Society, VOL. LIX. 1915.

PERLIN, E. *Déscription des royaulmes d'Angleterre et d'Écosse.* Paris 1558. Translations in *Antiquarian Repertory,* IV (1784), and Brown, *Early Travellers,* q.v.

The Perth Hammermen Book, 1518-68, ed. C. A. Hunt. 1889.

PITCAIRN, R. *Criminal Trials in Scotland from 1488 to 1624.* 4 vols. 1833.

Port Books = Exchequer and King's Remembrancer, Port Books. MS in Public Record Office.

POSTHUMUS, N. W. *Inquiry into the History of Prices in Holland.* Leiden 1946.

P.S.A.S. = Proceedings of the Society of Antiquaries of Scotland.

RAIT, R. S. *History of Scotland.* 1929.

Register of the Great Seal = Registrum magni sigili regum Scotorum, The Register of the Great Seal of Scotland. VOLS. VI-VIII, ed. J. M. Thomson. 1890-5.

Register of the Kirk Session of St Andrews, ed. D. H. Fleming. 2 vols. Scottish History Society, VOLS. IV, VII. 1889-90.

ROBERTS, M. *Gustavus Adolphus.* VOL. II. 1958.

ROBERTSON, D. and WOOD, M. *Castle and Town: Chapters in the History of the Royal Burgh of Edinburgh.* 1928.

ROBERTSON, H. M. *Aspects of the Rise of Economic Individualism.* 1935.

— "Sir Bevis Bulmer," in *Journal of Economic and Business History,* IV (1931).

ROBERTSON, W. *The History of Scotland during the Reigns of Queen Mary and King James VI.* 2 vols. 1794.

ROGERS, C. *Memorials of the Earl of Stirling.* 2 vols. 1877.

ROOSEBOOM. M. P. *The Scottish Staple in the Netherlands.* The Hague 1910.

ROWSE, A. L. *The England of Elizabeth.* 1953.

R.P.C. = *Register of the Privy Council of Scotland.* 1st ser., VOLS. I-XIV, edd. J. H. Burton and D. Masson, 1877-98; 2nd ser., VOLS. I, IV, VI, edd. D. Masson and P. Hume Brown, 1899-1905.

RUDDIMAN, T. *An Introduction to Mr James Anderson's Diplomata Scotiae.* 1773 edn.

RUDING, R. *Annals of the Coinage of Britain and its Dependencies.* 2 vols. 1840.

SAMUEL, A. M. *The Herring: its Effect on the History of Britain.* 1918.

SCOTT, W. R. *Joint-Stock Companies = The Constitution and Finance of English, Scottish, and Irish Joint-Stock Companies to 1720.* 3 vols. 1910.

SCOTTISH TEXT SOCIETY. *Miscellany Volume.* 3rd ser., VOL. IV. 1933.

S.H.R. = *Scottish Historical Review.*

SINCLAIR, G. A. "The Scottish Trader in Sweden," in *S.H.R.,* XXV (1928).

SKENE, W. F. *Celtic Scotland.* 1890.

SLAFTER, E. F. *Sir William Alexander and American Colonization.* Boston 1873.

Sound Toll Registers = Tabeller over Skibsfart og Varetransport genem Øresund, 1497-1660, ed. N. E. Bang. Copenhagen 1922.

South Leith Records, ed. D. Robertson. 1911.

SPEDDING, J. *Bacon = The Life and Times of Francis Bacon.* 2 vols. 1878.

State Papers and Miscellaneous Correspondence of Thomas, Earl of Melros, ed. J. Maidment. Abbotsford Club. 1837.

The Statistical Account of Scotland, ed. Sir J. Sinclair. VOL. X. 1796.

Stirling Records = Extracts from the Records of the Royal Burgh of Stirling, 1519-1666, ed. R. Renwick. Scottish Burgh Records Society. 1889.

TAYLOR, J. *The Pennyles Pilgrimage, or The Moneylesse Perambulation of John Taylor, alias the King's Majesties Water-Poet.* 1618.

TAYLOR, J. *The Works of John Taylor*, ed. C. Hindley. 1876.

TERRY, C. S. *The Scottish Parliament, its Constitution and Procedure, 1603-1707.* 1905.

"Testimonialis Grantit be ye Bailies [of Aberdeen] 1589-1603," ed. L. B. Taylor, in *Miscellany of the Third Spalding Club*, VOL. II. 1940.

THOMSON. D. *The Weaver's Craft.* 1903.

TROCMÉ, M. and DELAFOSSE, M. *Le Commerce rochelais à la fin du moyen âge.* Paris 1952.

TUCKER, T. "Report" = "Report upon the settlement of the revenues of Excise and Customs in Scotland, A.D. 1656," in *Miscellany of the Scottish Burgh Records Society.* 1881. Also Bannatyne Club, 1824.

Tudor Economic Documents, edd. R. H. Tawney and E. Power. 3 vols. 1924.

USHER, A. P. "General course of wheat prices in France, 1350-1788," in *Review of Economic Statistics*, XII (1930).

WARRACK, J. *Domestic Life in Scotland, 1488-1688.* 1920.

WAUS, SIR P. *The Correspondence of Sir Patrick Waus*, ed. R. V. Agnew. 1887.

WEBER, M. *The Protestant Ethic and the Spirit of Capitalism.* 1930.

Wedderburne Compt Buik = *The Compt Buik of David Wedderburne, Merchant of Dundee*, ed. A. H. Millar. Scottish History Society, VOL. XXVIII. 1898.

WILLCOCK, J. *Sir Thomas Urquhart of Cromartie.* 1899.

WILLSON, D. H. *King James VI and I.* 1956.

WILSON, C. "Treasure and trade balances," in *Ec.H.R.*, II (1949).

WINCHESTER, B. *Tudor Family Portrait.* 1955.

YAIR, J. *An Account of the Scotch Trade in the Netherlands.* 1776.

INDEX

Aberdeen: food supply, 3, 107; trade and shipping of, 22, 45, 57, 155, 159, 171, 179, 182, 187, 227, 241, 244, 245; population of, 29, 117; grants money, 35; government of, 62; harbour at, 96, 133; bridge at, 96; money and prices at, 99, 108, 109, 111; social regulations at, 123, 253; Shipmaster Society of, 134; relieves captives, 191; natives abroad, 194. *See also* UNIVERSITIES.

Acheson, John: exports lead ore, 55; and currency, 102; and the finance of trade, 163.

Adventurers: in Ireland, 68.

Aeneas Sylvius: on Scotland, 142.

agriculture: general state of, Chap. I *passim*; townsmen engaged in, 124. *See also* CATTLE; HORSES; SHEEP; SWINE.

alarm-clock: imported, 174.

alchemy: 34, 103.

ale: making of, 9; prices, 110. *See also* BREWING.

Alexander, Sir William, Earl of Stirling: achievements and colonial enterprises, 71-4.

Algerines: piracy of, 191.

Amsterdam: prices at, 32; Scottish affairs with, 132, 239, 240, 241.

Anstruther: ships and trade of, 155, 218, 230.

Antwerp: Scottish affairs with, 235, 237, 246.

Arbroath: harbour at, 96; population of, 118.

Argyll: hardiness of cattle in, 11.

Armstrong: Border family, 197.

Association of the Lord Treasurer: and fisheries, 60.

astrology and superstition: 120-1.

Atkinson, Stephen: on gold and silver production, 54-6.

Atlantic: Scottish ventures across, 66, 70-4.

Ayr: trade and shipping of, 58, 69, 155, 181, 190, 191; prosperity of, 64; loans at, 105; prices at, 111; size of, 117.

Ayrshire: coal-mining in, 48, 69.

Bacon, Francis: on usury, 105; and Union, 200, 205-6.

Bailie, George: 124.

Balcanquell, George: maritime activities of, 135, 229-30.

Balfour, Sir James: on tanning, 44; on coal-owners, 48; on wine trade, 172; on Borders, 198.

Balloch: wine-cellar at, 189.

Baltic: Chap. V *passim*; grain from, 17, 18, 19, 20, 21, 32; raw materials from, 39, 46, 62, 64; exports to, 51, 58, 240.

Banff: 132.

Banffshire: 3.

Barclay, William: defends tobacco, 86.

barter: 114, 140.

bark: imports of, 224.

beer: imports of, 224. *See also* BREWING.

Bell, James: affairs in Netherlands, 125, 241, 242, 243.

bells: imported, 241-2.

Berne, John: 131.

Berwickshire: 6.